THE INLAND WATERS
OF ENGLAND

Books by L. T. C. Rolt

NARROW BOAT

HIGH HORSE RIDERLESS

SLEEP NO MORE

WORCESTERSHIRE

GREEN AND SILVER

INLAND WATERWAYS OF ENGLAND

HORSELESS CARRIAGE

THE THAMES FROM MOUTH TO SOURCE

LINES OF CHARACTER (with *Patrick Whitehouse*)

RAILWAY ADVENTURE

WINTERSTOKE

THE CLOUDED MIRROR

RED FOR DANGER

PICTORIAL HISTORY OF MOTORING

ISAMBARD KINGDOM BRUNEL

THOMAS TELFORD

GEORGE AND ROBERT STEPHENSON

THE CORNISH GIANT

GREAT ENGINEERS

JAMES WATT

THOMAS NEWCOMEN

A HUNSLET HUNDRED

TOOLS FOR THE JOB

THE AERONAUTS

THE MECHANICALS

NAVIGABLE WATERWAYS

WATERLOO IRONWORKS

BEST RAILWAY STORIES (editor)

VICTORIAN ENGINEERING

THE MAKING OF A RAILWAY

LANDSCAPE WITH MACHINES

POTTERS' FIELD

FROM SEA TO SEA

THE INLAND WATERWAYS OF ENGLAND

By L. T. C. ROLT

London
GEORGE ALLEN & UNWIN
BOSTON   SYDNEY

FIRST PUBLISHED IN 1950
FIFTH IMPRESSION 1970
SECOND EDITION 1979

GEORGE ALLEN & UNWIN LTD
40 Museum Street, London WC1A 1LU

© *George Allen & Unwin (Publishers) Ltd*, 1950
Introduction © Charles Hadfield 1979

British Library Cataloguing in Publication Data

Rolt, Lionel Thomas Caswall
   The inland waterways of England.
   1. Inland navigation – England – History
   I. Title
   386'.0941   HE664   78–41242

ISBN 0-04-386006-0

Dedicated to the Memory of
JAMES BRINDLEY of Tunstead
JOHN RENNIE of Phantassie
THOMAS TELFORD of Westerkirk
Countrymen, Engineers, Architects, Master Craftsmen
1718–1834

022745940

"I admire commercial enterprise; it is
the vigorous outgrowth of our industrial life: I admire everything that gives
it free scope, as wherever it goes,
activity, energy, intelligence—all that
we call civilization—accompany it; but
I hold that the aim and end of all ought
not to be a mere bag of money, but
something far higher and far better."
THOMAS TELFORD

42048294 6

PRINTED IN GREAT BRITAIN AT THE
UNIVERSITY PRESS, CAMBRIDGE

FOREWORD

BY
CHARLES HADFIELD

TOM Rolt's original Preface to *The Inland Waterways of England* is dated from his converted narrow boat *Cressy* at Banbury in 1948, only thirty years ago. Yet, as he said then, it was the first book ever to 'give the general reader a picture of the history, construction and working methods of the waterways'.

It was written in the year when canals and river navigations, owned each by a private waterway or railway company, were gathered together by nationalisation. In that sense it marked the end of an era. Of a greater divide Tom Rolt himself was only partly aware, that the life of the working boats and boat people that he described so vividly and pictured so truly was almost ended. He envisages it continuing, but sees a parallel growth of pleasure cruising in junior partnership, perhaps, by inland waterway lovers rather like himself.

L. T. C. Rolt had converted his *Cressy* and taken to the canals in 1939, and his adventures live for us in his book *Narrow Boat*. Therefore by 1948 he had lived and travelled on the canals alongside working boaters for ten years using *Cressy* as a base for his war-time jobs. When, therefore, in 1946, four of us became the first officers of the newly formed Inland Waterways Association, he alone had the waterways knowledge and experience to become the Association's first Secretary.

Soon afterwards, he and I exchanged confidences: he intended to write a book about the canals as he knew them, I a general history. Both books were published in 1950, and both were 'firsts'. But whereas my *British Canals* has been revised and enlarged again and again to take account of subsequent research, his *The Inland Waterways of England* remains exactly as he wrote it then, a perfect picture not only of the canals as Tom Rolt then knew and experienced them, but of a world that has gone. There is no other book like it.

Look at his pictures. Apart from his own *Cressy* (e.g. in Plate I) and himself at work—he is energetically using a Calder & Hebble handspike at the foot of Plate X—only one picture shows a cruiser. Working boats and boatmen inhabit the book because they shared Tom Rolt's life, not because they were picturesque survivals. So it is in his text. The life of the working canals spoke exactly to Tom's own condition. He valued a way of life that encouraged personal independence and the development of character. Moreover, an engineer by training, he had a natural sympathy for the eighteenth and early nineteenth century structures of the waterways, from great aqueducts and tunnels to humble locks or culverts. Each had been individually designed and built to do its own job, and on no two canals were the small structures exactly the same, because the men who made them, and the local traditions that had influenced them, had been different. Tom liked that.

A few years later, for reasons given in his *Landscape with Canals*, Tom had sadly to abandon *Cressy* and take to the land, to the Talyllyn Railway restoration by volunteers, and much else by which also he is remembered. I remained in the canal world, watching it, working in it, changing with it. What that world is now is described in several periodicals and documented in dozens of books. It is on the whole a good world, which I understand, and which suits me. But it wasn't Tom's. He and I lived near one another, remained good friends until he died, and often used to meet. When we did so, I told him what was happening and what I hoped would happen on the waterways, he told me about *Cressy* and how canal life was lived in the days before I myself had first taken out a canal cruiser.

L. T. C. Rolt's book has been reissued unaltered, because it is unalterable. That was how it was in 1948, and that was how a deeply perceptive man with a craft background and a love for the way of life he wrote about, then saw it.

Yet, that having been said, this book is still an excellent introduction to the canals that anyone may cruise today. Structures change only very slowly: the aqueducts and the tunnels, the locks and the bridges that he describes are still there, even to handspike-worked paddles on Calder & Hebble locks. Water supply problems and maintenance methods are much the same.

A man is fortunate who can find, as Tom did, a way of life that so exactly suits him, and doubly so if he can catch its spirit in print. Tom was more fortunate still, for he did it twice. In *Narrow Boat* (1944) and *The Inland Waterways of England* (1950), he gave us two books that will last as long as men and women love canals. November, 1978

6

CONTENTS

PREFACE   *page* 8

ACKNOWLEDGEMENTS   14

I.   *Early River Navigations*   15

II.   *The Canal Era*   37

III. *Locks, Aqueducts, Tunnels and Other Works*   68

IV. *Waterway Maintenance*   101

V.   *Boats and Boatbuilding*   122

VI. *Traffic Working and Motive Power, Past and Present*   139

VII. *The Boatman*   170

VIII. *Travelling by Waterway*   195

BIBLIOGRAPHY   210

INDEX   211

NOTE ON ILLUSTRATIONS

These illustrations are grouped in six insets which follow pages 32, 64, 96, 128, 160 and 192. At the end of the book there is a folded map of the Inland Waterways of England showing their ownership prior to January 1, 1948.

AUTHOR'S PREFACE TO THIRD IMPRESSION

THIS book was written in 1948 and first published in 1950. That the demand for it after twelve years should justify this new impression is heartening evidence of the continuing and ever growing interest in the inland waterways of England.

In 1948 responsibility for our waterways had but lately been vested in the British Transport Commission and the old canal companies which had reigned for so long had ceased to exist. It was obvious that many changes would follow upon this transfer of ownership and the object of this book was to put on record a picture of our waterways as they were under the old regime. I have thought it best to let it stand as such rather than revise it and tinker with tenses in an attempt to bring it up-to-date. In any case the moment is inopportune for revision since the ownership of our waterways is about to be transferred from the Transport Commission to a new British Waterways Board.

Readers are therefore asked to treat with reserve paragraphs which are written in the present tense. This applies particularly to Chapter VI where I refer to some boats and to some traffic movements which, alas, no longer exist. On the broad waterways commercial traffic has been maintained and in some cases increased, but on the narrow canals it has declined in the fourteen years that have passed since this book was written. The brutal fact is that despite the inherent economy of water transport, by current economic standards the 30 ton payload of the narrow boat is too small to justify the man hours which must be expended in working it. To anyone who has known the narrow boats and the people who worked them as long and as well as I have this decline is inexpressibly sad. The boats represented more than a mere means of transport; they were a way of life and the canals can never be the same without them.

There is consolation in the fact that many of the canals which have lost their traditional traffic are not falling into disuse but serving new purposes. The observation in the last chapter of this book that so few people use our canals for pleasure cruising is no longer true. More and more people are so using them every year and their tremendous amenity value in this over-crowded, traffic-jammed island of ours is becoming increasingly evident. More-over, much greater use is being made of canals as water supply channels and, as this book explains, these two uses do not conflict but are complementary, the one helping the other. Unlike its pre-decessors, the new British Waterways Board will be specifically charged to foster and develop such new uses of our canals. It is to be hoped, therefore, that this book will never become wholly a nostalgic memorial to things past. The quiet beauties of our waterways have become too widely prized a part of our national heritage for that to happen.

L. T. C. R.

March, 1962

AUTHOR'S PREFACE

In the remote dawn of history our ancestors were nomads. When the days lengthened they would leave their sheltered winter camping-grounds in the river valleys and move with their flocks and herds to the sweeter airs and fresh herbage of the upland pastures, leaving little behind them but the cooling ashes of their camp fires. Centuries of settled civilization now divide us from these ancestors, and yet there must be few who do not at times feel a restlessness which is no less than the old nomadic instinct astir within us. It is the same instinct which sent men in search of Hy Brasil and Far Cathay and which invests such simple words as "over the hills and far away" with the magic of an incantation.

It is for this reason, I believe, that of all the ingenious inventions which man has perfected, those connected with transport appeal most strongly to our imagination, and none more strongly than ships and railways. It may be that no work of man's hands can ever equal or surpass the grandeur of the tall sailing ship; but the fact remains that any ship, whether she be a great liner, a dirty little coaster or a fishing boat, fascinates us because she is imbued with the mystery and magic of the sea—the lure of those far horizons which lie beyond the flashing of the harbour lights. This magic is no romantic illusion of the landsman. The sea changes a man's nature unmistakably and binds him to her in such a way that no matter how he may complain of the hardships she imposes, the seaman can seldom bring himself to leave her.

It is more difficult to analyse the magic of the railway, but for all that it is no less real. There is no air of mystery about the steam locomotive, for she travels a steel road, man-made and circumscribed. When the small coaster slips down the estuary with the evening tide and we watch her till she is no more than a smudge of smoke against the sunset on the horizon's rim it is easy to believe her to be bound for the Hesperides. But we can harbour no such illusion as we stand on the platform of a London terminus and watch the departure of a northbound express. Her destination is certain, yet the fascination is there, and is even due to the fact that in addition to the romance of her swift, far journey, our imagination is captured by the magnitude of the engineering works and the complexity of the organization which makes that certainty possible. The winking tail lamps fade away over the gleaming mesh of rails; we can no longer hear the heavy exhaust beats; signal lights flick from green to red or amber. But still the mind's eye can follow the progress of the express as she gathers speed. We can imagine her thundering over lofty viaducts or plunging with a scream into long tunnels as she races north-wards, the glare from her open firedoor lighting up the flying steam. And always the signal lights herald her coming and guard her passing as the signalmen in their lonely boxes flash their message northwards and peg their block instruments to "Train on Line". Yes, the appeal of the railway is a composite one, not dependent wholly upon the locomotive, but compounded of every-thing that makes the railway system. It has captivated generations of laymen, while the railwayman, like the seaman, acquires a certain indefinable character and tradition. He lives in a world of his own.

Another world, far less widely known but combining some features common both to the sea and to the railways, is that represented by the Inland Waterways of England. The navigable river is the road to the sea, while the canals which connect these rivers resemble the railways with their important junctions, their main and branch lines, their tunnels and aqueducts. Yet however narrow, shallow and man-made these canals may be they seem to bring into the very heart of England something of the sea's magic. For they are water roads, and so their traffic is not bounded, in imagination at least, by those limitations which the tarmac or the steel rail impose. We may not appreciate this as we lean over the parapet of the old bridge at the foot of the village street and watch the ducks dabbling in the water or the small boys with net and jar fishing for stickleback. The canal looks as domesticated as a village duck pond. It is only when we notice that the little pub by the bridge bears the sign of "The Anchor", "The Navigation", or "The Lord Nelson" that we begin to realize that it represents a world beyond the small, ordered and centuries-old routine of village life; that if we were to follow the waterway where it curves out of sight between the high hedges, it would lead us eventually to the river, and down the river to the sea. Perhaps a boat will pass by, shattering the smooth mirror of the water, setting the reeds swaying, frightening the ducks, and exciting the small boys, but soon vanishing to leave everything as still and as tranquil as before. Her errand may be prosaic enough did we but know it, but if we have any imagination we may experience again something of that sense of wonder and surmise with which we watched the coasting steamer sail into the sunset.

Is it not surprising that so little has been written about this world of the waterways? Ships and the sea have inspired some of the greatest prose and poetry in our language, while a volume of railway literature pours from the presses in an ever-increasing spate to cover every minute detail of the subject from the design of locomotive nameplates to the most obscure abandoned branch line. Yet the literature of our inland waterways is confined to a handful of historical and technical works and to a few travel books which are primarily records of personal experience. Add to these the tabulated guide books of Westall, de Salis and Wilson and the catalogue is complete. It includes no book designed to give the general reader a picture of the history, construction and working methods of the waterways.

The amount of interest shown by the public in the Exhibition which the Inland Waterways Association staged in London in 1947 seemed to indicate the need for such a book, and the chapters which follow represent an attempt to supply it. While each chapter deals fairly comprehensively with a particular aspect of the subject, I make no claim that the result is a definitive and exhaustive work. Even if I were qualified to produce such a work, the subject is so large that each chapter would become a book in itself and the reader without specialized interest would find the result wearisome. What follows may therefore be described as a detailed introduction to the waterways, its object being to stimulate rather than satiate intelligent interest in a neglected part of our national heritage.

The greater proportion of our waterway mileage was a product of eighteenth-century engineering. If we except purely architectural works, no other monuments of that age survive upon a scale comparable with the canals. They were the cradle, not only of the civil engineering technique which built the railways, but also of that mechanical skill which launched the first iron hull and the first successful steam boat. They were the first cheap and efficient means of inland transport, and consequently they played a tremendous part in that great process of social, economic and industrial change which we call the industrial revolution. The waterways, in fact, represent an important chapter in our social history and for this reason the study of them is not, or should not be, a minutely specialized undertaking, but one capable of making a contribution to the general knowledge of our past.

Had I set out to write a book of similar character about our railway system I should have found ready to hand such a wealth of literature on every aspect of my subject that it would have been possible to produce a reasonably authoritative work without ever having seen a railway or travelled by train. But in this case, while I have made full use of written information, the sources available are so few that a great deal of this book is compiled from personal enquiry, observation and experience. When it is realized that the subject I am dealing with is a transport system of a size and complexity comparable with that of the railways and of greater diversity, I hope the reader will be disposed to forgive any inaccuracies or omissions which he may discover, and be stimulated by that discovery to carry out further research himself.

Soon after this book was begun the control of the majority of our independent waterways passed to the Docks and Inland Waterways Executive of the British Transport Commission, while responsibility for the railway controlled canals is in process of being transferred to them. This marked the end of an epoch in waterway history. The process of change under the new regime has already been set in motion, and whether its results be good or ill, it is certain that much knowledge of the old order of things as it existed until December 31, 1947, may soon be lost if it is not recorded. Consequently I have attempted to draw an accurate picture of the waterways as they existed prior to nationalization. If I have thereby succeeded in recording some features of the Inland Waterways of England which might otherwise have been forgotten, one object of this book will have been accomplished.

M.B. "CRESSY",   L. T. C. R.
Banbury, 1948.

AUTHOR'S ACKNOWLEDGEMENTS

I wish to thank both my friends on the canals and the members of the Inland Waterways Association who have assisted me, directly or indirectly, in the preparation of this book. I am particularly indebted to Messrs. C. N. Hadlow and E. C. R. Hadfield who not only gave me invaluable information and advice but also read portions of the book in manuscript and proof.

I must also acknowledge my gratitude to the following who supplied me with the photographs which illustrate the book: to Mr. C. J. Weaving of Alvechurch for Nos. 4 (*a*), 4 (*b*), 5 (*b*), 44 (*b*); to Mr. R. J. M. Sutherland for Nos. 5 (*a*), 13 (*b*), 22 (*a*); to Mr. W. C. Wright of Skipton for No. 6 (*a*); to Mr. Eric de Maré, A.R.I.B.A. for Nos. 6 (*b*), 10 (*a*); to Messrs. Glenfield & Kennedy Ltd., of Kilmarnock for No. 9 (*b*); to the Docks and Inland Waterways Executive for Nos. 12 (*a*), 12 (*b*), 14 (*a*), 18 (*a*), 28 (*a*), 28 (*b*), 29 (*a*), 29 (*b*), 38 (*a*), 42 (*b*); to Mr. C. N. Hadlow of Blisworth for Nos. 16 (*b*), 25 (*a*), 25 (*b*), 42 (*a*); to Mr. Charles Green of Foulridge for Nos. 24, 48 (*a*); to Mr. John Hey of Skipton for Nos. 26 (*a*), 26 (*b*); to Mr. H. R. Hodgkinson of Droitwich for No. 31 (*a*) and to *The Yorkshire Post* for No. 33 (*a*). All the rest of the photographs are by Angela Rolt, the majority being taken expressly for the purpose of illustrating my text.

The vignette on the title page is reproduced from an engraving by E. M. Wimperis which appears in Vol. I of *Lives of the Engineers* by Samuel Smiles. It depicts the northern entrance of Harecastle Tunnels.

L. T. C. R.

CHAPTER I

EARLY RIVER NAVIGATIONS

THE accounts of the raids carried out by the Danish invaders of Saxon England represent the first historical references to extensive inland navigation. The Danes are said to have sailed up the Severn to raid Worcester and Bridgnorth, and to have ascended the River Lea to Hertford in the year 894. They are also reputed to have navigated the Great Ouse to Tempsford when raiding Bedford. Such successful forays assume an element of surprise, and how this was achieved is a problem which appears to have escaped the notice of historians. It is true that at this time our major rivers were not artificially held up by weirs or locks so that the tide flowed far inland. Thus a part of what is now Malvern Chase between Tewkesbury and Worcester consisted of a great tract of tidal saltings often called "the Straits of Malvern," the last portion of which, Longdon Marsh, was not drained until 1872. Moreover, the fresh water flow of rivers was then undoubtedly much greater and more regular throughout the year. The extensive forests not only caused a higher aggregate rainfall, but by retaining moisture they replenished the subterranean water table and the springs which flowed from it, thus checking that rapid run off which was later to cause recurrent excessive floods and droughts with their accompanying evils of erosion, scouring and silting of channels.

Yet even when all this is taken into account, the achievements of the Danes are remarkable. On a spring tide and with plenty of "fresh" in the Severn, they might, under the conditions then obtaining, have made an uninterrupted passage to Worcester, but that they could have reached Bridgnorth in this way seems highly improbable. In the early days of river navigation, vessels travelled with the tides, depending upon their influence to lift them over fords and shallows. It has even been said that the sites of the ancient inns along Severn's bank may mark the stages over which craft could travel on successive tides. If the tides proved

15

insufficient, temporary dams of turf and brushwood were some-times thrown across the river astern of the boat to raise the water-level over the shallows. These expedients might serve well enough for the peaceable traffic of commerce, but one would have supposed that a fighting ship aground on a ford while her crew waited for the next tide or constructed a dam would have been singularly vulnerable to attack by the defending Saxon, and that any element of surprise would inevitably be lost.

In the early Middle Ages England consisted largely of self-supporting village communities. Long distance trade was very small and was chiefly confined to local markets and fairs. There was consequently little general trade on our rivers at this time and probably their most notable use was to convey building stone. To build the monastery, the church, the castle or fortified manor, water transport was used whenever possible, even small streams being pressed into service such as the Thames tributaries, Windrush, Colne and Evenlode. Even when due allowance has been made for the greater flow in those early days, the job of transporting stone on rafts or "flottes" along these streams must have been slow and arduous and only practicable at all under favourable conditions, yet it was doubtless easier than lengthy land carriage through a country devoid of metalled roads. Where such small streams were tributaries of tidal rivers, tidal influence frequently helped, for even if the tide did not run up the tributary it assisted indirectly by backing up the fresh water. Thus the tide in the Severn made possible the navigation of the Salwarpe, the Teme and the Avon for short distances, while there is a tradition that Tewkesbury Abbey was built of Caen stone shipped up the Severn and conveyed to the actual site up the Swilgate brook on spring tides.

As the Middle Ages advanced, commerce, and consequently river trade, increased considerably. But because there were as yet no serious attempts to aid navigation by artificial means apart from the occasional "scouring" of channels, the extent of such traffic was still governed by the natural suitability of the river.

The River Thames was already London's highway, but above Richmond the navigation was slow and became obstructed by numerous fish "kiddles" and mill weirs which proved a frequent source of dispute. Nevertheless, in 1432, in the course of her journey from France to Warwick, the Countess of Warwick was able to travel from Windsor to Abingdon by barge at an average speed of fifteen and a half miles per day. Such a journey, however, was doubtless dependent upon a good flow in the river, and it was not until 1624 that the river became regularly navigable up to Oxford.

Undoubtedly the greatest water highway in medieval times was the River Severn. In the fourteenth century it was navigable by large vessels from the Port of Bristol to Bewdley and by smaller craft as far upstream as Shrewsbury. In the seventeenth century the upper limit was extended to Welshpool. No other English river provided so great a length of regularly navigable course. The great tides of the Bristol Channel not only assisted navigation as they swept far up the river, but their scouring action prevented the estuary from completely silting up. This latter trouble, irremediable at this period, proved fatal to navigation on other rivers, notably the Dee, where traffic practically ceased for this reason in the fifteenth century.

The pre-eminence of the Severn was duly recognized. Normally, only the tidal portions of rivers were freely navigable. Above the tidal limit the waterway became the property of the holders of the land upon its banks. But "the King's High Stream of Severn" was a "free river" throughout its navigable length. The King's subjects might travel freely upon it, no man having the right to levy tolls. In the seventeenth and early eighteenth centuries this freedom was to contribute greatly to the growth of the industrial Midlands by giving them a decisive advantage over Continental manufacturers hampered by crippling river toll monopolies. Consequently, in the seventeenth century, the Severn was carrying a greater traffic than any river in Europe with the sole exception of the Meuse. Nevertheless, this freedom of the river was a continuous source of dispute which at times almost amounted to civil warfare between the towns on Severn's bank.

As early as 1412 the men of Bewdley had acquired a reputation not only as watermen and boatbuilders but as pirates who, by raiding and pillaging other craft, attempted to secure a monopoly of traffic. The citizens of Bristol and Gloucester petitioned Parliament praying that their craft might pass Bewdley without let or hindrance. But Bewdley was a town to be reckoned with in those days. It was a manor of the Mortimers and its fortunes prospered with those of the white rose. It became a royal borough, and its arms display to this day the sword and fetterlock of Plantagenet. As a reward to the men of Bewdley who fought beside him at Tewkesbury, Edward IV confirmed Bewdley's freedom from all tolls and tributes on the river. Three years later, to defray the cost and maintenance of the bridges which they had built across the river, Worcester and Gloucester claimed the right to exact tolls from all passing craft. This the Bewdley boatmen refused to pay despite every attempt to hinder or obstruct their passage, and although the two cities appealed to the Star Chamber against the Act of 1503 which confirmed Bewdley's freedom, the Act was upheld. Meanwhile Bewdley retaliated by once again forcibly seeking to gain a monopoly of up-river traffic. The other river towns at once protested to Parliament against this interference, claiming that: "before this time there hath been common and free passage on the water of Severn from the town of Bristowe unto the towns of Glowster, Worcester, Bewdley and Shrewsbury with botes and shutes as well as to carry wyne and all other victailes and merchandises as well as for the sustenation of the people of the said towns as of all the people of the shires in the mean wayes."

In the reign of Henry VI it was Tewkesbury's turn to have trouble. The townsfolk complained to Parliament that their barges of wheat, malt, flour and other divers goods, as they passed by the coast near the Forest of Dean, were set upon by the men of Dean "with great riot and strength, in manner of war, as enemies of a strange country," and that the "marauders not only despoil them of their merchandise, but destroy their vessels, and even cast the crews overboard and drown them." This complaint was settled by an Act of Parliament in 1430 which declared: "Because the Severn is common to all the king's liege people, to carry and re-carry within the stream of the said river to Bristol, Gloucester and Worcester, all manner of merchandise, as well in trows, or boats as in flotes, commonly called drags, and many Welshmen and others dwelling near the said river having lately assembled, arrayed as in war, and taken the drags and hewed them in pieces, and beaten the men in them, to the intent that they should hire of the said Welshmen for great sums of money their boats etc., it is ordered that all such persons so offending shall be proceeded against according to the course of the common law."

Besides revealing the perils of inland navigation in the Middle Ages, these quotations are of interest because they indicate the variety and extent of river trade at that time.

Other troubles occurred in famine years when towns would seize cargoes of foodstuffs destined for places further upstream. For this purpose Gloucester placed a chain across the river at the end of the sixteenth century and for several years held up traffic until a complaint to Parliament brought about its removal.

Because the Severn was a free river, the only Acts of Parliament concerning the river which were passed from the sixteenth to the early nineteenth century relate to the towing path and the tolls chargeable upon it. The first path, on which tolls were fixed by Act of Henry VIII in 1531, permitted haulage by gangs of men, and it was only by Act of 1811 that a continuous horse towing path was completed from Shrewsbury down to Gloucester. Prior to this the heavily laden trows were hauled up the river by gangs of bow-hauliers assisted by sail if the wind favoured. As the grooves worn in the iron under the arch of the iron bridge at Coalbrookdale indicate, the towing line was attached to a point high up on the mast of the trow on account of the steep river banks. At Blackstone, just below Bewdley, navigation further upstream became a highly skilled and arduous job owing to the numerous fords and shallows, the fall of the river between Bridgnorth and Blackstone being greater than that in the whole distance from Blackstone to the sea. Knowing this treacherous stream "like the backs of their hands" it was therefore not without reason that the Bewdley men claimed a monopoly of up-river traffic. Consequently, the masters of trows proceeding above Bewdley were accustomed to hire a local gang of hauliers at "The Mug House" inn on Bewdley Quay. Bargains were customarily sealed with a mug of beer, and it is said that a bow-haulier's bad bargain was the origin of the saying "had for a mug."

A start on this up-stream journey was usually timed to coincide with the working of the mills on the tributary streams above Bewdley because the flush from their tailraces provided a greater depth of water over the fords. If this proved insufficient, planks were arranged between the boat and the shore in such a way that the stream built up against them sufficiently to enable the boat to be hauled over. Horse haulage on the Severn provoked bitter opposition from the bow-hauliers, just as in the 1860's the horse-men were to protest against the introduction of steam tugs.

Besides trows, and probably dumb barges, there were the large rafts called "flotes" or "drags" which handled heavy or bulky cargoes. By means of these rafts, remarkable loads were floated down the river when there was plenty of "fresh." As late as the eighteenth century, the great beam engine cylinders, cast by John Wilkinson at Coalbrookdale for Boulton & Watt, and destined for the Cornish tin mines, were floated down Severn in much the same way, no doubt, as the stone had travelled which went to the building of the great medieval churches on its banks.

After the Severn, the most considerable mileage of inland navigation in medieval England was that comprising the Fossdyke, the Rivers Witham, Trent and Yorkshire Ouse and portions of their tributaries, Swale, Ure, Wharfe and Derwent. Edward IV appointed the Mayor and Aldermen of York conservators of the Yorkshire Ouse as well as of the Aire, Wharfe, Derwent, Dunn and Humber in 1462. Subsequent Acts passed by Lord Protector Cromwell and by William III for improving the navigation of the Ouse to York indicate its ancient origin.

The Trent was nominally navigable to Burton-on-Trent, but in practice navigation on this river above the tidal limit was very uncertain owing to gravel shoals, being altogether impracticable in summer on the upper reaches. It was not until 1777 that the state of the river was improved somewhat below Wilden Ferry as a result of the construction of the Trent & Mersey canal to join the river at that place.

The Fossdyke and the River Witham from the Trent at Torksey, through Lincoln to the sea at Boston, together form a very ancient line of navigation. The Fossdyke is believed to have been a Roman work, and although originally constructed primarily for drainage purposes and subsequently deepened and widened, it may fairly claim to be the oldest artificial line of inland naviga-tion in England. The Witham is said to have been a tidal naviga-tion for seagoing vessels as far as Lincoln before the Conquest, while in 1121 Henry I instigated the scouring of the Fossdyke to enable boats to pass between Lincoln and the Trent. In the late Middle Ages the navigation deteriorated, and by the end of the sixteenth century the Fossdyke had become practically un-navigable. The poet John Taylor (1580–1653) in his *A Very*

Merrie Wherry-Ferry Voyage, gives us a graphic description of the condition of the canal at that time, and one that readers of this book who have navigated some of our semi-derelict waterways will find painfully familiar and topical:

> From thence we past a Ditch of Weeds and Mud,
> Which they doe (falsly) there call FORCEDIKE Flood:
> For I'l be sworne, no flood I could find there,
> But dirt and filth, which scarce my Boat would beare,
> 'Tis 8 miles long, and there our paines was such
> As all our travell did not seeme so much,
> My men did wade and draw the Boate like Horses,
> And scarce could tugge her on with all our forces:
> Moyl'd, toyl'd, myr'd, tyr'd, still lab'ring, ever doing,
> Yet were we 9 long hours that 8 miles going.
> At last when as the Day was well-nigh spent
> We gat from FORCEDIKES floodlesse flood to TRENT.

To this poem, Taylor adds the following explanatory footnote:

It [the Fossdyke] is a passage cut thorow the Land eight miles from LINCOLNE into TRENT, but through either the peoples poverty or negligence, it is growne up with weedes, and mudde, so that in the Summer it is in many places almost dry.

It was not until 1671 that an Act to amend this state of affairs received the assent of Charles II. The preamble to this Act reads as follows:

Whereas there hath been for some hundred of yeares a good navigacion betwixt the burrough of Boston and the river of Trent by and through the citty of Lincolne, and thereby a great trade mannaged to the benefitt of those parts of Lincolneshire, and some parts of Nottinghamshire, and Yorkshire, which afforded an honest employment and livelyhood to great numbers of people. But at present the said navigacion is much obstructed and in great decay by reason that the rivers or auntient channells of Witham and Fosdyke, which runn betwixt Boston and Trent are much silted and landed up and thereby not passable with boats and lyters as formerly, to the great decay of the trade and intercourse of the said citty and all market and other towns neare any of the said rivers, which hath producet in them much poverty and depopulation. For remedy whereof and for improvement of the said navigacion, may it please your most excellent Majestie that it may bee enacted. . . . etc.

The Act went on to empower the Mayor and Corporation of Lincoln to improve the navigation of the Fossdyke and the Witham and to levy tolls upon these waterways. Nevertheless, the Corporation appear to have confined their activities to the Fossdyke. Nearly a hundred years were to elapse before the

River Witham was improved by virtue of an Act of 1762 "for restoring and maintaining the Navigation of the said River from the High Bridge, in the city of Lincoln, through the borough of Boston, to the sea."

The River Lea in Hertfordshire also appears to have been navigable in medieval times, for in 1430 Henry VI passed an Act "to scour and amend" the channel of the river. Acts of 1561 and 1739 authorize further improvement, but it was not until 1767 that an Act was passed for the construction of the present navigable cuts.

In 1514 Henry VIII passed an Act regulating tolls upon the Canterbury Stour which continued in force until 1820, while in 1539 the same monarch sanctioned "the amending of the River and Port of Exeter" which took the form of a short canal from the river to the city. In its original state, this canal was not protected by sea-doors and consequently resembled a short tidal creek.[1] In 1566, however, under the direction of John Trew of Glamorgan, the canal was extended to a deeper part of the tideway and the old entrance was blocked up. It is said that in the course of this work the first pound lock in England was constructed on this canal. Further improvements were carried out, however, in 1675 and 1697, while the Exeter Canal in its present form dates from an Act of 1819.

In 1571 Queen Elizabeth passed "an Act for making the River of Welland, in the county of Lincoln, navigable." Subsequent Acts for improving the river were passed in the eighteenth century, but like the majority of the waterways of eastern England, these were concerned primarily with drainage. Nevertheless, whereas to-day the river is only navigable to Spalding on spring tides, it was still navigable to Stamford in the early nineteenth century and was at one time extensively used for transporting stone from the famous quarries of Ketton and Collyweston.

This brings our survey down to the seventeenth century. During the sixteenth century a number of associated factors, the Tudor enclosures, the capitalization of land, and a widening of the gap between wages and prices, had compelled the English peasantry to turn increasingly from agriculture to industry to augment their slender resources. With the exception of the wool

[1] Some authorities doubt whether any appreciable work was actually done prior to 1566.

trade, this industry was very largely domestic, commercial enterprise in the modern sense of the phrase being confined to the
providers of raw materials and to the companies of merchant
venturers who marketed the products of the domestic workshop.
The latter class multiplied for a very good reason. Hitherto,
industry had existed to meet the demands of the consumer;
indeed it was the object of the Trade Guilds to regulate production upon this basis. Now, for the first time in England, there
arose an industry governed primarily by the necessity of the
producer to produce in order to earn a livelihood. It was thus
essentially competitive and expansive, and the old guild system
which had regulated supply according to demand broke down
before the irresistible pressure of the producer. Thus it came
about that the forces which generated the Industrial Revolution
were already potent in the seventeenth century. The fact that the
Revolution was destined to make comparatively slow progress
for another hundred years was probably due more to the lack of
adequate overland transport facilities than to any other single
cause. Industrial concentration, involving the changeover from
the domestic workshop to the factory was impossible on any
large scale so long as transport was unable to supply sufficient
food, fuel and raw material or to distribute the finished product.
Thus, while there was a considerable growth of industry during
the century, especially in that part of the Midlands which we now
call the Black Country, its development was governed by the
pack-horse trains which wound through the narrow miry ways
towards the river port of Bewdley.

In view of this obvious need for improved transport facilities
it may be wondered why more progress was not made in the
seventeenth and early eighteenth centuries. A number of rivers
were certainly made navigable during this period, but none of
these schemes could be called a work of great magnitude. There
are a variety of reasons for this tardy development. In the first
place there was neither the finance nor the civil engineering
ability available. In the latter respect, England lagged behind the
other nations of Europe. The only great engineering achievements of the seventeenth century, the draining of Hadfield Chase
and of the Great Level of the Fens, and the embanking of the
Thames, stand to the credit of the Dutch "Adventurers," notably
Sir Cornelius Vermuyden, assisted by the labour of Holland and

Flanders and the capital backing of the merchants of Amsterdam. Englishmen such as Andrew Yarranton or Captain Perry whose names might have ranked with those of Telford or Stephenson in another age were either restricted to propounding paper schemes or found an outlet for their skill in other countries.

The complex network of waterways in the Great Levels of the Fens, in the construction of which Sir Cornelius Vermuyden played so notable a part, were cut primarily for the purpose of land drainage and reclamation. But because the great majority of these cuts and canalized river channels were also used for navigation, some brief mention of them must be made here.

The Great Level, sixty to seventy miles in extent from north to south and from twenty to thirty miles wide, is physically an enormous sump into which the waters of the Midland shires drain via the rivers Witham, Welland, Glen, Nene and Great Ouse. Until the Middle Ages the area was an inland sea in winter and a reedy swamp in summer. Through this swamp the rivers meandered, frequently changing their courses owing to the silting of their outfalls. All through history the Great Level has been the scene of an endless struggle between man and water. Gradually the drowned lands were reclaimed and converted into rich farm lands, often well below sea level, but this ascendancy over the waters can still only be maintained by constant vigilance as the disastrous floods of 1947 revealed only too clearly. Paradoxically, owing to silting at the outfalls, the higher levels are those nearest to the Wash. These, the areas called Marshland and South Holland, were reclaimed by the Romans. But if, as is generally believed, Carr Dyke was a work of Roman origin, they also made an attempt to mitigate fresh water flooding over the whole area. Carr Dyke, traces of which may still be seen, was a great cross "catchwater" drain 60 ft. wide and 40 miles long which extended from the Nene to the Witham along a winding course beneath the higher lands which form the western boundary of the Great Level. When John Rennie was making the survey of the Fens which resulted in his great scheme for reclaiming the Wash, he examined Carr Dyke and paid high tribute to his Roman predecessors. "A more judicious and well-laid-out work I have never seen" he wrote in his report, and went on to attribute much of the flooding which was then occurring in the North Level to the neglected condition of the ancient dyke.

In the Middle Ages, the lonely islands in the reedy wastes of the Great Level, Ely, Crowland or Croyland, Ramsey, Thorney and Spinney, all became religious settlements, and most of the reclamation work carried out during this period was sponsored by these monastic communities. Prior to the thirteenth century Wisbech was on the sea at the mouth of the estuary of the Great Ouse, but thereafter a cut at Littleport diverted the waters of the Great Ouse to King's Lynn via the bed of the Little Ouse, and the old estuary silted up. In the reign of Henry VII, at the instigation of John Morton, Bishop of Ely, a canal 40 ft. wide and 40 miles long was cut from the Nene at Peterborough through Guyhirne and Wisbech to the sea. This was the first major work carried out in the Great Level, its object being the reclamation of part of the North Level. As a result, Wisbech acquired the waters of the Nene in exchange for the Great Ouse, and it is interesting to note that, thanks to the extensive works recently carried out upon the Nene, the town has once more become a port although it is now twelve miles from the sea. Bishop Morton was the pioneer of the principle, adopted ever since, of making straight artificial river cuts, and his canal became known as Morton's Leam.

Monastic stewardship ceased at the dissolution, drainage works and outfalls were neglected, and in the reigns of Elizabeth and James I disastrous floods occurred which reduced great areas of reclaimed land to their original state. In 1605 James commissioned Chief Justice Popham and a company of Londoners to undertake drainage work. Their efforts were inadequate and unsuccessful though they have been perpetuated by the names of two drains then cut, "Popham's Eau" and "the Londoners' Lode." A portion of Popham's Eau became a part of the Middle Level Navigations.

Little effective work was done until 1629 when the Commissioners of Sewers of Norfolk in session at King's Lynn resolved to ask Sir Cornelius Vermuyden to undertake the drainage of the Great Level. Vermuyden's successful work in Hadfield Chase, Malvern Chase and Sedgemoor was well known, but the appointment of a foreigner created such an outcry that the contract made with Vermuyden was abrogated and Francis Earl of Bedford was appointed undertaker in his stead. Nevertheless, the Earl could not dispense with the superior knowledge of Vermuyden and his

Fleming labourers, and it was by them that the works on what became known as the Bedford Level were then carried out. The most important of these were: the Old Bedford River 21 miles long and 70 ft. wide from Earith to Salter's Lode on the Great Ouse with three sluices at Old Bedford, Earith and Salter's Lode; Bevill's Leam, 10 miles long, from Whittlesea Mere to Guyhirne; Sam's Cut, 6 miles long, from Feltwell to the Ouse. There were numerous smaller cuts such as Sandy's Cut, near Ely, Peakirk Drain, New South Eau and Shire Drain. Various sluices were erected to keep out the tides, one type, known as a "clow," opened and closed vertically on the portcullis principle and was therefore the ancestor of the "guillotine" lock gate of the type introduced recently on the river Nene. Despite the great labour expended upon them, these works proved unsuccessful because insufficient attention was paid to deepening and improving the river outfalls.

In 1634 Charles I himself resolved to undertake the drainage of the levels, and once again Vermuyden was put in charge of the works. As a result, Morton's Leam was embanked on the south side, King's Dyke was cut from Whittlesea to Stanground and a navigable sluice erected at the latter place, while a new cut was made on the Nene below Wisbech from the Horseshoe to the sea. Vermuyden's works were still in progress when the Civil War broke out, and the Parliamentarians employed the King's project as a political weapon. It was alleged that the motive of Charles' work in the Fens was to enrich his exchequer and so enable him to rule without a parliament. This propaganda aroused the Fenlands, and it was upon the tide of revolt which was thus engendered that Oliver Cromwell, member for Huntingdon, was swept to power. The Fenmen proceeded to destroy the drainage works, cutting through the embankments and damming up the drains so that the reclaimed lands were drowned once more. Despite this overwhelming catastrophe, and in a country torn by Civil War, the indomitable Vermuyden continued to advocate his drainage plans until at last, in 1649, his opportunity came when William Earl of Bedford was authorized to proceed with the drainage works in the Great Level. With the aid of a thousand Scottish prisoners taken at the Battle of Dunbar, Vermuyden went to work once more. The works necessary to complete his long-laid plans were very extensive, and in order to complete them

Vermuyden was forced to finance them himself by selling the reclaimed lands he had acquired elsewhere. The works were declared complete in 1652, and a year later a thanksgiving service to celebrate their successful conclusion was held in Ely Cathedral. They included the embanking of extensive reaches of the rivers Welland, Nene and Great Ouse; Smith's Leam which improved the navigation between Wisbech and Peterborough; the Forty-foot Drain or Vermuyden's Eau from Welch's Dam to the Nene near Ramsey Mere; Hermitage and Denver Sluices and the New Bedford River. The latter was cut from Earith on the Ouse to Salter's Lode, reducing the length of the river between these points by 20 miles. Its course was nearly parallel with that of the Old Bedford River, and Vermuyden utilized the ground between them as a flood reservoir or "washland" by erecting high floodbanks on the south bank of the new and the north bank of the old rivers. The Bedford Level Corporation was constituted in 1663, and the area divided into North, Middle and South Levels in 1697.

Vermuyden's work, though it resulted in the reclamation of 40,000 acres of fenland, was by no means perfect, and floodings still occurred. In 1713 a violent tide, rushing up the Ouse, burst Denver Sluice, with disastrous results. The sluice was rebuilt in 1748 by the Swiss architect Labelye. Throughout the eighteenth century engineers were making improvements in the Fens, and it was left to John Rennie to complete the work of reclamation, for he it was who perceived most clearly that the secret of success lay in maintaining deep and well-regulated outfalls. Nevertheless, the pioneer work of Sir Cornelius Vermuyden, carried out by crude methods in a period of civil war, should not be forgotten. Many of the navigable waterways in the Great Level remain to this day as a monument to the skill and resolution of this indefatigable Dutch engineer.

How extensively the Fenland waterways were used for navigation is evident from the remarks of the Recorder of Lynn in 1725. Describing the rivers Ouse, Cam, Lark, Little Ouse, Wissey and Nene, he says: "The tide putting up so far into all these rivers, and filling them twice in every twenty-four hours, they were not only competently supplied with water from the sea in the driest seasons to serve for the Inland Navigation, which by means of so many branches is the most extensive in England; so that commerce and trade was constantly maintained up the River Nene to Well, March and Peterborow, above fifty miles from Lenne [Lynn] into Northampton, Rutland, Lincoln, Nottingham and Leicestershires, with vessels of fifteen tuns which easily passed up loaden in the driest seasons. And up the River Ouse could sail with forty tuns freight thirty-six miles at least from Lenne at ordinary neip tides; and a great and constant commerce was held to Cambridge, Bedford, &c. and between Cambridge and St. Ives, Huntingdon, St. Neot, Bedford and places adjacent, with a burden of fifteen tun, which is ninety miles from Lenne by water." Undergraduates frequently travelled to and from Cambridge by water, and the merchandise destined for the great Stourbridge Fair travelled there directly from the Channel ports.

Works undertaken upon the upper reaches of rivers for the express purpose of navigation involved more formidable technical and legal problems and met with greater opposition from vested interests than did the Fenland drainage works. Vermuyden's difficulties were mainly due to political and racial prejudice. The only vested interest to oppose his work was that of the "Fen-slodgers," the native population of the Great Level whose livelihood of fishing and wild-fowling was threatened by fen drainage. It is doubtful whether this opposition would have proved very formidable had it not been deliberately fostered by the Parliamentarians. The seventeenth-century river "navigators," on the other hand, were confronted by the obstacles of numerous fords, mill weirs and fish weirs or "kiddles" each of which represented a powerful and conflicting vested interest apart from the practical difficulties which they involved. Moreover, rivers were deemed private property above the tidal limit so that any scheme of river improvement legally infringed the rights of the property-holders. Hence the necessity for the undertakers to obtain some authority in the form of an Act of Parliament or a grant of letters patent. Although a number of Acts relating to rivers were passed by the Stuarts, much river improvement was carried out under letters patent which often gave the holder wide powers. For example, in 1628, upon the strength of work which he had already "been at great charge in making" upon the Great Ouse, a certain Arnold Spencer of Cople applied for and obtained a patent authorizing him to make rivers navigable for a period of eleven years. He was to enjoy the profits of such rivers for a period of eighty years, and in return to pay to the Crown the sum of £5 a year for eleven years and an additional £5 for each river which, "by the sole use of his own engine," he made navigable. These patent rights could be, and frequently were, assigned wholly or in part to others, a proceeding which led to complex part ownership. This in turn led to disputes over the ownership of sluices or the right to levy tolls which, as in the case of the Great Ouse patents, culminated in protracted litigation. In addition to these disputes between themselves, these early "navigators" were involved in endless conflicts with local mill-owners over water rights, or with parties who feared that an improved navigation would diminish their trade, increase flooding or erode their fields. As these objectors frequently resorted to physical violence, it will be appreciated that the path of river improvement at this period was generally far from smooth.

Owing to the general nature of these grants of letters patent, and the later acts passed by Charles II "for making divers rivers navigable," it is by no means easy to determine the exact chronology of river navigation development in the seventeenth century. It seems probable, however, that in the Great Ouse and the Essex Stour we have the first considerable lines of inland navigation in which artificial cuts were made expressly for navigation purposes, and a number of staunches and sluices constructed. The work on both these rivers was carried out by Arnold Spencer under his patent of 1628, and its extent is indicated in the following preamble to the renewal of this patent which was granted to him in December 1638:

Charles by the grace of God, King . . . whereas . . . Arnold Spencer, gentleman, hath informed us that by virtue of our letters patent dated the 3rd day of January in the third year of our reign he hath made the river of Ouse navigable from St. Ives to St. Neots in the county of Huntingdon and from thence within four miles of our town of Bedford in our county of Bedford to the great ease and benefit not only of the inhabitants of the said counties but also of divers other counties adjacent to the said river; and hath also provided for making navigable the river of Stour leading from Sudbury in the county of Suffolk to Manningtree in the county of Essex which is likely to prove no less commodious to the inhabitants of divers several towns in the said counties; and whereas by our said letters patent we granted to the said Arnold Spencer and his assigns power and authority for the term of eleven years to cut and make locks, sluices, bridges, cuts, dams and other inventions not repugnant to our laws, for the making of rivers and streams navigable in all places convenient within our realm of England, dominion of Wales and town of Berwick. . . .

The document later refers, in considering the tolls taken, to the "boats, barks, keels, lighters or other vessels which shall pass, sail or go through the said sluices." There was undoubtedly considerable trade on the river at this period up to Great Barford, and it is recorded that in the six months from October 20, 1627, to April 23, 1628, one trader alone carried 2,120 tons of coal through the sluices. During the Civil War the state of the navigation deteriorated and trade declined, it being no longer possible to navigate beyond St. Neots. It was not until the last quarter of the century that the navigation was restored and extended to Bedford by the enterprising Henry Ashley and his son. Ashley was one of the litigants in the long dispute which arose as a result of the assignment and leasing of portions of Spencer's original patent. His son, described as "Henry Ashley, Esq. of Eaton Socon" was later responsible for making the River Lark navigable from Mildenhall Mill to Bury St. Edmunds under the authority of an Act of 1700.

It would almost seem as if the navigation of the Great Ouse was fated throughout history to become the subject of dispute and litigation. In 1893 the upper navigation between Holywell and Bedford, which was in a bad state of repair, was bought by L. T. Simpson, Esq., of Sevenoaks, for the sum of £420 plus £5,750 as discharge of a mortgage. This gentleman commenced to repair the locks at considerable expense, but when flooding occurred in November 1894, the gates of Godmanchester lock were forced open by the local inhabitants and considerable damage done. When this happened a second time, the owner took legal action and the case finally came before the House of Lords. The Lords' decision upheld the right of the people, by virtue of an Act of Charles I, to open the lock gates in time of flood. Mr. Simpson then abandoned work on the navigation which lay more or less derelict until the 1930's when reconstruction was commenced by the local authorities assisted by the Ouse Drainage Board and a Government grant. To-day, the river is used chiefly for sugar-beet traffic.

Spencer's work upon the Great Ouse was soon followed by that of other pioneers in different parts of the country. John Malet was at work upon the navigation of the Tone and Parret between Ham

Mills and Bridgwater, while in 1635 William Sandys of Fladbury launched a project to make the Warwick Avon navigable from Tewkesbury to Stratford. An Order in Council from Charles I established a Royal Commission to advance the work, and operations began in March 1636. Forty miles of river were involved, and it is related that Sandys carried on his works "through foul and low bottoms, and especially through the deep vale of Evesham, purchaseing with excessive charge mills, meadows, and other grounds to cut in some places a course for this watry work to have a way through firm land besides the main channell." It will be noted that the costly procedure, also adopted by Spencer on the Ouse, of buying off opponents such as the local mill-owners, was already established. In 1640, Sandys obtained a patent entitling him to levy a toll of 12d. per chaldron on coal carried on the river, but it does not appear that his work was ever satisfactorily completed, particularly on the upper reaches, and it was left to his successors, Andrew Yarranton and Lord Windsor, to perfect the navigation.

In 1651 a number of undertakers, headed by Sir Richard Weston, commenced the important work of making the River Wey navigable from the Thames to Guildford. The work was completed two years later, and unlike many other undertakings of the period it has proved to be of lasting value, though it was not until 1760 that the navigation was extended to Godalming.

During the Civil War and throughout the period of the Commonwealth there was little progress in the extension of inland navigation, and although a number of theoretical schemes were propounded little practical work was done. For example, in 1656 a certain Francis Mathew addressed Cromwell and his Parliament on the advantages of making an inland water communication between London and Bristol by making the Rivers Isis and Bristol Avon navigable to their sources and connecting them by a short canal.

The Restoration heralded a resumption of activity which was authorized by Acts of 1662 and 1664 "for making divers rivers navigable." These rivers included the Itchen from Alresford to the sea, undertaken by Sir Humphrey Bennet; the River Wye from Hay to Chepstow, including also part of the Lugg; the Rivers Salwarpe and Stour in Worcestershire; the River Medway to Maidstone and Aylesford, and the Hampshire Avon from

"New Sarum" to Christchurch. Acts for making navigable the Brandon and the Waveney and the section of the Great Ouse from St. Neots to Bedford followed in 1670.

Little of this work proved satisfactory or wholly successful. Some navigations worked for a time but were subsequently abandoned, some, such as the Medway Navigation, were reconstructed in the eighteenth century, while others, notably the Hampshire Avon and the Salwarpe, proved completely abortive. In the case of the former, a disastrous flood swept away the works. The Salwarpe had been navigable to Droitwich in the Middle Ages, for in 1378 Richard II granted to the bailiffs of that town the right to levy tolls on the river. But by the seventeenth century the river had become impassable, and in 1665 the alternative proposals of constructing a canal from the Severn or improving the river were put forward. The latter having been decided upon, Lord Windsor, in conjunction with Andrew Yarranton, undertook to build six locks on the river only to find the project impracticable after five had been completed.

Andrew Yarranton of Astley, near Stourport, was undoubtedly the most enthusiastic and far-sighted advocate of inland waterways of this period, but his ambitious schemes made little headway owing to lack of the necessary financial support. Thus his work of locking the Stour from the Severn, through Kidderminster to Stourbridge, was only a small part of a much bolder project for linking the Severn with the Trent. Of this work Yarranton wrote: "The River Stoure, and some other rivers, were granted by an Act of Parliament to certain persons of Honour, and some progress was made with the work, but within a small while after the Act passed it was let fall again. But it being a Brat of my own, I was not willing it should be Abortive; therefore, I made offers to perfect it, leaving a third part of the inheritance to me and my heirs forever, and we came to an agreement. Upon which I fell on and made it completely navigable from Sturbridge to Kederminster; and carried down many hundred Tuns of Coales, and laid out near one thousand pounds, and there it was obstructed for want of money, which by Contract was to be paid." It is recorded that the first boatload of coal was brought to Kidderminster by Yarranton's navigation on March 9, 1665.

The stimulus to the improvement of the Stour was the rise of the iron industry in the district which at this time accompanied

PLATE I.—A TYPICAL EARLY RIVER NAVIGATION
(*a*) A cut on the River Kennet near Sulhampstead, Berks.
(*b*) A turf-sided lock, River Kennet   INSET I

PLATE II.—RIVER LOCKS, ANCIENT AND MODERN
(a) Navigation Weir or Flash Lock, River Avon, Cropthorne
(b) A typical modern lock on the River Thames

PLATE III.—
WHERE THE CANAL
SYSTEM BEGAN

(*a*) The Old Basin at Worsley, Bridgewater Canal, showing one of the entrances to the underground canal system

(*b*) Worsley Basin: a small boat of the type originally evolved by Brindley for use on the underground canal system

PLATE IV.—TYPICAL SCENES ON THE MIDLAND CANALS
(a) Stratford-on-Avon Canal: looking over Bearley Aqueduct, near Wootton Wawen
(b) Shrewley Tunnel on the Warwick & Birmingham Canal

PLATE V.—FORGOTTEN
WATERWAYS

(*a*) Looking east from Tid-
combe Bridge, Grand Western
Canal, Devon

(*b*) East Portal, Sousant Tunnel,
Kington & Leominster Canal

PLATE VI

(*a*) Northern Waterway: The Leeds & Liverpool Canal at Skipton, Yorkshire

(*b*) "Gone were the days of the old contour canal." Tyrley Cutting on Telford's Birmingham & Liverpool Junction Canal

PLATE VIII.—
NOTABLE
STAIRCASES

(*a*) Foxton Staircase, Grand Union Canal, Leicester section

(*b*) Bingley "Five Rise," Leeds & Liverpool Canal

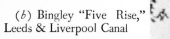

the decline of that trade in Sussex. Another and more modest work of Yarranton's in the same neighbourhood was to lock the Dick Brook from its junction with the Severn to the boundary of Astley and Shrawley parishes for the purpose of serving an ironworks situated in Shrawley woods. Here a long artificial cut with towing path, 18 ft. above the level of the brook at its terminus in a basin on the site of the ironworks, and the ruins of the locks, survive to show that at this early date Yarranton had virtually perfected the art of canal construction. The rectangular lock chambers, massively constructed of local sandstone, still stand to reveal how far in advance of his day Yarranton was. Had the times been more propitious, Yarranton and not Brindley might be remembered as the progenitor of the English canal system. One curious feature to be noted is that compared with the narrow and very tortuous channel of the brook below the cut, the lock-chambers are disproportionately large even when due allowance is made for the changes in the channel wrought in nearly three hundred years. This prompts the suggestion that Yarranton employed very small boats, locking them through in gangs of two, three or four, and transhipping to and from trows on the Severn. If this was the case, Yarranton anticipated the principle of the Shropshire Tub Boat Canals which will be mentioned subsequently. My authority for the statement that the Dick Navigation supplied an ironworks is the late Mr. R. C. Gaut's *History of Worcestershire Agriculture and Rural Evolution.* Local tradition asserts that a pottery and not an ironworks existed in Shrawley woods, and that china clay was carried up the brook from the Severn. Which of these theories is correct, or whether a pottery succeeded the ironworks is a matter for further local research.

Meanwhile the north was not idle, for in the last year of the century William III passed an Act to render the Rivers Aire and Calder navigable from Leeds and Wakefield to Weeland, this being the first link in a chain of development which eventually resulted in that network of broad waterways, part canal, part canalized river, which was destined to spread across the West Riding to connect the new industrial cities of Sheffield, Leeds, Huddersfield, Halifax and Wakefield with the Humber and so provide a tremendous stimulus to their growth. Work on the Derwent to New Malton was authorized in 1701, and on the Don from Tinsley to Doncaster in 1726. Finally, on the eve of the canal era the Calder and Hebble Navigation was constructed under Acts passed in 1758 and 1769 by John Smeaton the famous engineer of the Eddystone lighthouse and of the Forth & Clyde Canal. The confluence of these waterways, Calder, Aire, Trent, Derwent, Don and Yorkshire Ouse created the port of Goole in the same way that the construction of the Staffordshire and Worcestershire Canal was to create Stourport-on-Severn. Soon the canals were to climb and burrow through the formidable barrier of the Pennines to make these waterways part of trunk west to east routes, but for the present the pack-horse trains from Lancashire still wound their way over the moors to Sowerby Bridge where their goods were shipped down the Calder.

In the Eastern counties the navigation of the River Cam between Cambridge and Clayhithe Ferry was authorized in 1702 and that of the Nene from Peterborough to Northampton in 1714. The Idle Navigation from East Retford to Bawtry was sanctioned in 1720 and the Rivers Bure, Yare and Waveney improved by Act of 1722.

In the north-west, navigations were being extended and improved. The River Douglas Navigation from the estuary of the Ribble to Wigan was authorized by an Act of 1720. This was later acquired and superseded by the Leeds & Liverpool Canal, with the exception of the short tidal section between the Ribble and the junction of that Company's Rufford Branch. An Act of 1700 had resulted in the long overdue improvement of the River Dee to Chester, while the year 1720 also saw Acts authorizing the navigations of the Mersey & Irwell to Manchester and the extension of the Weaver Navigation from Frodsham Bridge to Winsford Bridge. The proprietors of the former soon found themselves challenged by Brindley's canals, but the latter proved to be the first chapter in a story of steady development which has resulted in one of the most efficient waterways in this country. In 1734 the Weaver Trustees were appointed; in 1807 the navigation from Weston Point to Frodsham Bridge was improved, while the present navigation with its large locks was the fruit of an Act of 1866.

Returning to the South of England, a curiosity of this period was the Stroudwater Navigation project. An Act had been passed in 1730 for making the Stroudwater navigable from Framilode to Stroud, but nothing was done. In 1759, however, some gentlemen named Kemmett, Wynde, Pynock and Bridge obtained a further Act. These ingenious individuals proposed to overcome the inevitable opposition of the mill-owners by constructing a waterway without locks of any sort. Goods were to be transhipped from one boat to another between each of a series of level pounds extending from mill to mill, and for this purpose Thomas Bridge devised a special type of pivoting, compensating double jib crane which was to be erected at each transhipment point. Its purpose was to lower cargo into the hold of one boat while it raised it out of the other. It is scarcely necessary to add that this curious project came to nothing and nearly ruined its promoters. The present Stroudwater Canal was the product of an Act of 1776 and was completed on July 24, 1779.

Moving still further south, we find that the ancient navigation of the Bristol Avon was improved to Hanham Mills by Act of 1700, and an extension to Bath authorized in 1712. Three years later the first Act was passed for the construction of the Kennet Navigation from Reading to Newbury. This last named work is notable in two respects. Firstly, it was a very ambitious undertaking for the period of its construction, being of considerable length and including many locks and artificial cuts; secondly, it aroused the most violent and active opposition from the townspeople of Reading who feared that they would thereby lose their trade. A full account of what amounted to a miniature civil war between Reading and the navigators is to be found in *Kennet Country*, by F. S. Thacker (1932). In 1720 a mob three hundred strong marched out of Reading and destroyed part of the works. But despite this and other similar hazards, the navigation was completed in 1723, boats loading 100 tons trading up to Newbury. This success inspired a fresh outbreak of violence in 1725 when organized mobs damaged boats and locks and obstructed navigation by drawing the mill sluices and draining all the water from the pounds. In July of that year a mob, encouraged by the Mayor, Recorder and Aldermen of Reading attacked the lock at Sheffield Mill where workmen were building a new weir. "At 7 o'clock in the morning deponents saw several numbers of men with axes, large sticks and clubs on the road going to the same mill; also saw great crowds of people returning back again towards Reading about 7 in the evening dancing with music before them."

Both the Bristol Avon above Hanham Mills and the Kennet Navigation were later to be taken over by the proprietors of the Kennet & Avon Canal, but the latter remains to this day substantially unaltered, including, like the Wey Navigation, some of the original turf-sided locks.

This brings our historical retrospect down to the dawn of the canal era, the natural stream of Severn and the elaborately canalized Kennet representing the extent of the technical progress so far made. In the latter, the technique of canal construction, though crude, was already in being. The next step only required an engineer of boldness and resource with the necessary capital backing by a far-sighted promoter. That combination was soon forthcoming. The Kennet Navigation may in this respect be compared with Newcomen's steam engine or the horse tramway. For just as it took a Watt and a Boulton to perfect Newcomen's crude "fire engine," or the partnership of Stephenson and Edward Pease to father the railway, so it required the genius of James Brindley, allied to the wealth and conviction of Francis Egerton, Duke of Bridgewater, to inaugurate the canal era in England.

CHAPTER II

℈

THE CANAL ERA

ALTHOUGH we are in the habit of attributing all those innovations and developments which have profoundly influenced the course of civilization and the structure of society to the unaided genius of some particular individual, in fact this is seldom or never the case. The old adage that necessity is the mother of invention is very true. Particular social and economic conditions create the necessity or pose the problem with the result that several pioneers, working independently of each other, frequently arrive at the same solution at approximately the same time.

In the last chapter we have seen how the growth of industry and the demand for transport which it created resulted in the development of the elaborately canalized river. But the conditions which initiated this original development in the latter half of the sixteenth century were intensified in the eighteenth by a fresh wave of agricultural enclosure and a further widening of the gap between wages and prices. South Lancashire, the West Riding and the Midlands were already established as industrial areas, but the river navigations were inadequate to serve their pressing needs. Apart from the fact that their traffic was liable to be delayed by floods or droughts, they stopped short at the barriers of the watersheds. Between the navigations of the Irwell and the Calder rose the formidable backbone of the Pennines to isolate west from east. The Midlands industrial area itself was perched upon the central watershed of England over 400 ft. above sea level, and its growing traffic must needs be transported over land to Bewdley on the Severn, to Winsford on the Weaver and to Burton or Wilden Ferry on the Trent. In the south, the Bristol Avon, the abortive Stroudwater Navigation project, and the navigations of Kennet and Isis pointed probing fingers towards each other from west and east, fingers that were forced apart by the rolling chalk downlands of Wiltshire and by the ridge of Cotswold that reared like a petrified wave above the Severn plain.

To connect the eastward and westward flowing rivers and to link the Midlands with the Mersey, Severn, Thames and Trent as a hub is linked by spokes to the rim of a wheel, this was the obvious solution of the transport problem. Schemes of this nature had long been advocated, but their execution called for feats of civil engineering that were hitherto unprecedented and generally considered impracticable. The technique of straightening a river channel by means of a series of short artificial cuts was well understood, but to construct a wholly artificial waterway of great length across country beset by natural barriers and to keep it supplied with water was a much more formidable undertaking.

In 1755 an Act was passed "for making navigable the River or Brook called Sankey Brook, and three several Branches thereof from the River Mersey below Sankey Bridges, up to Boardman's Stone Bridge on the South Branch, to Gerrard's Bridge on the Middle Branch, and to Penny Bridge on the North Branch, all in the County Palatine of Lancaster." In 1762 an Amendment Act enabled the undertakers to vary the line of the navigation so that it joined the Mersey at Fidler's Ferry. Despite the wording of the Act, this waterway was wholly artificial, the brook being used as a feeder only, and in later years the navigation became known as the Sankey or St. Helens Canal. It can therefore claim to be the first English canal, while it is possible to say that John Eye of Liverpool, the engineer of the Sankey Canal, should receive the credit usually accorded to James Brindley. In the same way there are those who uphold the prior claim of Newcomen to Watt's invention, or who would transfer the credit for the invention of the locomotive engine from Stephenson to Trevithick, Hedley or Matthew Murray. But in this case there can really be little doubt as to whom the honour is due. For whereas John Eye sinks into obscurity and the Sankey Canal remains to this day unconnected with the rest of the canal system except via the tidal Mersey, the modest canal executed by James Brindley for the Duke of Bridgewater from the latter's coal pits at Worsley to Manchester was destined to extend until it became a small part of a great network of inland water communications.

It was an unsatisfactory love-affair with Elizabeth, one of the three beautiful Gunning sisters and subsequently Duchess of Argyle, that induced Francis Egerton, 3rd Duke of Bridgewater, to forsake London society and to apply himself for the rest of his life to the development of his estates at Worsley. There was coal at Worsley, and the problem of transporting it to Manchester had already exercised the mind of his father who, in 1737, had obtained an Act to enable him to make the Worsley brook navigable. He had never used these powers, and Francis, when he reconsidered the scheme, decided to abandon it and to embark upon a more ambitious plan. The result was the historic Act of 1759 which was entitled: 'An Act to enable the Most Noble Francis Duke of Bridgewater, to make a navigable Cut or Canal from a certain place in the township of Salford, to or near Worsley Mill and Middlewood in the manor of Worsley, and to or near Hollin Ferry in the county palatine of Lancaster."

James Brindley, born near the hamlet of Tunstead in the Peak District of Derbyshire in 1716, was at this time practising as a millwright at Leek in North Staffordshire. Brindley, self-taught and remaining practically illiterate until the end of his life, was a natural genius and a man of extraordinary resource. A millwright in those days was by no means a specialist; he was the forerunner of both the civil and the mechanical engineer. By evolving a mechanical flint mill for the pottery trade, building an improved silk mill at Macclesfield and an atmospheric steam engine for the Walker Colliery at Newcastle-under-Lyme, Brindley had already acquired a great reputation in the North Staffordshire district. So much so that when a proposal for a canal from the Mersey to the Trent was first put forward by Earl Gower, Josiah Wedgwood and others, they commissioned Brindley to make the survey. It so happened that the brothers Thomas and John Gilbert were agents for Earl Gower and the Duke of Bridgewater respectively, and it was in this way that news of Brindley's achievements came to Worsley. On John Gilbert's recommendation, the Duke instructed Brindley to make a survey of the proposed line from Worsley to Manchester, and so the great collaboration began.

Under the Act of 1759 it was proposed that the canal should cross the Irwell on the level at Barton, locking down the slopes on either side. After what Brindley described in his diary as an "ochilor servey or a ricconitoring," he recommended that the canal should be carried over the river by an aqueduct, a course which would secure an unbroken level throughout. Such a proposal must at that time have seemed almost as fantastic as a rocket flight to the moon, and it speaks volumes for the confidence which Brindley inspired in his patron that the Duke agreed to his suggestion and obtained the necessary powers in 1760. Under this Act the proposed branch to Hollin Ferry was abandoned and a short branch to Longford Bridge substituted.

Measured by the scale of later works, the canal from Worsley to Manchester was a modest project, only 10½ miles long and level throughout. The only works of note were the embankments over Stretford Meadows and Trafford Moss, and the aqueduct at Barton. In the former case, Brindley's specific of clay-puddle confounded the sceptics who foretold that such embankments could never hold water. The projected aqueduct was ridiculed as a "castle in the air," but when the first boatload of coal sailed across it on July 17, 1761, it was acclaimed as a marvel. A contemporary called it "perhaps the greatest artificial curiosity in the world" and stated that "crowds of people, including those of the first fashion, resort to it daily."

The Duke's confidence in his engineer was triumphantly justified. In constructing his canal, Brindley solved many minor problems by means of weirs, culverts, stop gates and other contrivances which were to become the commonplaces of canal construction. Nor was his ingenuity confined to the waterway itself but extended to the boats that travelled on it and to the handling facilities at the terminals. From the basin at Worsley a tunnel was driven into the hillside which communicated directly with the coal face and became the nucleus of a network of underground waterways which eventually extended for 40 miles. These subterranean canals not only brought water transport to the coal face, they also drained the pits and supplied the main canal with water. The engineer ventilated these tunnels by means of a "water bellows," a current of air being induced by the rush of water through a large pipe or "trunk."

At its Salford terminal, the canal basin was situated at the foot of a steep hill. To save the labour of dragging the coal up this hill, Brindley again carried his canal underground a short distance so that the loaded boats could run beneath a vertical shaft. The coal was not loaded in bulk in the boats but in boxes for ready handling, and these boxes were drawn up the shaft to the surface by a crane powered by a water wheel 30 ft. in diameter which was driven by the River Medlock. To-day, when one may still see bulk-loaded coal discharged from the hold of a canal boat by means of the shovel and wheel-barrow, it is salutary to reflect that an improved method of handling such cargo was evolved by James Brindley nearly two centuries ago. Moreover, "container boats" of this type are in use to this day on the Bridgewater Canal. Examples of the small boats especially built for use on the subterranean canal system are also to be found. The tunnels themselves are no longer used, though they still drain the pits and thus feed the canal.

So far, the Duke's schemes had encountered no serious opposition, but when he proposed an extension from Longford Bridge to the Mersey at Hempstones to improve the communication between Manchester and Liverpool, the proprietors of the old Mersey & Irwell Navigation realized that their monopoly was seriously threatened. The Bill for the new extension met with the most determined opposition organized by "the old navigators" as they were called. Nevertheless, the necessary Act was passed in 1762 after a long and costly fight.

Four years later, while this extension to the Mersey was still under construction, Earl Gower, Josiah Wedgwood and their fellow promoters of North Staffordshire were granted powers to build the canal surveyed by Brindley from the Mersey at Runcorn to the Trent at Wilden Ferry. It was therefore agreed that the line of the Duke's canal should be altered to join the Trent & Mersey at Preston Brook and the Mersey at Runcorn instead of running to Hempstones. The Runcorn line was not finally completed until 1773, while in 1795 a further extension of the Duke's canal was sanctioned from Worsley to Leigh where it was later joined by the Leeds & Liverpool Canal.

The Bridgewater Canal was a bold and unique achievement especially when it is realized that it was not the product of an army of engineers backed by a body of wealthy shareholders, but the work of two men only, one of whom staked his reputation and the other the whole of his fortune upon what their contemporaries regarded as a fantastic enterprise. Its successful completion brought to Brindley immortal fame as the first great English Civil Engineer, and to the Duke an immense fortune. Its effect upon the growth of Manchester can scarcely be over-estimated, in fact it may be said that in partnership with the steam engine and the spinning jenny, the Duke's canal launched the factory phase of the Industrial Revolution in South Lancashire.

Yet compared with the projected waterway from the Mersey to the Trent, the Bridgewater Canal was a minor work of only local importance. In fact, the Trent & Mersey Canal was itself only the master link in a still bolder scheme, surveyed and envisaged in its entirety by Brindley. Without accurate maps or surveying equipment, and in an England almost devoid of metalled roads, Brindley had planned to link Mersey, Severn, Thames and Trent by means of a great silver cross consisting of over 260 miles of canals. Because it formed both the north-western and north-eastern arms of this cross, the Trent & Mersey was the key to the whole plan. Brindley realized this when he urged the promoters to call it, not "the canal from the Trent to the Mersey," but "The Grand Trunk."

Climbing out of the Cheshire plain in a south-easterly direction, and piercing the central watershed at Harecastle to join the upper valley of the Trent, the line of the Grand Trunk took the form of a broad V drawn across the North Midlands. It was from the southernmost point of this V at Great Haywood and Fradley in Staffordshire, that Brindley planned the connecting links to Severn and Thames; the Staffordshire & Worcestershire Canal to Stourport, and the longer line of the Coventry and Oxford Canals to the Thames at Oxford.

The Staffordshire & Worcestershire Canal followed a short and comparatively easy course through the valleys of the Penk, Smestow and Stour with a 10-mile summit level from Gailey to Compton near Wolverhampton. It was originally projected to join the Severn at Bewdley, but the inhabitants of that thriving inland port disdainfully rejected what they called "the stinking ditch," and the engineer was not loath to follow the easier route down the Stour valley throughout, a course which soon resulted in the eclipse of Bewdley and the rise of Stourport. Apart from aqueducts over the Trent, Penk and Stour, a certain amount of rock cutting and a short tunnel at Cookley, there were few works of much magnitude involved. Consequently it was the only section of his great project which the engineer lived to see completed. The Act for the Staffordshire & Worcestershire had been obtained in 1766, the same year as the Grand Trunk Act, and it was opened for traffic in 1771. On the 27th of September in the following year, James Brindley died at his home at Turnhurst, near Golden Hill, from the effects of a chill caught while he was surveying the Caldon Branch of the Grand Trunk. He was fifty-six. After his death, the works upon which he was engaged were completed by his brother-in-law, Hugh Henshall, clerk of the works of the Grand Trunk, and by his able pupil Robert Whitworth.

Brindley saw his Grand Trunk finished with the exception of Harecastle Tunnel. A tunnel 2,897 yards long was a work which involved a feat of civil engineering that was quite unprecedented, and, like the Barton Aqueduct, it was christened "Brindley's Air Castle" by local punsters. It was finally completed in 1777 after eleven years of unremitting labour. As at Worsley, so at Harecastle, branch tunnels were driven to the workings of the Golden Hill collieries and performed the three-fold function of transporting the coal, draining the pits and supplying the summit level of the canal.

Meanwhile the long line from Fradley Junction to the Thames was still far from complete. The Acts for the Coventry and the Oxford Canals had been obtained in 1768 and 1769, but progress was slow. After the first 17 miles of the Coventry Canal from Coventry to Atherstone had been constructed, the Company ran short of funds and after a disagreement Brindley resigned from his position as engineer. The canal was continued as far as Fazeley where work finally came to a standstill until 1782. In that year the proprietors of the Grand Trunk and of the projected Birmingham & Fazeley Canal agreed to complete between them the remaining 11 miles of the Coventry Canal from Fazeley to Fradley. This portion was opened for traffic in July 1790, by which time the Birmingham & Fazeley Canal was also completed. The Coventry Company subsequently acquired the 5½-mile section constructed by the Grand Trunk from Fradley to Whittington Brook, but the other portion remained a part of the Birmingham canal system.

The Oxford Company also became financially embarrassed and had to obtain powers to raise additional funds. Napton was reached in 1775 and Banbury in March 1778. Work then ceased until April 1786, and so it was not until January 1790 that Oxford was reached and the first boatload of Coventry coal sailed on to the Thames. Meanwhile many other canal projects had been successfully launched and in some cases opened for traffic, but Brindley's great work of uniting the four rivers had formed the skeleton of the Midland canal system and determined the course of future development so that others, emboldened by the success of the Bridgewater Canal, followed where he had led.

In addition to the waterways already mentioned, Brindley was consulted on many other canal projects, including that for a canal from Leeds to Liverpool. He was also engineer of the Birmingham, Droitwich and Chesterfield Canals. Of these the first named was the most important, for, by linking Birmingham and Wolverhampton with the Staffordshire & Worcestershire Canal at Aldersley Junction, it brought water transport to the heart of the Black Country. It was completed in 1771, and in the same year the Droitwich Barge Canal down the valley of the Salwarpe to the Severn was opened for traffic. The 45 miles of canal from Chesterfield to the Trent at West Stockwith, including a long tunnel at Norwood (opened May 9, 1775), were a more formidable proposition which was carried to completion in 1776 by Hugh Henshall.

These early canals executed by Brindley reflect their engineer's policy which was to concentrate the locks together wherever it was practicable and to provide long level pounds between. In the pursuit of this policy, and in order to reduce earthworks to a minimum, his surveys followed the contours with the result that his canals are often very circuitous. He argued that such a course, serving a wide area, would be more valuable than a short route between terminals, and there is no substance in the legend that the devious windings of his canals were due to the fact that the contractors were paid by the mile or that the promotors had an eye on the mileage tolls! In Brindley's day, when the ancient rural economy of England had not yet foundered under the impact of industrialism, there was much to be said for this argument. But he did not foresee how soon the Industrial Revolution which he helped to foster would suck the life and trade out of the countryside into the new towns and by so doing change the trade routes. The future demand was to be for improved communications between the new industrial areas and the ports. So soon did this demand arise that even before the railway age dawned, portions of Brindley's canals had already been straightened while others had seen much of their traffic pass to more direct routes. Probably the most characteristic example of Brindley's contour canal work still in use is the tortuous summit level of the Oxford Canal between Marston Doles and Claydon.

To any observant traveller who passes through one of Brindley's canals it will be plainly apparent that the engineer's methods were purely empirical. Like all pioneers, there was no accumulated fund of experience upon which he could draw, no cut-and-dried formula to aid him. His canals show no evidence of that "cut and fill" principle which has become a commonplace of modern surveying whereby levels are chosen in such a way that the amount of soil excavated in cuttings equals as nearly as possible the amount required to form the embankments. The minute exactitude with which his waterways follow the natural contour reveal a policy of avoiding the slightest earthwork, and where a cutting or embankment becomes unavoidable the work was considered in isolation as the grass-grown spoil mounds and excavations reveal. Lacking precise knowledge of critical slopes in varying soil formations, Brindley played for safety. He built his embankments of massive breadth and chose to tunnel rather than excavate a cutting of any considerable depth. For example, his tunnel on the Oxford Canal at Fenny Compton, now opened out, could scarcely have been more than 40 ft. below the surface at its deepest point. Nevertheless, these works of Brindley are the solid and enduring foundations of that great civil engineering technique which his successors were destined so soon to perfect with such mighty results.

The historical parallel which may be drawn between the periods of canal and railway construction in England is extraordinarily exact. Just as the old river navigations paved the way for the canals which superseded many of them, so the canals in their turn stimulated feeder tram roads, the Sirhowey, the Leicester & Swannington and the Peak Forest, for example. The canal proprietors little reckoned that these puny plate-ways would so soon grow into steel monsters which would threaten the life of their parents. Both eras began with modest projects, constructed in an atmosphere of scepticism and ridicule, in the same north-western corner of England. In each case this small beginning was followed by a brief period of more ambitious construction which was soon succeeded by a fever of promotion as the success of the new form of transport became apparent.

Smeaton (in the earlier phase), Whitworth, Henshall, Outram, Jessop, Rennie and Telford were the foremost engineers of the canal era which followed the success of Brindley's work. From 1770 onwards the number of new canal promotions gradually increased and culminated, in 1792, in a riot of speculation comparable with the "railway mania" of 1845. Typical of the events of this memorable year is John Latimer's[1] description of the canal mania in the West Country.

On the 20th November a meeting to promote the construction of a canal from Bristol to Gloucester was held in the Guildhall, when the scheme was enthusiastically supported by influential persons, who struggled violently with each other in their rush to the subscription book. A few days later, a Somerset paper announced that a meeting would be held at Wells to promote a canal from Bristol to Taunton. The design had been formed in this city [Bristol], but the promoters sought to keep it a secret, and bought up all the newspapers containing the advertisement. The news nevertheless leaked out on the evening before the intended gathering, and a host of speculators set off to secure shares in the undertaking, some arriving only to find that the subscription list was full. The third meeting was at Devizes, on the 12th December. Only one day's notice was given of this movement, which was to promote a canal from Bristol to Southampton and London, but the news rapidly spread, and thousands of intending subscribers rushed to the little town, where the proposed capital was offered several times over. The "race to Devizes" on the part of Bristolians, who had hired or bought up at absurd prices all the old hacks that could be found, and plunged along the miry roads through a long wintry night, was attended with many comic incidents. A legion of schemes followed, Bristol being the proposed terminus of canals to all parts of the country, and some of the projected waterways running in close proximity to each other. A pamphlet published in 1795, narrating the story of the mania, states that the passion of speculation spread like an epidemical disease through the city, every man believing that he would gain thousands by his adventures. The shares which were at 50 premium today were expected to rise to 60 tomorrow and to 100 in a week. Unfortunately for these dreams, the financial panic to be noticed presently caused a general collapse, and the only local proposal carried out was the comparatively insignificant scheme for uniting the Kennet with the Avon.

The fact that this story was to be repeated exactly in 1845 would certainly seem to confirm the gloomy dictum that mankind does not profit by the example of history.

While the events of the railway era have been very fully recorded, a detailed history of the canal period, the herculean labours of the constructors, the conflicts between the promoters

[1] John Latimer, *The Annals of Bristol in the 18th century* (1893).

and their opposers or with each other, and the many fanciful schemes which were dangled before gullible speculators, this has still to be written. All that can be done in the space of this chapter is to notice briefly the most notable canals which were built in each district of England during the heyday of construction, with a side glance later at a few of the abortive or short-lived schemes.

In the North, the most pressing need was obviously for a waterway which would cross the barrier of the Pennines to unite the industrial areas of Lancashire and Yorkshire, and this the Leeds & Liverpool Canal fulfilled. Originally projected and surveyed by a Mr. Longbotham of Halifax, the promoters called in Brindley to re-survey following the success of the Bridgewater Canal, and construction began in 1770. But it was a very formidable undertaking. Not only did the canal pass through difficult country, but the distance from the junction with the Aire & Calder Navigation at Leeds to Pall Mall Basin at Liverpool was 127 miles, the longest single main line of artificial waterway ever constructed by one company in the British Isles. Through the easier country near its western and eastern terminals, the work proceeded rapidly. The section from Liverpool to Newburgh was opened in 1775, and that from Leeds to Holmbridge in June 1777. The crossing of the central watershed, however, was a very different proposition. The work far exceeded the original estimates and it was not until October 1816, forty-six years after construction began, that the last section between Blackburn and Johnson's Hillock was opened for traffic. The most difficult and expensive section of all had been the $17\frac{1}{2}$ miles from Foulridge to Enfield which included Foulridge Summit Tunnel, Gannow Tunnel, and the great embankment and aqueduct over the valley of the Calder at Burnley. In its later stages the work was directed by Robert Whitworth who re-surveyed and departed from the original line in many places. Furthermore, by agreement between the two companies the Leeds & Liverpool obtained what would be described in railway parlance as "running powers" over 11 miles of the Lancaster Canal, South End, from Johnson's Hillock to Wigan top lock. Finally, in the same year that saw the completion of their main line, the Company obtained powers to construct a branch from Wigan to join the Leigh branch of the Bridgewater Canal. This gave them a route to Manchester, and linked their main line with the Canal system of the Midlands.

In 1794, while the Leeds & Liverpool was still far from complete, two further trans-Pennine routes were promoted. These were the Rochdale Canal, engineered by Rennie, from the Bridgewater Canal terminus at Castlefield, Manchester, to the Calder & Hebble Navigation at Sowerby Bridge, and the Huddersfield Canal. The latter was planned to connect two canals which had already been wholly or partially constructed; the Ashton Canal from Ducie Street, Manchester, to Ashton-under-Lyne on the west, and Sir John Ramsden's Canal from the Calder & Hebble at Cooper Bridge to Huddersfield on the east.

Samuel Smiles, in his biography of John Rennie, gives the following graphic description of the Rochdale Canal:

From the rugged nature of the country over which the canal had to be carried—having to be lifted from lock to lock over the great mountain-ridge known as "the backbone of England"—few works have had greater physical obstacles to encounter than this between Rochdale and Todmorden. A little before the traveller by railway enters the tunnel near Littleborough, on his way between Manchester and Leeds, he can discern the canal mounting up the rocky sides of the hills until it is lost in the distance; and as he emerges from the tunnel at its other end, it is again observed descending from the hilltops by a flight of locks down to the level of the railway. In crossing the range at one place, a stupendous cutting, fifty feet deep, had to be blasted through hard rock. In other places, where it climbs along the face of the hill, it is overhung by precipices. On the Yorkshire side, at Todmorden, the valley grows narrower and narrower, overhung by steep, often almost perpendicular, rocks of millstone-grit, with room, in many parts, for only the waterway, the turnpike road, and the little river Calder in the bottom of the ravine. At some points, where space allowed, there were mills and manufacturing establishments jealous of their water-supply, which the engineer of the line had carefully to avoid. It was also necessary to provide against the canal being swept away by the winter's floods of the Calder, which rushed down with immense violence from Blackstone Edge. Large reservoirs had to be carefully contrived to store up water against summer droughts for the purposes of the navigation, as well as to compensate the numerous mills along the valley below. One of these, fourteen feet deep, was dug in a bog on Blackstone Edge, and others, of large dimensions, were formed at various points along the hill route. But as these expedients were of themselves insufficient, powerful steam-engines were also erected to pump back the lockage water into the canal above, as well as into side-ponds near the locks to serve for reservoirs, and thus economize the supply to the greatest extent. No more formidable difficulties, indeed, were encountered by George Stephenson, in constructing the railway passing by tunnel under the same range of hills, than were overcome by Mr. Rennie in carrying out the works of this great canal undertaking. The skill and judgement with which he planned them reflected the greatest credit on their designer;

and whoever examines the works at this day—even after all that has been accomplished in canal and railway engineering—will admit that the mark of a master's hand is unmistakably stamped upon them."

Whereas the Rochdale was a broad canal with 74 ft. × 14 ft. locks, the Huddersfield was built to the narrow, Midlands gauge of 70 ft. × 7 ft. It climbs to the highest canal summit level in England, 644 ft. above sea level, and the chief obstacle to its completion was the cutting of the tremendous 3-mile tunnel beneath Standedge. Outram was the engineer responsible.

The object of both these waterways was to provide a more direct east to west route than that which was afforded by the circuitous Leeds & Liverpool. The fact that both were completed some years before the latter must have occasioned the Leeds & Liverpool proprietors some chagrin. Yet in this case the years have vindicated the wisdom of Brindley's policy, for the considerable saving in mileage which the Rochdale, and the still more direct Huddersfield, certainly achieved, was more than offset by the extremely heavy lockage. They amount to nothing more than ladders of locks ascending and descending the watershed. This is particularly true in the case of the Huddersfield. The locks on the Leeds & Liverpool, on the other hand, are concentrated in flights and divided by long levels of 18, 23, 8, 10, and 29½ miles on the Brindley plan, an arrangement which makes for easier working and supervision. The Leeds & Liverpool is still a busy waterway to-day, while the Rochdale no longer carries trade and the Huddersfield has been abandoned. The latter was particularly unfortunate in the choice of gauge, for the locks on Sir John Ramsden's Canal and on the Calder & Hebble Navigation were built short and wide to suit Yorkshire keels, with the result that only very small boats 58 ft. × 7 ft. could pass from one canal to the other.

While these three east to west routes were building, canal construction was proceeding apace on both sides of the Pennines. The Barnsley and Dearne & Dove Canals, engineered by Jessop and Whitworth respectively, linked Barnsley and each other with the Aire & Calder near Wakefield, and the River Don Navigation at Swinton. The latter was also provided with a more direct link to the Trent by means of the Stainforth & Keadby Canal.

West of the Pennines, the Lancaster Canal was promoted in 1792, John Rennie being the engineer, and its course to be from

Wigan to Kendal via Preston and Lancaster. Constructional and financial difficulties prevented completion of the section of this canal from Walton Summit northwards to Preston South Basin, and until 1857, when it was abandoned, a tramroad connected these two places. The North End remained isolated from the rest of the canal system, having only a connection with the sea via its Glasson Dock Branch near Lancaster. The southern portion was eventually leased by the Leeds & Liverpool Company, who, as has been already mentioned, used the greater part of it as a section of their main line. A broad canal, the Lancaster is notable for its long level of 43 miles from Preston to Tewitfield and for the fine aqueduct over the River Lune completed in July 1796.

In 1794 the Peak Forest Canal was promoted by Samuel Oldknow, Outram being appointed engineer. This canal extended from the Ashton Canal at Dukinfield to a terminus at Bugsworth and was completed on May 1, 1800. It includes a notable aqueduct at Marple, which, with its pierced spandrels, seems to bear the hallmark of Smeaton's designs although that engineer died in 1792. Later, this waterway was to be connected with the Cromford Canal in Derbyshire by the remarkable Cromford & High Peak Railway engineered by Jessop.

Further south, the Chester Canal, a broad waterway from the Dee at Chester to Nantwich, was authorized in 1772 and completed in 1780. In 1793 the Ellesmere Canal, a much more ambitious project, was launched, and Thomas Telford, who was at the same time executing the canal from Donnington to Shrewsbury, was appointed engineer. The main line of this canal was to extend from the Mersey at Netherpool (or Ellesmere Port as it was later to be called) to the Severn at Shrewsbury. There were to be numerous branches, of which the more important were as follows: From Pont Cysyllte, near Ruabon, to Llangollen and (as a navigable feeder) to Llantisilio; from Welsh Frankton to Ellesmere and Whitchurch; from Lockgate Bridge to a junction with the Eastern Branch of the Montgomeryshire Canal (promoted 1794) at Carreghofa. The main line traversed the difficult country of the Welsh Marches, and Telford planned the works on a magnificent scale. He drove a tunnel complete with a towing path at Chirk and built great aqueducts which spanned the valleys of the Dee and Ceiriog. But alas, depression followed the rosy prospects of the boom years, and money ran short. The section from Chester, through Ruabon to Pont Cysyllte, was never executed, neither was the long tunnel which was to take the canal through the high ground between Weston Wharf and the Severn at Shrewsbury. Apart from the section from Netherpool to Chester, which was connected to the Chester Canal, the whole line, including the Montgomeryshire Canal to Welshpool and Newtown, was isolated from the rest of the canal system. To remedy this, in default of the original scheme, the Company obtained powers in 1801 to extend the Whitchurch branch from Whitchurch to a junction with the Chester Canal at Hurleston near Nantwich.

Turning now to the Midlands, we find canals extending like spokes from the hub of the Black Country towards the Severn and the original canals of "the cross." The Wyrley & Essington Canal (1792) connected the Cannock Chase coal-field with Lichfield and with the Coventry Canal at Huddlesford Junction. Next, moving in a clockwise direction, came the Birmingham & Fazeley which has already been mentioned. The Warwick & Birmingham (1793) and the Warwick & Braunston (1794) linked Birmingham more directly with the Oxford Canal. In 1796, however, the latter obtained powers to carry their canal to Napton instead of to Braunston. In 1791 the Worcester & Birmingham Canal was projected to provide Birmingham with a more direct route to the Severn. This proved an arduous and costly work involving much tunnelling and lockage, while apart from these natural difficulties the luckless proprietors became financially embarrassed by costly disputes over water rights and extravagant compensation demands. Consequently the canal was not completed until 1815. The Stratford Canal from the Worcester & Birmingham at King's Norton to the Upper Avon Navigation at Stratford provided yet another link between Birmingham and the Severn and was also joined, after some dispute between the two companies, with the Warwick & Birmingham at Kingswood. The proprietors of the Dudley Canal (1776) had access to the Severn in the west via the Stourbridge Canal, which was authorized in the same year, from the Staffordshire & Worcestershire at Stourton Bridge to Black Delph. But in 1785 and 1793 they obtained powers to extend northwards to the Birmingham Canal through Dudley Tunnel, and eastwards to join the Worcester & Birmingham at Selly Oak by Halesowen and Lappal Tunnel.

Elsewhere in the Midlands, Robert Whitworth constructed the Ashby Canal, 30 miles long, from the Leicestershire coal-field to the Coventry Canal at Marston, and remarkable for the fact that it was built without a lock. Between them, the Coventry, Oxford and Ashby Canals thus made up an unbroken level of 70 miles extending from Atherstone to Hillmorton, Coventry and Moira respectively, the longest canal level in England. Further eastward, the Derby, Nutbrook, Cromford, Erewash and Nottingham Canals linked the two county towns with the River Trent and the Nottinghamshire coal-field, while through the rich vale of Belvoir the Grantham Canal (1793–97) meandered on its leisurely course from Trent Bridge. The River Soar, canalized by the Loughborough and Leicester Navigation Companies, connected these towns with the Trent. In 1793 the Leicestershire & Northamptonshire Union Canal was authorized but, like the Ellesmere Canal, it never reached its objective. A broad canal, it was projected to run from the Soar at Leicester to the Nene near Northampton, but it never got further than Market Harborough and was later referred to as "The Old Union." William Jessop was the engineer responsible for most of the waterways in this part of England.

So far, the only link between this growing network of Midland waterways and London was the tortuous line of the Oxford Canal and the River Thames. Thus the most important project of this boom period was that of the Grand Junction Canal, launched in 1793. The main line of this canal was to run from the Oxford Canal at Braunston to the Thames at Brentford with branches to the Nene at Northampton, to Buckingham, Newport Pagnell, Aylesbury, Wendover and Paddington. It tunnelled through the ironstone ridges at Braunston and Blisworth, and climbed the Chilterns to its summit level near Tring, taking a course which was later to be closely followed by the London & Birmingham Railway. A Mr. Barnes carried out the original survey, but several other engineers, including Telford and Jessop, assisted in the work, and the line was opened throughout by the completion of the Blisworth Tunnel in 1805.

In the South of England, as in the North, interest chiefly centred upon communications between east and west coasts. The first of these routes was the Thames & Severn Canal, from the Stroudwater Navigation at Wallbridge, near Stroud, to the Thames at

Inglesham near Lechlade. Originally surveyed by Brindley, the Act authorizing construction was not passed until 1783, and Brindley's pupil Robert Whitworth was the engineer. The canal ascends the Golden Valley by a flight of 28 locks to the great summit tunnel, over 2 miles long, at Sapperton which pierces the ridge of the Cotswolds. This proved the chief obstacle to the completion of the canal, the tunnel in places requiring no lining, so solid were the beds of limestone rock through which it was driven. The borings met on April 20, 1789, and on the 19th November following the first boat travelled from the Severn to the Thames amidst much local rejoicing.

The second east to west route was the Kennet & Avon Canal (1794) from Newbury to Bath engineered by John Rennie. Rennie's survey avoided lengthy tunnelling, but he experienced considerable trouble in securing a watertight bed for the canal on the 15-mile level over the chalk and sand of the Vale of Pewsey between Wootton Rivers and Devizes. He also had difficulty in the valley of the Avon where the canal bed is terraced on a steep slope above the river. Here heavy rain caused serious slips in the clay, a trouble which was only overcome by an elaborate system of drainage culverts driven into the hillside. The canal was opened for traffic in 1810, and the Company subsequently acquired the Kennet Navigation from Reading to Newbury, and a controlling interest in the Avon between Bath and Hanham. In 1811, a canal from Bath to Bristol was proposed but never executed.

The connection of these waterways, and those of the Midlands, with the Severn, greatly increased the traffic on that river and stimulated an ambitious proposal to bypass the dangerous and circuitous tidal section between Berkeley and Gloucester by means of a ship canal. This was a project of unique magnitude. The canal was to be 70 ft. wide and 15 ft. deep, and it was to extend for $18\frac{1}{4}$ miles on one level from the Severn at Berkeley Pill to Gloucester. The Act authorizing its construction was passed on March 28, 1793, but so formidable was the work that it was not until 1827 that England's first ship canal was opened for traffic and has proved itself of the greatest value ever since. In the period which elapsed between authorization and completion, several further Acts were passed relating to the canal. Its maximum depth was increased to 18 ft., its course was varied and, although the canal has retained its original title, the southern terminus at Berkeley Pill was abandoned. Instead, a less favourable junction with the river at Sharpness Point reduced the length of the waterway to 16½ miles. In 1874 a new and larger entrance lock and an extensive new dock were opened at Sharpness, and the company then called itself the Sharpness New Docks & Gloucester & Birmingham Navigation Company.

Between the Thames & Severn and the Kennet & Avon Canals ran the system of the Wilts & Berks Canal which was authorized in 1795. Unlike its neighbours, the Wilts & Berks was a narrow canal with a main line running from the Thames at Abingdon through the Vale of White Horse to Swindon and thence through Wootton Bassett, Laycock Abbey and Melksham to join the Kennet & Avon Canal at Semington, below the Devizes locks. There were short branches to Wantage, Longcot, Calne and Chippenham. It was opened throughout on September 22, 1810. The Company subsequently acquired the North Wilts Canal (1813) which ran from their canal at Eastcot, Swindon, to the Thames & Severn at Weymoor Bridge near Cricklade. It was also proposed to effect a direct link with the Grand Junction by means of a canal from Abingdon to Aylesbury via Thame, but this project never materialized. The Wilts & Berks, though it can scarcely be numbered among the abortive schemes, proved a luckless undertaking, and it was finally abandoned in 1914.

Serving predominantly rural areas, the canals of the South never enjoyed the same degree of prosperity that rapid industrial development brought to the proprietors of the waterways of the Midlands and the North. Although it has never been legally abandoned, and still carries traffic at its eastern end, the history of the Basingstoke Canal from the Wey at Woodham to Basingstoke has been similar to that of the Wilts & Berks. Proposals for connecting its western end with the Andover and Kennet & Avon Canals were never carried out.

The canal boom, which reached its peak in 1793, was followed by the inevitable slump, a slump which was aggravated by the adverse economic and social conditions created by the Napoleonic wars. Canal companies authorized in the boom years struggled to complete their lines in the face of rapidly rising costs, while between the years 1795 and 1825 there were only three new canal promotions which were destined to become important and lasting links in the system. These were the short Sheffield Canal from the River Don at Tinsley (1815), the Grand Union and the Regent's Canals (1810 and 1812).

The Grand Union Company's main line extended from the Grand Junction at Norton near Long Buckby to a junction with the Old Union Canal at Foxton near Market Harborough. By thus bridging the gap left by the failure of the Leicester & Northants Union Company to finish their line to the Nene, the Grand Union opened up a direct water route between London, Nottingham, Derby and the Trent. The works, planned by Bevan, one of the engineers of the Grand Junction, were ably executed upon the Brindley model, the Watford and Foxton locks being concentrated at each end of a 20-mile summit level which included two considerable tunnels at Crick and Husbands Bosworth. Unfortunately, however, 7-ft. locks were built, and these constitute a bottle-neck in an otherwise all wide route from London to the Trent. The canal was amalgamated with the Grand Junction in 1894, and for a time the Foxton locks were superseded by the short-lived Foxton Lift.

Although only 8½ miles long, the Regent's Canal is one of the most important and best known canals in England because it brought water transport into the heart of London. Generations of North Londoners have had their imagination stirred by the strange spectacle of boats moving over this narrow ribbon of water amid the London streets; a momentary glimpse from the top of a bus, perhaps, or a more comprehensive view in the green oasis of Regent's Park. Yet very few know the course of London's canal. It commences at a junction with the Paddington branch of the Grand Junction Canal near the point where Warwick Avenue and the Harrow Road unite, and the short Maida Hill Tunnel carries it beneath the Edgware Road in the direction of Regent's Park. Originally, by means of a branch ending in a Basin at Cumberland Market, the canal made a complete semicircle round the Park, but this branch has now been filled in and built over, and the main line leaves the park by an acute turn after it has passed the zoological gardens, describing another and more northerly loop through Camden Town. Passing a little to the north of King's Cross Station and under the Caledonian Road, it disappears into another and longer tunnel at Islington. The line of this tunnel passes beneath Islington High Street just north of the "Angel," and its eastern portal is by Graham Street off the City Road. Here is City Road Basin which, in the past, witnessed the arrival and departure of generations of "fly-boats." Heading due east beneath innumerable bridges, the canal reaches Victoria Park where it swings south, passing under the Old Ford, Mile End and Commercial Roads to reach its terminus and London River at Regent's Canal Dock, Limehouse. In this course there are twelve locks, falling to Limehouse and in duplicate, the first being at Hampstead Road. As originally projected, the Regent's Canal apparently included some curious devices for economizing water. I have discovered no description of them, and they were evidently a failure, for Priestley comments: "To have described the cassoon locks and other mechanical inventions made use of to save the expenditure of water upon this canal, would answer no purpose as they have been exploded, and the usual and more simple means adopted." Presumably one device was a form of inclined lift, as the company were authorized to construct such lifts by their original Act.

In 1855 the Regent's Canal Company acquired the short Hertford Union or Sir George Duckett's Canal (opened 1824) which linked their waterway at Old Ford with the River Lee Navigation at Stratford Marsh. Finally, in our own day, the Regent's Canal became a part of the Grand Union system.

Throughout this period the majority of the established canal companies were basking in the cloudless sunshine of a brief hey-day of unexampled prosperity. The fortunate shareholders in these undertakings reaped profits of a magnitude which may be judged from the following typical list of share selling prices in 1824[1]

Canal	Price of Issue	Dividend	Selling Price
Trent & Mersey	£100	£75	£2,200
Loughborough Nav.	£100	£197	£4,600
Coventry	£100	£44	£1,300
Grand Junction	£100	£10	£290

But their monopoly was soon to be threatened. The year 1825 began another period of speculation which was to culminate in the railway mania, and the Liverpool & Manchester Railway proposal in that year shook the canal proprietors out of their

[1] As quoted by Westall and others.

complacency. To counter the new railway threat, expensive improvements to certain of the old trunk routes were put in hand and new direct cut-off canals were promoted. Thomas Telford was the engineer concerned with nearly all these schemes.

In 1827 Telford successfully completed Harecastle New Tunnel which relieved traffic congestion in Brindley's restricted tunnel on the summit of the Trent & Mersey. Between 1824 and 1834 he carried out a complete reconstruction of the main line of the Birmingham Canal between Birmingham and Aldersley Junction. By means of a deep cut at Smethwick, spanned by graceful high-level overbridges in the cast-iron of which he was such a master, Telford reduced the length of the main line by 8 miles, and eliminated 9 locks and 3 pumping stations. Brindley's old main line then became a series of loops and branches. Similar improvements were carried out on the main line of the Oxford Canal between Hawkesbury and Napton in the years 1829–34. Here, a series of embankments and deep cuts reduced the length of Brindley's old contour canal between these points by no less than $13\frac{1}{2}$ miles.

Meanwhile the need for more direct routes between the Midlands and the north-west led to the promotion, in 1826, of the Birmingham & Liverpool Junction and the Macclesfield Canals, Telford being the engineer in each case. The former ran from the Staffordshire & Worcestershire Canal at Autherley, half a mile from the junction of the Birmingham Canal at Aldersley, to the terminus of the Chester Canal at Basin End, Nantwich, and so made a very direct canal from the Black Country to Ellesmere Port which avoided the heavy lockage of the longer Trent & Mersey route. The Macclesfield Canal, from the Trent & Mersey at Hardingswood through Congleton and Macclesfield to the Peak Forest Canal at Marple, provided an equally direct communication between the Potteries and Manchester. Anyone travelling over either of these waterways cannot fail to be struck by the directness of their course and the magnitude of the earthworks which made this possible. Gone were the days of the meandering contour canal of which the summit level of the Grand Union between Watford and Foxton was the last example to be built. Telford had mastered the "cut and fill" technique, and the canyon-like cuttings and towering embankments of his Birmingham & Liverpool Junction Canal are comparable in their magnitude with the earthworks of the first railways from London to Birmingham and Bristol whose engineers, still doubting the power of friction between smooth wheel and rail, spared no expense to build a level road. Straight as the blade of a rapier piercing the green folds of the landscape, the long levels of the Birmingham & Liverpool symbolize the arrogance and the engineering mastery which the new century brought to birth. Yet in strange contrast to the scale of the earthworks and the width of the channel, the depth of water on these lately built waterways of Telford's is less than that on many earlier canals, while the locks are of narrow gauge. A branch from Norbury through Newport (Salop) to Wappenshall connected the new Birmingham & Liverpool with the Shrewsbury Canal and the tub-boat system of industrial Shropshire.

In 1827 the Chester and Ellesmere Companies (who had amalgamated in 1813) were empowered to construct a branch from the Chester Canal at Barbridge to the Trent & Mersey at Wardle Lock, Middlewich. This also was carried out by Telford, and it is to this day referred to as the "New Cut" by the boatmen who work the Trent & Mersey. On account of the saving in lockage it was, and is still, used by boats travelling between Wolverhampton and Manchester in preference to the Trent & Mersey route.

Before passing on to consider the fate of the canals in the railway age, mention must now be made of some of those canals which enjoyed only a brief career, were never completed, or which never developed beyond the paper stage. This is a fascinating subject which has been sadly neglected. A study of early records combined with field work would produce results of great interest besides rescuing from oblivion and recording for posterity forgotten waterways which often include civil engineering works of considerable magnitude and merit. Owing to the habit of early cartographers or writers on canals such as Philips or Priestley of treating projected canals as though they were accomplished facts, it is often impossible to discover, without practical research in the field, whether work was actually commenced or how far it was carried. Such research should commend itself to the attention of local archaeological societies whose members, having plotted every prehistoric or medieval trackway and Roman road in their area, frequently remain completely unaware of the existence of water roads which were constructed centuries later. As a result of this absorption with the remote past, much valuable information concerning the early stages of the Industrial Revolution—in many respects the most significant period in human history—has been, and is being, altogether lost. Some of these old waterways will be found marked, wholly or partly, upon Ordnance Survey sheets, but even where they are not marked, it is a simple matter to plot the approximate course on the Survey map by reference to the historical large-scale canal maps of Priestley or Bradshaw.

For the reason already mentioned in connection with the Wilts & Berks and Basingstoke Canals, the South and West of England is the most fruitful source for these lost causes. The Thames & Medway Canal was opened in 1824 when the long tunnel between Higham and Rochester was at last completed after vast labour and expense. Its career was brief, for in 1845 the concern was acquired by the Gravesend & Rochester Railway & Canal Co. who converted the tunnel section into a railway which is now part of the Southern system.

Further west, the Wey & Arun Junction Canal (authorized 1813) had a very brief career. It extended from the Wey at Shalford near Godalming, to the Arun Navigation at Newbridge, a distance of 18 miles, its object being to open a communication between the Thames and the south coast which would obviate the passage of the Foreland. Apart from the effect of steam competition on land and sea, the Wey and Arun suffered from an inadequate water supply to its summit level on the Surrey Weald. J. B. Dashwood in *The Thames to the Solent by Canal and Sea, or the Log of the Una Boat "Caprice"* (1868) describes the semiderelict and waterless state of the canal at that time. *Caprice* may well have been the last boat to pass from the Wey to the Arun, for in the same year that Dashwood made his voyage the canal was abandoned.

Two even more ill-starred projects in this south-eastern corner of England were the Portsmouth & Arundel and the Weald of Kent. In conjunction with the Wey & Arun, the former provided an inland route from London to Portsmouth. It was promoted in 1817, but although the work was completed and opened with great éclat, the section between Hunston Bridge and the Arun was closed as early as 1853. The concern was finally wound up in 1892. The Weald of Kent Canal, which never materialized, was to run from the Medway at Brandbridges, East Peckham, to the Royal Military Canal at Appledore. The latter, extending from Shorncliffe and Hythe to Rye, Winchelsea and Cliff End, was authorized for strategic reasons in 1807 as a precaution against Napoleonic invasion.

It was not only the coming of railways which brought about the early death of these waterways but the application of steam power to seagoing vessels. Steam boats made light of the once hazardous passage round the North Foreland which both the Wey & Arun and the Weald of Kent had been primarily designed to avoid. Similarly, in the West of England the new power affected the fortunes of the Grand Western Canal (1796) from Topsham to the Tone at Taunton, and of the later English & Bristol Channels Ship Canal project from Colyton to Bridgwater Bay, both of which were designed to obviate the passage round Land's End. Only the 11-mile summit of the Grand Western, including the Tiverton Branch, was ever opened to traffic, while the Ship Canal never got beyond the paper stage.

An even more optimistic product of the boom years was the Bristol and Taunton scheme for a canal running roughly parallel with the coast line of the Bristol Channel, which would have given the Grand Western an inland link with the rest of the canal system. Only that portion which now forms the Bridgwater and Taunton Canal was completed.

Further east, the Somerset Coal Canal was projected and partially constructed to connect the Somerset coal-field with the Kennet & Avon. Part of this line was eventually built as a tramway which ultimately became a section of the Somerset & Dorset Railway. From Widbrook, near Trowbridge, likewise on the Kennet & Avon, the Dorset & Somerset Canal was to run to join the Stour at Gains Cross near Blandford, but the only portion ever dug was a section of the Nettlebridge branch where, at Mells, near Frome, a patent "Fussell's Balanced Lock" (presumably a form of lift) with a fall of 21 ft. was erected and tried.

Another short-lived southern waterway was the Andover Canal down the valley of the Test from Andover through Stockbridge to Southampton Water at Redbridge. This waterway was completed, Robert Whitworth being the engineer, but in 1858 it was converted into the Andover & Redbridge Railway.

Southwards from London ran the Croydon Canal, its terminal

basin on the site of the present West Croydon Station being linked by tramway with the old Surrey Iron Railway, while northwards the London & Cambridge Junction Canal was projected from the Stort at Bishops Stortford to the River Cam at Clayhithe Sluice. Both Whitworth and Rennie surveyed this line, but no construction work was ever done.

Further to the north a line of water communication actually built but destined to have a very brief career consisted of the Oakham Canal from Oakham to Melton Mowbray and the Rivers Wreak & Eye Navigation from Melton to the Leicester Navigation of the Soar.

Two unfortunate waterways in the Severn area were the Hereford & Gloucester and the Kington & Leominster Canals. Both were costly lines involving heavy engineering works carried through the rural areas of the Welsh Marches. Consequently they proved unremunerative because they soon felt the adverse effect of that change from an agricultural to an industrial economy which the waterways of the new manufacturing areas hastened. The 34 miles of the Hereford & Gloucester, including three tunnels at or near Hereford, Asperton and Oxenhall, took many years to complete. The canal was vested in the G.W.R. in 1870, and nineteen years later the last boat passed through to the Severn. Subsequently, with the exception of Oxenhall Tunnel, that part of the canal between Gloucester and Ledbury was usurped by the present branch railway.

The career of the Kington & Leominster was even less fortunate. Only the central portion of the canal was ever opened for traffic, coal from the Mamble pits being conveyed from Frith Common wharf to Tenbury and Leominster. The Great Pensax Tunnel and the flight of locks which were to bring the canal to the Severn above Stourport Bridge were never completed so that the canal remained isolated. Had it reached Kington, a tramway was to have been constructed from thence to Hay, thus forming, via the Hay Railroad, a connection with the Brecon & Abergavenny Canal at Brecon.

With the completion of Telford's canals in the north-west, the era of canal expansion in England virtually came to an end. If we exclude the great Manchester Ship Canal, construction was thereafter confined to a number of short branches and connecting links in the Black Country network, to the Droitwich Junction Canal

(1851), now abandoned, and to the Slough Branch of the Grand Junction which was opened in 1883.

The downfall of the canal industry in the face of the competing railway was as swift as its meteoric climb to prosperity. To suppose that this downfall was due merely to the fact that the canal boat, like the stage coach, was made obsolete by the steam locomotive is a popular misconception. For the expeditious transport of passengers the rail certainly possessed unquestionable superiority and the canal "packet boats," like the road coaches, were naturally doomed. But for the carriage of heavy goods water transport possessed, and in fact still possesses, certain positive advantages over any form of land carriage which might have enabled our waterway system to hold its own against both rail and road competition. That it did not do so was due to a number of causes which are by no means widely appreciated. In the first place the waterway system was composed of a number of projects promoted to satisfy local needs at different periods, often without regard for the fact that they might eventually form important links in a trunk route. There was thus a lack of uniformity of width, depth and gauge of locks not only between different companies' lines but even on a single line of canal such as the Leeds & Liverpool or the Trent & Mersey. With the exception of the G.W.R. with its 7-ft. gauge, the railways avoided the mistakes of their predecessor. The canal companies also suffered grievously from the unimproved and archaic state of the old river navigations with which their waterways connected and upon which they often depended for their traffic. Navigation on the Severn was probably more uncertain than it had been in medieval times and improvements were belated, Tewkesbury lock not being completed until 1858. On the Thames and Trent the situation was even worse. A succession of navigation weirs of the paddle and rimer type obstructed the Thames between Oxford and Inglesham despite the pressure of the Thames & Severn Company to obtain improvement. It was not until the 1920's that the last of these weirs were superseded by locks, an improvement which came too late to save the Thames & Severn. On the Trent conditions were no better. Owing to gravel shoals there was a minimum draught of only 2 ft. between Newark and Nottingham, a state of affairs which was only amended by the construction of new locks by Nottingham Corporation between 1909 and 1928. By the time these belated river improvements were made, the position had been reversed, the connecting canals having become archaic by comparison. Lack of uniformity has thus been perpetuated in our own day.

Although these rivers were outside the jurisdiction of the canal companies, there can be no doubt that had the latter co-operated promptly in face of the railway threat much could have been accomplished, both physically and financially, to facilitate competitive through traffic working. That they did not do so was one of the chief causes of their downfall. In many cases the companies had raised their tolls during the period of their monopoly, and the fact that the Bridgewater Canal rates between Liverpool and Manchester were trebled between 1795 and 1810 was a stimulus to the promotion of the railway between these two towns. Some companies levied extortionate tolls on short sections of waterway forming part of a through route, while others exacted "bar" tolls on all traffic entering their canal from another waterway of later date as compensation for possible loss of traffic. In this way the Oxford Company netted a quarter of a million in twenty years from a bar toll levied at Napton Junction. When the railways were fairly established and competition had set in, these tolls came down with a run. But it was too late; the canal companies had exploited their monopoly too long and too arrogantly and had forfeited public sympathy and support in consequence.

There was another respect in which the canals were ill equipped to meet rail competition. Unlike the railway companies, the canal proprietors were not carriers but merely toll-takers. Until an Act of 1845 enabled them to act as carriers they were prohibited from doing so upon the grounds that, by failing to charge the statutory toll to themselves, they would gain an unjust advantage over other carriers. A canal was thus in the same position as the turnpike road of the period, the owners charging tolls for its use by the public. The great majority of canal carriers at that time were small traders operating over particular waterways. This state of affairs made expeditious through traffic working and the quotation of through rates virtually impossible.

In the first years of their existence the new railways tended to concentrate upon passenger and parcels traffic and to disdain the less remunerative bulk goods. So for a time, while the stage coaches and canal packet boats rapidly disappeared, canal goods traffic held its ground and the canal proprietors enjoyed a temporary respite and a false sense of security. But as the railways grew and competition between one railway and another developed, the new companies found that they could no longer afford to select their traffic. The war of the freight rates between rail and canal then began in earnest, and its outcome was never in doubt. Apart from the factors already outlined which crippled the waterway, in order to break its rival, the railway could afford to quote an uneconomic goods rate and look to passenger traffic receipts and to high rates on non-competitive routes to recoup the loss. For the canal there was no such redress. That the result was catastrophic for the canal companies the single example of the Loughborough Navigation will show. Until 1836 the rate charged on this waterway was 2s. 6d. per ton, but thereafter it fell rapidly to 4d. per ton. Meanwhile the value of the shares in this undertaking had fallen from £4,600 in 1824 to £1,500 in 1838. By 1872 their value was less than £200. Panic seized the industry. Many canal companies sold their undertakings to the railways either by agreeing in return to withdraw their opposition to the railway schemes or by threatening to promote rival railway projects. For example, in 1846 the combined Ellesmere, Montgomeryshire, Shrewsbury, Chester, and Birmingham & Liverpool Junction Canal Companies, formed The Shropshire Union Railways & Canal Company with powers to build railways or to convert their canals into railways. The only railway actually promoted by the Shropshire Union, however, was the line from Stafford through Newport to Wellington, for in the following year the undertaking was leased in perpetuity to the L. & N.W.R. Other companies, notably the Birmingham Canal Navigations, while they did not actually sell their undertakings, surrendered the controlling interest to a railway company in return for a guaranteed dividend. By such means the railway companies obtained control over a third of the total inland waterway mileage of the country. In three years alone, 1845, 1846 and 1847, 948 miles of waterways fell into railway hands. As these waterways included trunk routes such as the Kennet & Avon, Thames & Severn, Shropshire Union, Trent & Mersey, Macclesfield and Huddersfield Canals, as well as the Birmingham Canal Navigations which formed the hub of the Midlands "cross," all hope of the development of a homogeneous system of inland waterways vanished. For it was manifestly not in the interest of the railway

PLATE IX.—GUILLOTINE
LOCK GATES, ANCIENT AND
MODERN

(*a*) King's Norton stop lock,
Stratford-on-Avon Canal

INSET II

(*b*) Billing Lock, River Nene
Navigation

(*a*) Bottom gate paddle, Worcester & Birmingham Canal

(*b*) Top ground paddle, Worcester & Birmingham Canal (The lock "stopped off" for repairs, revealing mouth of culvert)

PLATE X.—
TYPES OF LOCK PADDLE
GEARING

(*c*) Shutter type gate paddle with horizontal rack, Stroudwater Canal, Saul

(*d*) Top ground paddle worked by wooden handspike, Calder & Hebble Navigation

PLATE XI.—THE ANDERTON
VERTICAL LIFT

(*a*) Side view of the lift, showing one caisson descending

(*b*) Interior view at the lift bottom, gates raised for boats to emerge

PLATE XII.—THE FOXTON INCLINED PLANE LIFT

(*a*) Ascending and descending caissons with boats

(*b*) Boats emerging from the top of the lift

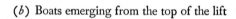

PLATE XIII.—AQUEDUCTS
OF STONE

(*a*) A typical Brindley aqueduct carrying the Staffordshire
& Worcestershire Canal over
the Trent at Great Haywood

(*b*) Marple Aqueduct, Peak
Forest Canal

PLATE XV.—
THE BARTON SWING
AQUEDUCT

(*a*) Boats crossing the aqueduct

(*b*) The aqueduct swing-ing over the Manchester Ship Canal

PLATE XVI.—CANAL TUNNELS

(a) The Marsden end of Standedge Tunnel, Huddersfield Narrow Canal
(b) An early photograph of Blisworth Tunnel, Grand Union Canal, showing leggers emerging

companies to improve their canal property or otherwise facilitate traffic when such improvement would automatically benefit the surviving independent canal companies with which they still competed. On the contrary, traffic was actively discouraged in a variety of ways; by neglecting maintenance; by diverting water supplies; by raising tolls; by prohibiting Sunday working and power driven craft; and by closing waterways for lengthy periods on the pretext of carrying out repairs.

A mere catalogue of waterways owned or openly controlled by railway companies does not reveal the extent of the influence which they acquired over the waterway industry by means of secret agreements, by control of tolls and by securing majority representation on the boards of supposedly independent canal companies such as the Sheffield & South Yorkshire Navigation. Always able to recoup competitive losses on other non-competitive routes and traffics, the railways held the whip hand, and despite successive Acts of Parliament which were designed to amend this state of affairs, it has persisted down to our own day, both canal owners and traders being completely dominated by their more powerful rival.

The Act of 1845 which empowered canal companies to act as carriers also enabled them to facilitate through traffic rates by varying tolls or by leasing them to one another. The railway companies, however, as canal owners, took advantage of these powers to further their own ends. For example, in 1851 the London & North Western, Midland, and Lancashire & Yorkshire companies between them secured a 21 years' lease of the tolls of the Leeds & Liverpool Canal, raised them to a figure which prohibited competition, and thus dealt the waterway a blow from which it has never fully recovered. The Rochdale Canal suffered a similar fate. In this way a legal instrument designed to assist the canals was turned against them with deadly effect.

The Railway and Canal Traffic Act of 1854 which stipulated that all reasonable facilities for through canal traffic should be provided, remained a dead letter for lack of definition. A similarly titled Act of 1873 defined these facilities, insisted that all railway owned canals should be properly maintained, and prohibited the railways from making toll agreements under the 1845 Act. These provisions were either circumvented or ignored, and in 1888 a further Act established the Railway and Canal Commissioners with powers to fix through tolls, to forbid railway companies to acquire any more canals, to order effective maintenance and to set up a canal clearing-house. This body proved singularly ineffective; a canal clearing-house was never set up while the railway companies continued to flout the proper maintenance clause of the 1873 Act.

It is safe to say that the legislators of this period were no more successful than the canal industry itself in countering the activities of astute and powerful railway companies. In fairness it must be said that it was no easy task as the example of the fate of the Upper Avon Navigation shows. In 1860 this navigation was purchased by a certain Mr. Boulton. This gentleman proved to be an official of the Oxford, Worcester & Wolverhampton Railway Company which subsequently "repaid" him the purchase money. In 1863 the O.W. & W.R. was acquired by the Great Western Company, and ten years later the Upper Avon became impassable. In 1877 Messrs. Foster Brothers, Bargemasters of Gloucester, appealed to the Railway & Canal Commissioners to exercise their powers to compel the Great Western to restore the navigation to order. This application was dismissed because the appellants were unable to prove ownership, the navigation being in fact owned by the "man of straw" who was the railway company's nominee.

It would be wrong to convey an impression that the railways at once killed the traffic on all the waterways which they acquired. In certain cases, where it suited their policy, they worked them vigorously, and consequently these cases are always advanced to refute the allegation that the railways were responsible for "strangling" the canals. On the Shropshire Union system the L. & N.W.R. operated their own fleet of boats for the reason that almost the entire system lay within the territory of rival companies, the Cambrian and Great Western, and not in their own. Again, on the Birmingham Canal Navigations, though nothing was done to improve facilities for through traffic by increasing the gauge of locks or by other means, a very heavy short-distance traffic was worked to feed the railway depots, and to this end the system was considerably extended during the period of railway control.

Despite all the disadvantages and difficulties and the losses of route mileage through abandonments, the total annual tonnage carried by inland waterway throughout the nineteenth century did not show any very substantial decrease. The relative fall, however, was very great because railway tonnage increased enormously in the same period. Furthermore, towards the end of the century, an increasing proportion of the water-borne tonnage total was accounted for by the few independent waterways, notably the Weaver Navigation and the Aire & Calder, where the normal process of development and growth was not checked. These waterways are the only bright spots in an otherwise gloomy picture of slow decline.

So far, the twentieth century has provided a similar story of good intentions yielding little result. A growing interest in waterways at the beginning of the century culminated in the appointment of a Royal Commission whose report, advocating considerable canal development, makes interesting reading. Its recommendations were never acted upon, and the first world war soon supervened.

The most important positive development of the between war years was the formation of the Grand Union Canal Company as a result of the amalgamation of the Regent's, Grand Junction, Warwick & Napton, Warwick & Birmingham, and Erewash Canal Companies and the Leicester and Loughborough Navigations. This unified the trunk routes between London, Birmingham and Nottingham, and an extensive widening and improvement scheme was carried out which, had unification been wider in its scope, might have been devoted to better effect by securing a less heavily locked route between London and Birmingham.

To sum up, with certain notable exceptions, the story of the canals from the beginning of the railway era down to the present day is a sorry one. In fact, it speaks volumes for the inherent economy of water transport that, in the face of such adverse circumstances, so many should have survived so long. Few traders, however, realize how deeply indebted they are to the canal that passes through their town, even though they never use it and may even be unaware of its existence. For it is that real economy of water transport which has been responsible for keeping down the freight rates levied by the rail and road. It remains to be seen whether, under the new transport regime, the system of waterways developed by our great civil engineers will be properly utilized or whether it will continue to be squandered.

CHAPTER III

⚘

LOCKS, AQUEDUCTS, TUNNELS
AND OTHER WORKS

THE most characteristic and familiar feature of the inland water-way is the lock. Whether it is set among the willows and rich water-meadows of the river valley or forms one of a serried ascending flight through the higher fields where the canal climbs the hill, the ponderous outspread arms of the balance beams have become an accepted part of the English landscape. There can be few of us who have not paused to look at a lock at some time or another; perhaps to rest on the lock-beam on a hot summer's day, lulled by the murmur of the water that trickles past the gate or over the weir; perhaps to hurry at the sound of the rattle of a paddle and the sudden surge and thunder of water from the sluices to watch a boat pass through. Yet few of us realize that the pound lock, like the wheel, was an invention of profound historical importance.

There is an old tradition that the lock was a Dutch invention, and that the principle was introduced to England from Holland by Sir Richard Weston, the undertaker of the Wey Navigation, in 1645. It is almost certain, however, that the invention was a fruit of the Italian Renaissance, and Leonardo da Vinci is often named as the inventor. Whether this is true or no, pound locks were certainly employed in Italy by Philippe Marie Visconti in 1440, whereas knowledge of lock construction does not seem to have penetrated north of the Alps until the latter half of the sixteenth century when pound locks were used on the Canal de Briare.

Several authorities state positively that the first pound lock in England was constructed in 1564–66 on the Exeter Canal by John Trew of Glamorgan, though even here there seems to be an element of doubt. In the seventeenth century the terms "lock," "sluice" and "turnpike" are loosely used by contemporary writers to describe both pound locks and flash locks or navigation

68

weirs. Consequently it is difficult to trace with certainty the existence of the earliest pound locks or the extent to which the principle was employed in seventeenth-century river improvements.

When terms of definition became more precise, the flash lock became generally known as a staunch in eastern England and as a navigation weir in the west. It consisted of a dam or weir built across the river which had a removable portion to allow for the passage of craft. It was of two types. The simpler, cheaper, and probably earlier form was a wooden structure built out from each bank, the navigable space between being closed at will by the insertion of vertical planks and posts called respectively paddles and rimers. In the case of the other more elaborate type, the weir was built of masonry and was equipped with a gate, swinging on rides and equipped with movable paddles, which could be opened against the flow of the river by means of a winch on the bank. The purpose of these flash locks was twofold. When closed they raised the water level in the reach above them until there was sufficient draught to enable boats to proceed upstream. When the paddles were drawn, the release of the pent up water produced a flush or "flash" upon which craft either rode downstream over the shallows below the weir or were drawn upstream through the weir by means of winches. As may be readily imagined, the passage through such flash locks was often a hazardous business, while if the difference of level to be overcome was considerable, it entailed great delay and wastage of water.

Long before many of our rivers were used for navigation their waters had been held up by weirs for the purpose of capturing fish or for driving mills or for both. Some of these weirs were of considerable height. Monmouth weir on the Wye had a fall of 11 ft., while the Medway weirs of 1600 had an average fall of 6 to 8 ft. These were the obstacles with which the navigation undertakers had to contend, and they encountered bitter opposition from the owners of the weirs who feared that the passage of boats would prejudice their interests. Either the undertakers were forced to buy out the weir owners or else the owners retained control over the use of the weirs. The latter arrangement generally proved highly unsatisfactory. Mill or weir owners levied an exorbitant toll for a "flash" from their weirs, and if water was short they would often refuse to draw the weir at all with the result that laden barges would be stranded on the shallows below for perhaps weeks on end.

These troubles were very largely overcome by the introduction of the pound lock. The first cost of the pound lock was, of course, much higher than that of the flash lock, and consequently its early use on some rivers appears to have been confined to surmounting those weirs where the greatest fall took place. Thus, while navigation weirs continued to exist on the Thames until the present century, pound locks were built at Iffley, Sandford and Culham under the Act of 1623–24. That these were pound locks of modern type is established without doubt by the description of them given by Plot in his *Oxfordshire*. After describing the principle of the flash lock he continues:

But where the declivity of the Channel, and the fall of the water is so great, that few barges could live in the passage of them, there we have Turn-pikes, whereof there are three between Oxford and Bercot; one at Ifley, another at Sanford, and a third at Culham in the Swift-ditch, which was cut at that time when the River was made navigable; and all are thus contrived. First, there are placed a great pair of folding doors, or Flood-gates of Timber across the River, that open against the stream and shut with it, not so as to come even in a straight line, but in an obtuse angle, the better to resist and bear the weight of the water, which by how much the greater it is, by so much the closer are the gates pressed; in each of which Flood-gates there is a sluice to let the water through at pleasure, without opening the gates themselves. Within these there is a large square taken out of the river, built up at each side with Free-stone, big enough to receive the largest barge afloat; and at the other end another pair of Flood-gates, opening and shutting, and having sluices like the former. Which is the whole Fabrick of a Turn-pike.

From this description it is apparent that in the case of these early Thames locks the "pounds" consisted of vertical-sided rectangular chambers of masonry of the type with which we are familiar. In this respect they were of advanced design, for many of the pound locks constructed at this period, and even at a much later date, consisted merely of "pounds" having sloping earth banks, timber piling being used only in the neighbourhood of the lock gates. This type of lock was used, and may still be seen, on the River Wey Navigation and on the Kennet Navigation engineered by John Hore. Such locks suggest that, in certain areas at all events, the pound lock was evolved by the natural expedient of constructing two flash locks in close proximity to each other in such a way that the short reach of the river between them became an equalizing pound. This theory is strengthened by the fact that the first pound locks constructed on the River Ivel between Shefford and the Great Ouse at Tempsford possessed no gates but were enclosed by paddles and rimers after the fashion of the simpler type of flash lock. It would also account for the curious shape of the chambers of certain of the early river locks. For instance, the derelict Cherry Ground Lock on the Lark Navigation, 6 miles below Bury St. Edmunds, has a chamber the shape of a crescent moon, Wyre Lock on the Lower (Warwick) Avon is diamond shaped, Cleeve Lock on the derelict upper portion of the Avon is also diamond shaped, and Luddington Upper Lock chamber is circular. All have masonry side walls. The fact that the enclosure between the gates originally consisted merely of the embanked bed of the river, and that it influenced subsequent masonry work is surely the only rational explanation of such apparent eccentricity.

It is generally assumed that the pound lock superseded the flash lock and that its universal adoption was only retarded on the grounds of higher capital cost. A consideration of the Lower Avon (Warwick) Navigation, however, suggests that William Sandys constructed both pound and flash locks on that river for a reason connected with the working of the water mills. Between Tewkesbury and Evesham there are two flash locks or navigation weirs on the river at Pershore and Cropthorne. They are of the masonry weir and gate type. Both are workable, the former being still in regular use. Beside each of the pound locks on this section of the river, that is to say at Nafford, Pershore, Wyre and Fladbury, there is or was a water mill of ancient origin, but there is no evidence that mills ever existed by the sites of the navigation weirs. On the contrary, above them there are ancient fords beneath Pershore Bridge and Jubilee Bridge, Cropthorne, and it seems clear that their purpose was to raise the level of the water over these fords. Had Sandys used pound locks instead of flash locks for this purpose he would have adversely affected the working of the mills above and below. For example, had a pound lock been built on the site of Cropthorne Weir it would have caused the water to "back up" at the tail race of Fladbury Mill a little distance upstream and also reduced the length of the reach upon which Wyre Mill, the next downstream, depended for its supplies. In the case of the navigation weir, these conditions only obtain when the weir is "set" for the passage of craft; normally, the weir gate remains open so that the river is unobstructed.

With the disappearance in recent years of the flash locks on the Upper Thames and on the Nene and Great Ouse, the two Avon Weirs are now, to the best of my belief, the last examples of this ancient contrivance in England which are still in working order. They are therefore of the greatest historical interest, and it is to be hoped that their preservation for many years to come can be assured.

Because they are built in soft sand, the chambers of the two locks at Beeston on the Chester Canal section of the Shropshire Union main line are formed of cast-iron plates bolted together. With these exceptions, and those of the early locks on the rivers Wey and Kennet to which reference has already been made, lock pounds usually consist of rectangular chambers of brick or stone.

The side walls of these lock chambers are either vertical or they may be slightly inclined so that the chamber is wider at the top than at the bottom. In the case of James Brindley's early locks on the Trent & Mersey and Staffordshire & Worcestershire Canals this "batter" of the side walls is so great that it is readily apparent at a glance. Moreover, the axis of the lower gates is thereby so inclined that they always tend to swing open when free from water pressure. Brindley doubtless reasoned that walls so constructed would be better able to resist lateral thrust due to frost action or clay movement, and it is certainly true that the vertical walls of later locks appear to be more liable to "come in" after a severe winter.

Beside each lock chamber a side weir (generally pronounced "wire" on the canals) is constructed to convey any surplus water from the head to the tail or lower end of the lock. Hence the fact that when a canal is well supplied with water it is commonly said to be "running weir." These weirs are usually of a simple type; the water falling over a straight sill into an open leat or a closed brick culvert, but on the Staffordshire & Worcestershire Canal some of the side weirs are circular. Here the sill takes the form of a shallow saucer, the culvert entrance consisting of a vertical hole at the centre. The effect is that of an enormous funnel and they occupy much less space than a straight weir of equal capacity. Another advantage of these curious weirs is that tree branches or other floating debris tend to collect in the "saucer" whence they are easily removed, whereas in the case of the normal type of weir they either pass over the sill and choke the culvert or else remain to obstruct the canal. These advantages, however, scarcely outweigh the greatly increased cost of their construction.

The lock chambers are enclosed by swinging gates at each end. These are generally constructed entirely of timber, oak being most commonly used, although on the Oxford Canal Napton flight cast-iron gates with oak balance beams have been in use for many years. The gates at the lower end or "tail" of the lock are necessarily the larger and heavier because they must extend to the full depth of the lock whereas those at the upper end or "head" need only be the depth of the upper pound of the canal. On river navigations or barge canals double gates are invariably used, but on the 7-ft. locks of the narrow canal system, single top gates are always employed and occasionally single lower gates also. Both upper and lower gates, when closed, bed against a sill at the bottom of the canal. The inside of the upper sill is uncovered when the lock is empty, but the lower one is permanently submerged. While concrete has been widely used in the construction of these sills in recent years, the old type of sill is of wood built in two parts. A top sill of oak against which the gates fit is spiked down to a base sill which consists of a single block of elm keyed into the masonry of the lock walls. Alone of all the wooden components of the lock, some of these elm base sills have never been replaced since the canals were built. Just as the length and breadth of the lock chambers determine the length and beam of the craft which can pass through a canal so, no matter how much the channel may be deepened, maximum draught is governed by the depth of the gate sills below the surface of the water at weir level.

The vertical timbers of the gates furthest from their hanging are called breasts or mitre posts. They must fit snugly together or, in the case of single gates, against the rebate in the lock wall, in order to prevent leakage. The breasts of single top gates are generally extended upward to form what is called a "strapping post." The steerer of a boat entering a full lock passes a line or "strap" round this post thus pulling the gate shut behind him and checking the boat at one and the same time.

The vertical timber of the lock gate nearest to the lock wall is known as the heel post, and its outer surface is rounded to fit the "hollow quoin" in the masonry in which it partially rotates. Water pressure holds the heel post tightly into the quoin, so that only a comparatively light metal strap, keyed into the masonry, is necessary to locate the gate in position when it is free to swing. Before this simple but effective method was evolved, lock gates were hung like field gates on hooks and rides, examples surviving until recently on the River Lark and on the Essex Stour Navigations.

Besides providing the necessary leverage for opening or closing the gate the balance beam, as its name denotes, also acts as a counterpoise to the weight of the gate. In the case of some large locks, however, the weight of the gate may be supported directly by rollers working over traverse plates on the sills. Balance beams may or may not be used in addition. If not, the gates will be moved by manual or powered winches. The lock gates on Sir George Duckett's River Stort Navigation, though small, have no balance beams and must be swung by hauling directly on chains attached to the mitre posts.

An uncommon exception to the orthodox type of lock gate is the guillotine gate, examples of which can be found on the Old Shropshire Canal section of the Shropshire Union near Hadley Castle and at King's Norton Stop Lock at the junction of the Stratford-on-Avon Canal with the Worcester & Birmingham. The guillotine gate is raised and lowered vertically in guides which form a frame over the canal. Chains attached to the gate pass over pulleys mounted on the top of the frame and from thence to an operating winch and compensating weights. On navigations liable to flooding, guillotine gates are more readily controlled and less liable to damage than the orthodox type, hence their recent introduction on the Rivers Nene and Great Ouse.

The sluices which enable the lock chamber to be filled or emptied are generally known as "paddles" in the Midlands, "slackers" in the Fens, and "cloughs" in the North. "Gate paddles" are fitted on the lock gates while "ground paddles" are mounted beside the lock and admit the water through a culvert. In both cases the actual paddle consists of a block of elm, moving vertically in a frame, which closes the sluice aperture. The use of gate and ground paddles varies very widely. The majority of river locks, particularly on the older navigations, employ gate paddles only, while on the canals the most usual practice is to use gate paddles exclusively at the tail of the lock and a combination of ground and gate paddles at the head of the lock. The provision of ground paddles for emptying or "drawing off" locks is rare. Examples are to be seen on the wide locks constructed by the Grand Union Company between Napton and Birmingham and on the narrow locks of the Huddersfield Narrow Canal immediately west of Diggle summit. In these cases ground paddles are used exclusively.

The mechanism employed for lifting or "drawing" the paddles differs widely in detail. On the earliest river locks it consisted merely of a long rod attached to the paddle and perforated with holes at its upper end to allow for the insertion of a hand-spike with which to lever them up. This was simply an adaptation of the old method of drawing weir paddles from which the principle, and in fact the name, of the lock paddle was derived. Examples of these early hand-spike paddles may still be found controlling mill pond sluices and on the Avon Weir gates, but their use on locks has become extinct. Perhaps the nearest equivalents surviving in use are the paddles on the upper locks of the Calder & Hebble Navigation. Here a toothed paddle rod is levered up by means of a wooden "hand-spike."[1] In the eighteenth century this crude method of operation was superseded by a simple rack and pinion mechanism equipped with a pawl or other locking device to hold the paddle up in the drawn position. Subject to variations in detail this is still by far the commonest form in use on both river and canal locks. On some large locks the paddle gearing is enclosed and operated by hand wheels or even by electric motor, but the principle is the same. The only alternative method of operation is by worm and nut. The earliest examples of this type of paddle gearing are to be found on the ground paddles or "cloughs" of the Leeds & Liverpool Canal. Here the paddle rods are attached to the nut which is raised by turning a vertical wormshaft by means of a handle rotating in a horizontal plane. The original eighteenth-century drawing of this gear is preserved in the Company's office at Skipton. Worm and nut mechanism is also used to actuate the ground paddles of the new locks on the Grand Union Canal which have already been mentioned.

[1] Presumably, this type of paddle gear was evolved by Smeaton, because the paddles of the locks on the Forth and Clyde Canal, also laid out by this engineer, are very similar.

Here, however, the principle is reversed, the paddle being attached to the vertical worm and raised by rotating the nut.

Some paddles, instead of sliding vertically, swing on a pivot over the sluice aperture in a manner similar to that of the simplest type of camera shutter. Paddles of this type are operated either by a horizontal variant of the orthodox rack and pinion or directly by means of a long wooden lever. All the gate paddles on the Leeds & Liverpool Canal and on the Lancaster Canal at Tewitfield are of this type worked by rack and pinion, while on the former canal the majority of the top ground paddles west of Gargrave are of the swinging lever type. These pivoting paddles are peculiar to the North of England, for examples in the South are extremely rare. The lever operated top ground paddles of Newbury Lock on the Kennet & Avon Canal, and the rack type gate paddles of the old Junction Lock at Saul on the Stroudwater Canal are the only examples known to me.

The bottom gate paddles on the Staffordshire & Worcestershire Canal are actuated by fixed handles, but with this and a few other exceptions the lock paddles throughout the waterway system of the Midlands and the South are worked by means of a detachable handle or windlass which is carried by the boat crew and which fits over a square formed on the end of the pinion shaft. This wise precaution prevents meddlesome people from tampering with the lock and wasting water, a form of trouble which besets the Leeds & Liverpool and other northern waterways where fixed windlasses or levers are the rule. Here, on more than one occasion grown men have been summonsed by the canal authorities for opening "cloughs" and draining whole pounds merely for the pleasure of seeing the water rush out. Moreover, if it goes undetected, the unfortunate boatmen frequently get the blame for this unforgivable canal crime.

The largest lock in the British Isles is Irlam Lock on the Manchester Ship Canal which is 600 ft. long, 80 ft. wide with a fall of 16 ft. and 24 ft. of water over the sills. Like other large locks on this canal and elsewhere, the chamber can be subdivided by means of intermediate gates for the passage of small craft. The Manchester Ship Canal is unique in its magnitude and somewhat outside the province of this book. As a general rule, river locks are larger than canal locks, not merely because they were built to suit larger craft, but rather that the question of water supply was not a determining factor. The canal engineer, on the other hand, was confronted with technical problems of water supply and of abrupt changes of level which produced smaller and special types of lock.

The deepest narrow canal lock in England is the Summit Lock at Tardebigge on the Worcester & Birmingham Canal which has a fall of 14 ft. But this is exceptional for the reason that economy in the use of water is essential on a canal, and the deeper the lock the more water it will consume. Consequently the average fall of the canal lock is from 6 to 8 ft. Even so, methods of economizing water have been evolved, notably the principle of the side pond. This consists of a brick lined chamber adjacent to the lock at a level midway between the upper and lower pounds of the canal and communicating with the lock chamber by means of a culvert controlled by a ground paddle. The latter is known in this case as a "side-pond paddle." When a craft enters the full lock and the gates are closed, this side-pond paddle is first raised and the water discharged from the lock into the side-pond until the levels equalize with the lock half empty. The side-pond paddle is then closed and the rest of the water is released from the lock into the lower pound in the ordinary way. When a boat comes into the empty lock the side-pond paddle is again the first to be drawn whereupon the water from the side-pond half fills the lock, the remainder being drawn from the upper pound. By this means half a lock of water is saved at each lockage. A number of the wide locks on the old Grand Junction Canal main line between Brentford and Braunston are equipped with side-ponds, though unfortunately they do not effect any very considerable saving at the present time. To make full use of the side-pond involves more time in locking through. Consequently the boatmen who work the locks themselves and to whom time is money because they are paid by the trip, do not so use them despite notices threatening dire penalties if they fail to do so. If the side-pond paddle is touched at all it is only drawn at the same time as the gate paddles so that the amount of water entering or leaving the side-pond at each lockage is negligible. This, however, is no reflection upon the principle of the side-pond, but is a matter of working conditions and lock supervision which does not concern us in this chapter.

A variant of the side-pond consists of duplicate locks side by side, their chambers linked by an interconnecting ground paddle so that one acts as a side-pond to the other. Examples of these paired locks are to be found on the Trent & Mersey Canal between Middlewich and Harecastle Summit—the "Cheshire Locks" as they are usually known to canal folk—and on the Oxford Canal at Hillmorton.

Where the change of level to be overcome is particularly abrupt, a special type of lock sometimes called a "riser" is used. Here the top gates of one lock are also the bottom gates of the lock above and are consequently of great depth. A pair of such locks is usually termed a double lock, but where more than two are grouped in this way, the combination is called a staircase. The name is apt, for such a flight does in fact resemble a gigantic staircase. A notable example is to be seen at Foxton near Market Harborough where the Leicester Section of the Grand Union Canal descends from its 400 ft. summit level by means of two staircases of five locks each. There are no paddles in the intermediate gates of these locks, the water level in each chamber being controlled by a large ground paddle which communicates with a side-pond at each level. Another remarkable staircase is "Bingley Five Rise" on the Leeds & Liverpool Canal. Here there are no side-ponds, the water passing directly from chamber to chamber. The disadvantage of such staircases is that they cause delay if traffic is heavy because craft of a beam exceeding half the width of the lock chambers cannot pass each other on the staircase.

There is a very curious and unique flight of three locks on the Staffordshire & Worcestershire Canal at the Bratch, a few miles south of Wolverhampton. The change of level is steep, and to all intents and purposes the locks form a staircase. Yet they cannot be so described because each lock has its own gates although the top gates of the two lower locks are only a few feet from the lower gates of the locks next above. Side-ponds control the levels of the intermediate lock. At Botterham on the same canal, a few miles further south, there is a double lock or "riser" of normal type, while a little to the north is Compton Top, said to be the first lock to be built by Brindley. It therefore seems likely that Brindley thought out the principle of the staircase immediately after building the Bratch Locks.

Unlike river navigations where locks usually occur at widely spaced intervals often determined by pre-existing mills and weirs, considerable groups or "flights" of locks are often to be found on the canals. We have already noted how Brindley, in constructing his canals, aimed at such grouping which makes for more convenient working. The greatest concentration of locks in this country is the famous flight of thirty narrow locks at Tardebigge on the Worcester & Birmingham Canal. This is generally known to boatmen as "the thirty and twelve" because it is closely followed by a further twelve locks at Stoke Prior. It is almost equalled by a flight of twenty-nine wide locks on the Kennet & Avon Canal at Devizes which lifts the canal out of the upper valley of the Bristol Avon on to the 15-mile level through the Vale of Pewsey to Wootton Rivers. This is more impressive to the eye than the Tardebigge flight because a number of the locks are laid out only a boat's length apart and in a perfectly straight line. The capacity of the short intervening pounds at Devizes is increased by extending them laterally so that they form what can best be described as a series of water terraces down the slope. Without such enlargement, an ascending craft would draw too much water out of them to enable it to pass through to the next lock without first drawing water down into the pound from above. This is exactly what has to be done to-day because the railway owners of the canal have allowed the short pounds to become choked with reeds and mud.

The "thirty and twelve" flights on the Worcester & Birmingham Canal form part of a total of 58 locks in the 16 miles between the 420 ft. Birmingham level at Tardebigge Summit and the River Severn at Worcester. Other examples of heavy lockage per mile are to be found on the canals which cross the Pennines between Lancashire and Yorkshire; 92 locks in 32 miles on the Rochdale Canal between Manchester and Sowerby Bridge, and 74 locks in 20 miles between Ashton and Huddersfield on the Huddersfield Narrow Canal.

Before leaving the subject of locks, a word should be said about those which are not built for the purpose of overcoming a permanent change of level. These consist of flood or tide locks on navigable rivers, and stop locks on canals. Kegworth and Pilling's Flood Locks on the River Soar Navigation in the Loughborough neighbourhood are examples of the first type. They have to be used only in time of flood. Normally, all gates can be opened and craft pass straight through. There are many examples of Tide Locks on the rivers and drains of the Fen district, their purpose being to overcome differences in level between fresh and tidal waters. At such locks, the fall may be in either direction depending on the state of the tide and the level of the "fresh." Normally, as in the case of a flood lock, all the gates of a tide lock can be opened together twice at each tide; once on the flood tide, which is known as "the first level," and once on the ebb, or "back level." Naturally boats on such waterways always endeavour to work with the tides so as to take advantage of these levels and thus avoid the necessity of working tide locks.

The Stop Lock is often to be found at the junction of two canals owned by different companies, and its object is to prevent the interchange of water between the two so that if one canal gets short of water for any reason it will not draw water away from the other. As a rule the difference of level at a stop lock is only a matter of inches, but as in the case of the tide lock, it may be in either direction, and, like the latter, it is sometimes equipped with two sets of gates at each end which open in opposite directions.

During the period of canal construction, this question of effecting junctions was a frequent source of dispute and litigation between the two companies concerned which usually ended in an agreement whereby the newcomer was the loser. Thus for many years the Birmingham Canal Company would not allow the Worcester & Birmingham Company to make a junction with their canal in Birmingham. A narrow "bar" of masonry, which may still be seen, divided the two waterways, and over this all goods consigned from one canal to the other had to be transhipped from boat to boat. Eventually the matter was settled and a stop lock built, but to this day the junction is known as Worcester Bar or the Bar Lock.

Again, at Kingswood where the Stratford-on-Avon and Warwick & Birmingham (now Grand Union) Canals pass within a hundred yards of each other, it would have been possible to link the two waterways on the level. Instead, the short arm which connects the two canals includes a lock because the junction with the Stratford Canal is made at a higher level. In this case the Stratford was the newcomer, and the reason for the arrangement was that the Warwick & Birmingham exacted the price of a lock of water for every boat which passed over the junction as the condition of agreement.

There is an interesting example of these old water agreements between companies to be found at Aldersley and Autherley Junctions near Wolverhampton where, within a few hundred yards of each other, the Birmingham and the Shropshire Union Canals join the Staffordshire and Worcestershire Canal. There is no stop lock at Aldersley because, by ancient right, the Staffordshire & Worcestershire is entitled to the lock of water which comes down the Wolverhampton locks of the Birmingham Canal with every boat passing from one canal to the other. At Autherley Junction there is a stop lock, the level of the Shropshire Union being normally lower than that of the Staffordshire & Worcestershire. But for every boat passing from the Birmingham Canal to the Shropshire Union or vice versa, the latter canal is entitled to claim a share of the lockage water which the Staffordshire & Worcestershire receives at Aldersley. This right the Shropshire Union exercises by means of a special sluice and paddle which by-passes Autherley Stop Lock.

Ever since the period of canal construction, engineers have toyed with the idea of saving both time and water by substituting some form of mechanical lift for a flight of locks. A good argument can be made out for the lift, but in practice the capital cost is high, it must be under constant supervision, while the situations where a change of level sufficiently steep to justify a lift occurs naturally are very few. To create them artificially would involve very costly earthworks. The only canal lift still in use in this country is at Anderton near Northwich. This is of vertical type, and lowers boats from the Trent & Mersey Canal down to the River Weaver, a fall of 50 ft. It was designed by Sir E. Leader Williams. Each of the two caissons is capable of holding a pair of narrow boats, and owing to the displacement factor, their weights always remain the same whether the boats are loaded or empty. As opened in 1875, the Anderton lift worked hydraulically, a system of syphons reducing the weight of the ascending caisson sufficiently to enable it to be drawn up by the descent of its fellow. This was not entirely satisfactory, and the caissons now operate independently by electric power, the modification being carried out in 1912 by Mr. J. Saner, then engineer to the River Weaver Trustees. Craft are admitted to the lift at top and bottom through guillotine gates which seal off both caisson and canal. Towering above the shipping on the Weaver, the great black bulk of the Anderton lift makes an impressive sight, but never more so than in early morning or late evening when it looms indistinctly through the mists of the river and the fumes of the factories.

In 1900 a lift was opened at Foxton with the object of superseding the staircase of locks at that place which has already been described. The general principle of the Foxton Lift was the same as the Anderton, but in this case each caisson moved sideways on sixteen wheels and eight rails down an inclined plane 307 ft. long representing a vertical rise of 75 ft., steam providing the motive power. Trouble was experienced with the rails which subsided owing to the great weight of the caissons, while the volume of traffic did not justify keeping a boiler constantly in steam and an engine man in attendance. Consequently the lift was abandoned after only a few years' working. All that remains to-day are two derelict arms of canal at top and bottom, a crumbling concrete ramp over which a tangle of briars is fast creeping, and a ruined engine house.

Another and older ruined engine house stands prominently on a hilltop between Wellington and Oakengates in the queer little "black country" of Shropshire. It is a notable landmark. Standing by this engine house, in clear weather the eye can command a great sweep of country from Caer Caradoc and the Long Mynd in the south to Ruabon Mountain in the north. This airy ruin was the winding house for the Trench Inclined Lift of the old Shropshire Tub Boat Canal. The length of this plane, which can still be traced, was 227 yards and the vertical lift 73 ft. 6 in. Instead of floating into caissons, the tub boats were drawn up out of the water on trolleys running on the inclined rails. Here, therefore, there was no water displacement factor to equalize weights, and consequently more power was required to work the lift. Another complication was that while the rails could run straight down into the bed of the canal at the bottom, they had to surmount the bank of the canal at the top by means of a short opposing plane. Tub boats loaded with the products of neighbouring collieries and ironworks were lowered down this lift and their cargoes subsequently transhipped to narrow boats on the main line of the Shropshire Union.

On the Coalport Canal, another tub boat canal in the same district, a similar lift was constructed on the steep slope of the gorge which the Severn has carved through the hills at Coalport. This inclined plane was 300 yards long with a vertical fall of no less than 213 ft. There was never any actual union between the canal and the river at the foot of the lift, goods being transhipped from the tub boats into the barges which then plied on this part of the Severn. The Coalport Lift fell into disuse in 1902 while the Trench Lift survived for a few years longer.

No less than seven lifts were planned between Taunton and Loudwell on the abortive Grand Western Canal project. These were to be inclined plane lifts of similar pattern to those at Trench and Coalport except that instead of steam power an ingenious hydraulic compensating arrangement was evolved. While the ascending and descending trucks carrying the boats were connected by rope with each other, each was also connected to a bucket working in a vertical well of a depth equal to the fall of the lift, the bucket being at the top of the well when the truck to which it was connected was at the bottom of the incline. Obviously a descending truck carrying an empty boat could not draw up a fully loaded one. In these circumstances the bucket at the top was filled with water drawn from the upper pound of the canal until its weight was sufficient to send it down the well and draw up the loaded truck. When it reached the bottom a flap valve in the base of the bucket was tripped and the water drained away into the lower pound of the canal. Thus the ascending bucket was always empty.

Perhaps the most curious waterway ever actually constructed in this country was the Bude Canal, which was built on the principle evolved by the American engineer, Fulton. The first two miles from Bude sea lock to Helebridge were normal enough, but thereafter it became what can only be described as an amphibious tramway. All changes of level were accomplished by inclined plane lifts, but in this case the tub boats themselves had wheels which ran in channel rails on the inclines up which they were hauled by the power of waterwheels in some cases, and in others by buckets on the principle of the Grand Western lifts. This curious waterway extended to Druxton with branches to Blagdonmoor and Alfardisworthy, a total distance of 40 miles. It was abandoned in 1891.

It will have been observed that all these early canal lifts were of the inclined plane type. The first recorded example of a vertical lift of the type still in use at Anderton was designed by a Mr. Woodhouse and constructed at Tardebigge on the

Worcester & Birmingham Canal in 1809. Whereas the Anderton Lift employs two metal caissons originally designed to counterbalance each other, the Tardebigge Lift consisted of a single wooden caisson 72 ft. long, 8 ft. wide, and 4½ ft. deep, weighing 64 tons when filled with water. This caisson was supported by rods attached to chains which passed over cast-iron pulley wheels each of 12 ft. diameter. There were four of these pulley wheels on each side, each set revolving on a common horizontal axle mounted on an overhead framework. Counterbalance weights, consisting of masses of brickwork built on timber frames and weighing 8 tons each, hung by rods from the chains on the landward side of the pulleys. Chains of equal weight were hung beneath the caisson and the counterweight frames. This was an ingenious arrangement for, hanging suspended or lying slack on the ground as the lift was moved, they exactly counterpoised the weight of the suspending chains which would otherwise have thrown the lift out of balance as their length varied. The lift was operated manually by a windlass which rotated the pulleys through gearing. Gates enclosed the caisson and the canal at either end and a sluice valve admitted water to the space between each set in order to relieve the pressure and enable them to be opened. The Company contemplated using these lifts on the steep descent from Tardebigge to Stoke Prior, but after a brief period of working the experimental lift was abandoned in favour of locks, perhaps owing to the higher cost of construction and maintenance. The lift occupied the site of Tardebigge top lock, this being the reason why this lock is of such unusual depth.

When the canal engineers were confronted by changes of level which could not be overcome by lockage they carried their waterways over river valleys by lofty aqueducts, or burrowed long tunnels under the watersheds. Although they excited admiration and almost incredulous wonderment at the time they were built, these great achievements of the canal engineers were soon forgotten when the railway age dawned. While the railway constructors basked in a limelight of fulsome public praise, the earlier works of the great canal builders, Brindley, Telford and Rennie were undeservedly forgotten. Yet despite the rapid improvement of civil engineering technique, of tools and equipment and of structural metalwork, the railway engineers rarely surpassed the achievements of their forerunners. Few railway viaducts can equal, much less surpass the grace of Telford's great aqueduct at Pont Cysyllte or the classic proportions of Rennie's aqueducts at Limpley Stoke, near Bath, and over the Lune at Lancaster. Likewise it was many years before the railway men bored a tunnel which exceeded in length the 5,415-yard Standedge Tunnel which carries the Huddersfield Narrow Canal through the Pennines.

The first canal aqueducts constructed by James Brindley consist of a series of squat arches as massively proportioned as the arcades of an early Norman church, for they were called upon to support not only the waterway but also the tremendous weight of its bed of earth and puddled clay. They are thus little more than a series of enormous culverts beneath an embankment. A number of these early aqueducts are to be found on the Stafford-shire & Worcestershire and Trent & Mersey Canals, the best example being the aqueduct over the River Dove near Burton-on-Trent.

These aqueducts are not, and in fact could not be, of any great height, and when Thomas Telford was faced with the problem of carrying the Ellesmere Canal across the valleys of the Ceiriog and the Dee at a high level he was forced to evolve some new and less cumbersome method of construction. Already he had constructed a small cast-iron aqueduct on the Shrewsbury Canal at Longdon-on-Tern. At Chirk, he carried the canal 70 ft. above the Ceiriog by a stone aqueduct of ten arches each of 40–ft. span. He formed the bed of the canal of cast-iron plates flanged and bolted together and set in side walls of ashlar masonry backed by hard brick set in Parker's cement. The result was a massive but beautifully proportioned structure. The more formidable gulf of the Vale of Llangollen forced Telford to adopt an even lighter and more daring technique. Here he carried the use of metal a stage further. The trough carrying the waterway and the towing path platform were constructed entirely of cast-iron sections, and the masons' work was confined to the supporting piers. The result, completed in 1803, was Pont Cysyllte, over 1,000 ft. long and 120 ft. above the River Dee. Having compared Brindley's aqueducts with early Norman architecture then Telford's Pont Cysyllte can only be likened, in its airy lightness, to the full flower of the Gothic. The slender symmetry of Telford's aqueduct and of the great cathedral vault both display the exuberant craftsmanship of men who have won a new command over materials. Sir Walter Scott did not exaggerate unduly when he described Pont Cysyllte as the greatest work of art he had ever seen. To the Georgians this mighty work of Telford's presaged the dawn of an age of wonders, but alas, it stands to-day as the melancholy symbol of a promise never fulfilled. These first flowerings of the metal age were also the best, for it is an age that has led, not to a new Parthenon but to the "Pre-fab."

It was the custom of the canal builders to let out portions of the work to local contractors, a practice which was perpetuated by the railway builders. It sometimes happened that these local contractors were not equal to their commitments, the results being unfortunate for all concerned. J. Hassell in his *Tour of the Grand Junction* (1819) tells the sad story of the Ouse aqueduct at Wolverton. Anxious to complete the line of canal and so earn revenue, the proprietors of the old Grand Junction carried a temporary waterway down and across the river valley by means of ten locks. Meanwhile the work of constructing a permanent canal on the level by means of an embankment and aqueduct was entrusted to "some persons at Stony-Stratford." When this was eventually completed, the Company's engineer, a Mr. Bevan of Leighton Buzzard, predicted that it would not stand for twelve months. This gloomy forecast turned out to be only too true, for six months after completion the aqueduct, or rather the embankment above it, blew up. "Mr. Cherry, of Greenbridge Lock," writes Hassell, "was the first person to observe the disaster, and at eleven o'clock at night had but just time to pull up the stop gates and let off some of the waste water, before the embankment blew up. He sent off a messenger to apprise the inhabitants of Stony Stratford of the accident. The consternation soon became general, every inhabitant expecting momentarily his house to be insulated from the effects of the approaching element. The alarm, added to the time of night, caused a dreadful and awful suspense, which only subsided with the day-breaking, when it was observed the valley only was inundated; which cleared off its waters in about three days."

A local carpenter thereupon partially erased this blot from Stony Stratford's escutcheon by constructing a temporary wooden trough across the breach which successfully passed the traffic for twelve months until the present cast-iron trunk arrived from the

Ketley Bank Ironworks in Shropshire. It is interesting here to note that precisely the same technique of a temporary wooden trunk was successfully employed in modern times when deviation work on the Leeds & Liverpool Canal involved the removal of an aqueduct. Traces of the piers of the old Ouse aqueduct and of the temporary locks which were used while it was building can still be seen, while the presence of the single very shallow lock at Fenny Stratford at the south end of this pound is due to an error in the levels. Obviously, the first aqueduct was of the Brindley pattern, whereas its successor is of the type developed by Telford at Pont Cysyllte. Like the latter it must be kept free from solid ice in winter, otherwise the cast-iron trough might fracture with serious results.

In 1893 when the Manchester Ship Canal was built, Brindley's first aqueduct carrying the Bridgewater Canal over the River Irwell at Barton had to be destroyed. It was replaced by the famous Barton Swing Aqueduct designed by Sir E. Leader Williams to carry the Bridgewater over the Ship Canal which at this point follows the old course of the Irwell. This most impressive feat of engineering consists of a swinging span of steelwork 234 ft. long carrying a waterway 19 ft. wide and 6 ft. deep. When the aqueduct is opened to pass shipping on the lower waterway, gates at each end of the aqueduct and at each shore end are closed and the 1,600-ton span swings electrically. We may regret the passing of Brindley's first aqueduct, but it is an appropriate coincidence that its name should have passed to this, the latest aqueduct to be built in this country and one that is quite unique.

Canal tunnels are usually, though by no means always, to be found on the summit level. When the canal traveller has passed through the summit lock he sees the hills of the watershed ahead of him. For a time it may seem as though the canal will avoid them as it winds this way and that, but sooner or later the hills close in until, rounding a turn, the dark portal of a tunnel appears, shadowed, perhaps, by overhanging trees. It is a strange experience to travel through a long canal tunnel. All tunnels, like caves, have a mysterious and somewhat sinister quality which repels some people while it fascinates others. This is particularly true of canal tunnels, partly, perhaps, because of the lonely situations in which they are usually to be found, but chiefly because of their unsubstantial floor of dark water. This produces strange hollow echoes, and, since very few tunnels have a towpath through them, to the perpetual darkness is added a feeling of utter isolation. The traveller wonders what would happen to him if his boat were to sink in the middle of the tunnel.

The first canal tunnels to be built in this country were Preston-Brook, Barnton, Salterford and Harecastle on the Trent & Mersey Canal. Harecastle Old Tunnel carries the summit level of the canal under Harecastle hill which here forms the watershed between the valley of the Trent and the plain of Cheshire. It is 2,897 yards long but the bore is extremely small, only 9 ft. wide and 12 ft. high. Boats were thus unable to pass each other in the tunnel, it caused considerable delay to traffic, and was a fruitful source of disputes between the boatmen as to who should take the next turn. In 1824, this state of affairs was remedied by Thomas Telford's new tunnel which runs parallel with the old. This is of larger section and includes a towing path. It was completed in less than three years, a fact which illustrates the rapid strides made in civil engineering methods. For ninety years both tunnels were worked on a one-way traffic system, but subsidences due to colliery working eventually caused the older to be closed to traffic.

Even more restricted in size than Harecastle Old Tunnel is the bore of the great tunnel beneath Standedge on the Huddersfield Narrow Canal which in places is only 8 ft. 6 in. high with a channel width of 7 ft. 6 in. Standedge has a dual claim to distinction, for not only is it the longest canal tunnel in England (3 miles, 135 yards) but it is also situated upon the highest canal summit level in the British Isles—644 ft. 9 in. above Ordnance Datum for $4\frac{1}{4}$ miles between Diggle and Marsden. Although there has been no through commercial traffic on the Huddersfield Narrow Canal for many years, the tunnel is still open so that I was recently able to make a passage through it. In the course of my travels by waterway I have passed through nearly all the canal tunnels which are still navigable, but my journey beneath Standedge was a unique experience which I shall never forget. The tunnel is not brick-lined throughout, nor is it of uniform size. On the contrary, for the greater part of its length the walls and roof are of jagged rock which reveals to this day the shot holes of those intrepid "navigators" who blasted their way through the Pennines a century and a half ago. In places these rock walls recede and for a short space the narrow cave becomes a roomy cavern where boats were able to pass each other. In this respect Standedge is reminiscent, not of any other canal tunnel, but of the flooded workings of the Speedwell lead mine in Derbyshire. There are ventilation shafts at intervals, but these contribute only the faintest glimmer of daylight to the depths, for the shafts are any-thing up to 600 ft. deep, while their mouths are protected by stout timber stagings to guard against rock falls. Upon each side at a slightly higher level run the railway tunnels on the line from Manchester to Leeds, and at intervals there are subterranean galleries connecting the tunnels, for the railway engineers made use of the canal tunnel for construction work, drainage and ventilation. At the passage of an express the rocks reverberate with a dull thunder of sound and a sudden blast of air is soon followed by a blinding cloud of acrid smoke which bellies out from the cross galleries. Altogether a closer approximation of the legendary route to the infernal regions by way of the Styx it would be difficult to conceive. Our passage through the tunnel occupied over two hours, for we travelled extremely slowly owing to the risk of damaging the boat since it was impossible to avoid contact with the jagged side-walls. During this time the numbered cast-iron plaques which are fixed to the tunnel roof every fifty yards indicated our progress and seemed the only friendly link with the outside world.

Some of the longer canal tunnels are not merely disused but have become impassable also. For example, Sapperton Tunnel (3,808 yards) on the summit of the Thames & Severn Canal at the head of the Golden Valley, is waterless. For some years prior to its closing the canal suffered acutely from lack of water, and, to avoid the risk of getting stuck in the tunnel, boats often unloaded part of their cargoes into spare boats kept for the purpose at Daneway and Thames Head Wharves. Lappal Tunnel (3,795 yards) between Halesowen and Selly Oak on the Birming-ham Canal, Dudley Line No. 2, has been affected by mine sub-sidences like the Harecastle and is believed to have collapsed. The same applies to Norwood Tunnel (3,102 yards) on the Chester-field Canal and Butterley Tunnel (3,063 yards) on the Cromford Canal. Greywell Tunnel (1,200 yards) on the Basingstoke Canal near Odiham is also said to have fallen in. Tunnels such as

Oxenhall and Ashperton on the old Hereford & Gloucester, or Sousant and the legendary Pensax on the Kington & Leominster have been almost totally forgotten even in the locality, and they are often difficult to discover. An afternoon's search in the Teme Valley brought to light the eastern portal of Sousant, but I have failed to discover any trace of Pensax. Contemporary authorities disagree as to what had actually been accomplished before work on this tunnel was abandoned, and it is probable that it has vanished completely. There is a local legend that the tunnel suddenly collapsed, and that the men working in the shaft at the time are still buried there with their tools beside them. Some Teme Valley people, however, maintain that this story applies to Sousant Tunnel. Certainly the western end of Sousant, if it ever existed, has disappeared.

The longest canal tunnel still in regular commercial use is the Dudley Tunnel (3,172 yards) of the Birmingham Canal Navigations. This is one of the older tunnels of the Brindley period, and consequently it is of very restricted section being only 8 ft. 5 in. wide with a minimum height above water level of 5 ft. 9 in. Traffic congestion through Dudley Tunnel was considerably reduced by the construction of Netherton Tunnel (3,027 yards) which is situated on another arm of the same system. With a headroom of 15 ft. 9 in. and a width of 27 ft., including a towing path each side, it is as large as Dudley is small. It also has the unique distinction of being lit by electric light. It was the last canal tunnel to be constructed in England; work commenced in December 1855 and was completed two years and eight months later. Almost equalling these tunnels in length is Blisworth Tunnel (3,056 yards) on the Grand Union Canal in Northamptonshire. This tunnel occasioned the contractors a great deal of trouble, and during the years it was building the canal company carried goods over Blisworth Hill by means of a plate tramway, transhipping at each end.

Besides possessing the greatest flight of locks in England, the Worcester & Birmingham Canal also shares with the Trent & Mersey the distinction of possessing the greatest number of tunnels on any single line of canal. These, commencing at the Birmingham end, consist of Edgbaston (105 yards), West Hill (2,726 yards), Shortwood (613 yards), Tardebigge (580 yards) and Dunhampstead (230 yards). Of these the Tardebigge is said to have caused most trouble to contractors. It is cut through almost solid rock and only a small portion is brick-lined.

The short tunnel on the Oxford Canal at Newbold-on-Avon was constructed during the 1829–34 improvements, and supersedes an older and smaller tunnel the entrance to which can still be seen beside Newbold churchyard. Later, in 1868, the 1,200, yard summit tunnel at Fenny Compton was opened out, though to this day, after nearly a century, the resulting cutting is still called "the tunnel."

Tunnel portals and their abutments vary from simple utilitarian brickwork to elaborate affairs of ashlar masonry with Doric pilasters and flanking niches. West Hill Tunnel (completed 1797) is curious in this respect, for whereas the north portal is a pretentious affair, the south end is simply a hole in the ground, consisting merely of the ragged edges of the facing brick courses. This suggests either a lack of funds (from which the Worcester & Birmingham Company suffered acutely) or that the tunnel has at some period been reduced in length. The portals of Sapperton Tunnel are also strikingly dissimilar. Compared with the elaborate eastern entrance with its niches and classical columns, the western portal is a comparatively simple affair with a castellated top. Despite its modest length (502 yards) Savernake Summit Tunnel on the Kennet & Avon Canal boasts an imposing east entrance bearing a monumental inscription. This informs the beholder that the tunnel is named BRUCE in recognition of the support of the Right Honourable Thomas Bruce, Earl of Ailesbury, and Charles Lord Bruce, his son, in the noble work of linking the cities of London and Bristol.

The method of tunnel construction adopted by Brindley at Harecastle was to sink a series of vertical shafts down to canal level and then strike headings in each direction from the bottom of the shafts. Spoil was drawn up and water pumped out through these shafts by means of horse-gins, wind pumps and, later, "fire engines." This principle has been followed by all his successors. When the work was completed, the vertical shafts were either filled up or retained for ventilation in the case of the longer tunnels. Even where they have disappeared, their outlets on the hill-top overhead can usually be traced by the old grass-grown spoil mounds. For this constructional reason, canal tunnels are almost invariably straight so that if the atmosphere is clear it is

91

possible to see through all but the longest of them. Barnton (572 yards) and Saltersford (424 yards) tunnels on the Trent & Mersey Canal are exceptions to this rule, while Braunston Tunnel (2,042 yards) on the Grand Union Canal near Daventry has a slight S bend near its southern end which is generally believed to be due to an error on the part of the surveyor or contractor. Braunston Tunnel was completed on June 6, 1796.

None of the older canal tunnels, with the exception of Armitage on the Trent & Mersey which is extremely short, included a towing path, so that in the early days of horse haulage all craft had to be man-handled through while the horses went over the hill. Savernake Tunnel is provided with a chain along the wall for this purpose, but as a general rule the boats were shafted or "legged" through. Legging consisted of pushing with the feet against the tunnel walls, and to do this the boatmen, or frequently the boatman and his wife, lay at each end of a plank laid across the fore-end of the boat. This was a highly dangerous practice, for any sudden movement of one person might cause the other to be thrown into the water to drown or to be crushed between the boat and the tunnel wall. There were many such fatalities until special legging boards or "wings" were introduced which could be outrigged securely from the boat sides. A fully equipped narrow boat then carried two sets of these, "broad cut wings" and "narrow cut wings" to suit the different tunnel widths. At many of the longer tunnels professional leggers were available to handle the traffic. At Blisworth Tunnel, for example, there were two gangs of twelve leggers stationed at each end of the tunnel at Blisworth and Stoke Bruerne. These did not work both ways, the Stoke Bruerne men working northbound traffic and vice versa. Four men out of each gang took night duty. They were known as Registered Leggers, and were issued by the Grand Junction Company with brass armlets as their badge of office. Their wages were 1s. 6d. per trip. The hut where these leggers waited for boats still stands beside the canal at Blisworth, while the neighbouring bridge is still called Candle Bridge because it was here that the boatmen purchased tallow dips to light them through.

Before the middle of the nineteenth century, steam tugs had been introduced at Blisworth and many other canal tunnels, and the practice of legging was discontinued except in the case of boats carrying explosives. On canals where traffic was not sufficiently dense to justify keeping tugs in steam, however, legging continued down to modern times and until horse-drawn traffic ceased. Thus until 1939, occasional horse boats continued to work through the Leicester section of the Grand Union Canal which involved legging through Crick, Husbands Bosworth and Saddington Tunnels unless they were lucky enough to obtain a tow from a motor boat.

It is impossible to attach a towline to the stern-end "stud" of a horse-drawn narrow boat without fouling the "ram's head" of the rudder. Consequently the practice of tug haulage led to the provision of hooks mounted on the top strake at each side of the stern to which the towlines of following boats could be secured. These "tunnel hooks" as they are called may still be seen on the majority of the erstwhile horse boats which have now become "butties" to motor boats.

The widespread introduction of self-propelled craft on the canals in the last thirty years has brought about the discontinuance of many tunnel tug services. Diesel tugs still handle traffic through Maida Hill and Islington Tunnels on the Regent's Canal and through Tardebigge, Shortwood and Westhill on the Worcester & Birmingham, while a curious electric tug with overhead pick-up which hauls itself along on a submerged cable plies through Harecastle New Tunnel. But the steam tugs at Blisworth and Braunston on the Grand Union, at Preston Brook, Barnton and Saltersford on the Trent & Mersey,[1] and at Gannow and Foulridge on the Leeds & Liverpool were all withdrawn in in the 1930's.

Foulridge Tunnel (1,640 yards) is remarkable for the fact that a cow once swam through it to be rescued and revived with brandy by the tunnel keeper when she emerged. Though this occurred in 1912, the villagers of Foulridge recall and recount the event as though it had happened yesterday, while a portrait of the athletic cow hangs in the bar of the New Inn. Like all good stories it has improved with keeping, one version asserting that the cow met the tug with a tow in the tunnel and had to dive under them in order to pass.

Though its towing duties are over, this tug is still moored at Foulridge where it is occasionally used for ice-breaking. It is a

[1] These Trent & Mersey tugs mounted horizontal wheels which made contact with the tunnel walls.

curious "either way" vessel, a compound steam engine mounted amidships being permanently coupled to "push and pull" propellers by a propeller shaft running the whole length of the hull. Her original equipment included air bottles which were charged by an air pump driven by eccentric from the propeller shaft. These provided a fresh air supply for the crew. To-day, this may seem to be a needless precaution, but in the days of the steamers there was a very real danger of asphyxiation. Unlike railway tunnels, the canal tunnels were not built for steam traffic. Not only were they inadequately provided with ventilation shafts but the traffic through them did not induce the self-ventilating effect of the faster moving train. In still weather the longer tunnels can be murky enough to-day when the fumes of diesel engine exhausts hang long in the dank air, but in the days of steam they resembled Dante's inferno. I have travelled through Braunston Tunnel at that time in a choking fog of smoke so dense that we could scarcely see our own tunnel lantern. This state of affairs resulted in a grim tragedy at Blisworth soon after the tug service was started. The tug entered the tunnel, travelling light, but failed to emerge at the time expected. At long last she crawled out on the few pounds of steam remaining in her boiler and the crews of the waiting boats found that her steerer and engine man had both died of suffocation. After this, additional ventilation shafts were opened in the tunnel. The crew of a cargo-carrying steamer were similarly overcome in Foulridge Tunnel, but in this case they happily recovered. A curious feature of this mishap was that the son of the steamer's steerer was in charge of the "butty" in tow astern and was not only quite unaffected by the fumes but was not aware that anything was amiss until the boats emerged and the steamer rammed the bank at the first turn. The wide boat could not deviate from her course in the narrow tunnel, and the father, though insensible, had remained standing and grasping the tiller.

When, as in this instance, self-propelled craft operate through a "one-way" tunnel, some form of traffic control becomes necessary. At Foulridge the system employed is similar to that of single line railway working. No boat can enter the tunnel without collecting a ticket from the tunnel-keeper, and until that ticket is given up at the opposite end no oncoming craft can proceed. Preston Brook, Barnton and Saltersford on the Trent &

Mersey are also one-way tunnels. Here boats are admitted from either end only at stated times and must stop to await their turn if a red flag, or a red light at night, is exhibited at the tunnel mouth.

So far we have considered what might be called the major works of civil engineering, but it is probably the minor works, the over bridges and buildings, which contribute most to each canal's individual character and charm. Even the familiar and almost universal hump-backed bridge varies in shape and proportion from one district to another, and may be built in either brick or stone, depending on the region. Brick is the usual medium for all canal structural work throughout the Midlands, but stone appears in the North or where, as on the Oxford Canal south of Banbury, or on the Kennet & Avon near Bath, the waterway enters the limestone belt. All bridges are numbered, but those on the Staffordshire & Worcestershire Canal bear names—fascinating names such as "Coven Heath" or "Long Moll's"—in bold eighteenth-century lettering on oval cast-iron plates. It is characteristic of our age that where these old bridges have been superseded by modern structures, the nameplates have been destroyed. How simple it would have been to replace them on the new bridge and so preserve that continuity between past and present which we lack so sorely!

Certain canals affect peculiar types of over-bridge. Thus on the Stratford-on-Avon Canal there is to be seen a curious divided bridge. In this the carriage-way is carried on two cast-iron brackets which project from the brick abutments and which fail to meet at the centre by the space of an inch. There being no towing path under the arch, the horse boatman would have had to detach his towline but for this arrangement which enabled him to drop the line through the slot. On the Kennet & Avon and Leeds & Liverpool Canals there are many wooden swing bridges working on massive ball bearings, while wooden drawbridges are used extensively on the Oxford Canal south of Fenny Compton. These drawbridges have balance beams attached directly to the lifting platform, and pivot by means of a toothed segment of cast-iron. In the other type of canal drawbridge found on the Northampton and Welford Branches of the Grand Union, on the Welsh Section of the Shropshire Union, on the Stratford Canal north end, on the Brecon & Abergavenny Canal and elsewhere, the balance beams are mounted on stout uprights above the platform to which they are connected by chains or rods.

A unique type of drawbridge is to be seen on the Huddersfield Broad (or Sir John Ramsden's) Canal at Huddersfield. Here, by means of a geared winch and overhead pulleys, the whole platform of the bridge is raised vertically upward.

The graceful wooden swing bridges on the Gloucester & Berkeley Ship Canal are particularly pleasing to the eye. Owing to the width of the channel these bridges consist of two swinging portions; that on one bank is opened by a resident bridge-keeper while that on the other bank is opened by a travelling bridgeman who accompanies craft on a bicycle along the towpath. A tug towing a train of eight or more barges is allotted two travelling bridgemen because in places one man could not close a bridge after the last barge and be in time to open the next. The men employed in this unusual occupation are paid by the trip.

Three interesting steel swing bridges cross this canal as it enters Sharpness docks. Two carry both roads and dock railways and are opened by handwheel and hand capstan respectively, while the third forms the eastern span of the Severn Bridge carrying the Severn & Wye Joint Line. The bridges are of different heights above water level, the last named being the highest, and craft approaching them sound a warning of one, two or three blasts according to how many bridges must be opened to allow them to pass through. The Severn Bridge carries regular passenger train traffic and has a number of interesting features, which include elaborate safety precautions. An overhead control cabin houses duplicate sets of vertical boilers and horizontal steam engines to provide power for opening the bridge, and a small lever frame of orthodox railway pattern. The drive from the steam engines to the fixed crown wheel on the supporting pier is taken through ribbed steel friction drums, bevel gearing and vertical shafts. Although the cabin is in the middle of the railway block section between Sharpness and Severn Bridge Stations, it is equipped with block repeater instruments while the lever frame is electrically interlocked. One lever on this frame controls a pin which locks the handwheel which must be rotated before the bridge locks can be released. This means that the bridge cannot

PLATE XVII.—A CONTRAST IN TUNNEL PORTALS

(*a*) East portal, Sapperton Tunnel, Thames & Severn Canal
(*b*) West portal, Sapperton Tunnel

INSET III

PLATE XVIII.—CANAL TUNNELS

(a) Interior view of Blisworth Tunnel, Grand Union Canal

(b) Darkness to daylight; emerging from the south end of Westhill Tunnel, Worcester & Birmingham Canal

PLATE XIX.—TUNNELS ON THE
TRENT AND MERSEY CANAL

(a) South end, Preston Brook
Tunnel

(b) Electric tug emerging from the
north end of Harecastle New Tunnel

PLATE XX.—TYPES OF CANAL
OVERBRIDGES

(*a*) Divided bridge, Stratford-on-Avon Canal

(*b*) Wooden drawbridge, Oxford Canal

(*c*) Ornamental foot-bridge, Birmingham & Fazeley Canal

PLATE XXI.—TYPES OF CANAL OVERBRIDGES

(*a*) Cast-iron roving bridge, Oxford Canal, Braunston

(*b*) Steam-operated railway swing bridge, Gloucester & Berkeley Canal, Sharpness

PLATE XXII

(a) Types of canal bridge: Wooden swing bridge, Gloucester & Berkeley Canal

(b) Canal architecture: Bridgeman's cottage, Gloucester & Berkeley Canal

PLATE XXIII.—
CANAL ARCHITEC-
TURE

(*a*) Round tower lock house, Thames & Severn Canal

(*b*) Old warehouse at Shardlow, Trent & Mersey Canal

PLATE XXIV.—CANAL WATER SUPPLY: FOULRIDGE SUMMIT RESERVOIR,
LEEDS AND LIVERPOOL CANAL

be opened against the railway without the sanction of the signal-men at each end of the section. Two more levers operate "home" signals protecting each approach. Naturally, these signals are not mounted on the swing bridge itself and so there can be no positive link between lever and signal. Push rods on the bridge press against levers to which the signal wires are attached. Thus while the push rods can hold the signals to the "off" position when the bridge is closed to canal, when it is swung the signals must come to the "on" position. Another lever controls a semaphore signal of normal pattern mounted on the bridge itself. This is for the benefit of canal traffic. When the opening of the bridge has been sanctioned by the signalmen at Sharpness and Severn Bridge, the bridgeman can pull this signal "off" to advise the oncoming craft that the bridge is about to swing. This is the only case known to me where a railway signal operated by a railwayman controls canal traffic. In the event of a failure of the electrical interlocking, the bridge locks can only be released by means of a key held by the Sharpness station-master who must, in these circumstances, pilot all trains over the bridge.

Another very remarkable bridge is the steel swing road bridge over the Weaver Navigation at Northwich, constructed in 1899. It weighs 300 tons, and five-sixths of this weight is supported by a circular floating pontoon under the centre of gravity. Sub-sidences due to brine pumping prompted this form of construction which proved so successful that another of the same type was built at Sutton Weaver to carry the Chester–Warrington main road over the river. The bridge at Northwich has the added distinction of being the first to be operated by electric power in this country.

The period of canal construction coincided with that age of landscape gardening with which the name of "Capability" Brown is chiefly associated. Consequently, where a canal enters the vicinity of great estates it is often apparent that its presence there was only sanctioned upon the condition that the waterway must obey the directions of the landscape gardener. In this connection it is salutary to reflect that to-day hordes of "planners" are busying themselves with this same task of reconciling utility with beauty. As the memorials of our pre-industrial past eloquently demonstrate, there was once no need for such self-conscious effort for the simple reason that wherever man worked in co-operation with nature there could be no divorce between beauty and utility. But so soon as the relationship between man and nature changed from co-operation to conquest the two were divorced and the task of reconciliation became progressively more difficult. Thus the railway constructors, when faced with the same problem of appeasing the proprietors of parklands, could only solve it by concealing their "iron road," often at great expense, by varying their line, planting belts of trees, or by constructing "artificial" cuttings and even tunnels, as at Kemble on the G.W.R. Swindon–Gloucester line, or at Gisburn on the old Lancashire & Yorkshire line to Hellifield. But even the railway builders were better off than our planners of to-day who attempt the impossible task of inducing the ferro-concrete factory, the dual track highway, the "pre-fab" housing estate, the pylon and the power station to conform with the English scene. The canal builders, on the other hand, had an easy task. The scars of construction soon healed; the towpath hedge grew up; the wild flowering plants of marsh and stream soon graced the margins; trees extended their boughs over the water as though to gaze at their new-found reflections; the birds came: the stately swan; coot and moorhen; wild-duck; the bright enamelled kingfisher and the heron standing sentinel or flying over on slow-beating wings. Thus the natural world quickly adopted the new waterway and so, far from detracting from the landscape, it made a positive contribution to it. To make the canal conform to the whims of the eighteenth-century landscape gardener was therefore not a matter of concealment but merely one of adaptation or embellishment.

At Tixall, near the northern end of the Staffordshire & Worcestershire Canal, the waterway has been formed into an ornamental lake, while ornamental bridges of rusticated stonework with balustrades are to be found on many canals. A good late example carries the drive way to Chillington Park over the Shropshire Union Canal near Brewood, and others can be seen on the Grand Union. But the most curious of these ornamental bridges crosses over the Birmingham & Fazeley Canal near the latter place. It is a footbridge access to which is gained by spiral staircases housed in squat castellated towers on each bank.

Yet there is really little need for these conceits because the purely utilitarian architecture of the canals, like the waterway itself, is generally satisfying to the eye. It may possess no outstanding merit, but the cottages, inns and warehouses of canal centres like Shardlow or Stourport remind us in their solidity and good proportion that they belong to that late Georgian age when, though the shadows of Victorian night were already gathering, the sun of English architecture had not set. Architectural poetry has gone, but here we have still fine prose which, if we take pains to study it, reveals the distinction of its craftsmanship in meticulous detail; in roofing slates diminishing in size from eave to ridge; in round-headed windows set with slender cast-iron glazing bars; in an elegant date label; in a finely wrought lantern bracket or weather vane.

It is the lock cottage that reveals canal architecture in its greatest variety. The commonest type, examples of which can be seen throughout the Midlands, consists of a simple four-roomed cottage of mellowing brickwork, its pleasantly proportioned windows often framed in climbing roses, creeper or jasmine. But on some canals, notably the Shropshire Union, there is to be found a curious convention of low-pitched roofs having eaves projecting so far as to give the impression that the house is wearing a wide-brimmed hat. These are varied by single storeyed houses designed by Telford after the model of his toll houses on the Holyhead Road. Again, some canal companies adopted their own, often highly individual, style of lock house. Such are the cottages on the Stratford-on-Avon Canal with their odd but attractive barrel roofs and, stranger still, the round tower lock houses of grey Cotswold stone on the old Thames & Severn Canal. The former are embowered in all the richness of Shakespeare's Arden, but the latter, like watch towers or stranded lighthouses, stand stark and forlorn beside the dry bed of the old canal as it winds over the wolds on its course from Inglesham to Sapperton.

But perhaps the most typical and eloquent reminders of the age when the canals were built are the elegant little bridgeman's cottages on the Gloucester & Berkeley Canal, which, with their classical porticoes, recall the Regency as vividly as the stucco terraces of nearby Cheltenham. These canal cottages are merely what we would describe to-day as "workers' homes," yet they are also a last flowering of English architectural genius. How

99

could their builders have foreseen that their work would so soon be succeeded by the mean "back-to-backs" of the new industrial cities, and what would they think of our housing estates?

Canal architecture so soon became the monument of a lost tradition because the canals themselves were in a great measure responsible for those very changes which obliterated that tradition. It lingered on precariously until the dawn of the railway age, but the great Doric columns of Euston guard the entrance to its tomb. It has yet to be re-born. The subsequent chapters in our architectural history are told in the terra-cotta Gothic of St. Pancras, in the "Banker's Baroque" of a rebuilt Waterloo, and finally in the bleak, impermanent sterility of the concrete, steel and asbestos sheeting of our own day.

❦

CHAPTER IV

WATERWAY MAINTENANCE

On no other aspect of our inland waterways is public ignorance so profound as on the subject of waterway maintenance. This is an age which is inclined to take everyday things for granted without troubling to enquire into the why or wherefore, and as a result there are many intelligent people who imagine that a navigable river was conveniently provided by nature with a sufficient depth of water for commercial navigation, or that once the engineers had dug the channel of a canal, it obligingly filled with water like a well. They are surprised to learn that none of our navigable rivers are natural streams, or that the supply of water to a canal represents the maintenance engineer's biggest problem.

A navigable river is not merely a commercial highway; it is also a source of water supply, a great land drain and, like the farmer's fields, a source of food in the shape of the fish which live in its waters. The representatives of these varying interests may readily conflict with one another, and in fact, as the first chapter of this book reveals, the history of river navigation is a record of endless dispute between the navigators, the landowners, the owners of fishing rights and the mill owners who were then the chief water consumers. Then as now the only reasonable hope of compromise lay in placing the responsibility for river control and maintenance in the hands of a corporate body truly representative of all the interests involved. Yet in practice, methods of administration have moved but slowly towards this end. For many years river control continued to be either non-existent, ineffective, diverse, or representative only of a sectional interest.

The administration of the Great Ouse until 1930 affords a good illustration of the chaotic state of affairs which prevailed until recent times. No less than nine bodies were responsible for different portions of the river and its towing paths. These were:

L. T. Simpson, Esq., Sevenoaks (Bedford to Holywell).
The South Level Drainage & Navigation Commissioners.

The Bedford Level Corporation.
The Denver Sluice Commissioners.
The Conservators of the Ouse Outfall.
The King's Lynn Conservators.
The Lower Ouse Drainage Board.
The Ouse Haling-ways Commissioners.
The Ouse Banks Commissioners.

The rights and responsibilities of these bodies were often incredibly involved and complex. For example, the Bedford Level Corporation owned the site of Denver Sluice and appointed the sluice-keeper, but the Denver Sluice Commissioners maintained the fabric of the sluice and the sea doors, while the maintenance of the navigation doors was the responsibility of the South Level Drainage & Navigation Commissioners. Moreover, despite this formidable army of Boards and Commissioners, considerable portions of the river remained "open navigation," that is to say, they lacked any controlling authority. It will be obvious that such divided administration was especially harmful to navigation because the failure of only one of these bodies to fulfil their obligations could at once affect traffic over the whole river and its connecting waterways.

In 1930 river administration was simplified and reformed by a Land Drainage Act which was passed in that year. Under this Act forty-seven Catchment Boards were set up, the number increasing to fifty-three in 1943. But as the title of the Act denotes, these Boards were primarily concerned with drainage. Fishing interests had become the concern of the Fishery Boards which were constituted in 1923, while the maintenance of navigation often continued to be the responsibility of a separate body. Divided control was thus perpetuated. Where a Catchment Board became responsible for navigation this obligation was generally neglected, if not altogether abrogated, in the interests of drainage. This is particularly true of the rivers in the eastern counties, the River Nene Catchment Board being a shining exception.

With the eclipse of the water-mill the age-old conflict between the millers and the navigators has died a natural death, but the modern age has brought with it new problems of far greater magnitude. On the one hand mechanized farming and the use of artificials, by depleting the fertility and moisture-retaining power of the land, have induced a far more rapid "run-off" of rain water. This produces a steady fall of the level of the subterranean water table and at the same time an increased tendency to sudden and violent flooding accompanied and aggravated by the deposition of the washed away top soil as silt at the river mouths. Upon the other hand the concentration of a vastly increased population in industrial cities combined with the provision of piped water with all its attendant amenities has led to an unprecedented and rapidly growing demand for water. In addition there is the problem of the disposal of a tremendous volume of domestic sewage and industrial effluent.

Throughout the first expansive phase of the industrial revolution no measures were taken to check the pollution of rivers, and the inland fisheries of this country were dealt a blow from which they have never recovered. The River Pollution Prevention Acts of 1876 and 1893 were a very tardy recognition of the problem. The powers authorized by these Acts were exercised by Borough, Urban, Rural District or County Councils, but the Local Government Act of 1888 provided that a joint committee might be set up to deal with the pollution problem of a particular river or group of rivers. Only four such committees were actually formed, and of these only one, in the West Riding of Yorkshire, has to its credit any considerable achievement in redressing past wrong. This has been partly due to the fact that the powers granted under the Acts do not extend to the tidal portions of rivers. This omission has proved disastrous. A vast volume of untreated effluent is consequently discharged into river estuaries, a volume so great that it is often unable to escape but is washed to and fro by successive tides. This not only prevents fish from ascending the river and so nullifies any protective measures which may have been taken on the non-tidal portion, but the deposition of solids from the effluent increases the rate of silting in the estuary.

Sewage discharged into non-tidal waters must conform to a certain standard of purity, but this standard takes into account the very considerable self-cleaning power of a river and therefore assumes that the volume of effluent discharged is small in proportion to the normal flow of the river. Unfortunately this is no longer the case, for the volume of effluent has vastly increased since the Pollution Prevention Acts were passed. Not only are many sewage plants overloaded, with the result that their effluent does not conform to the standard of purity, but the volume of effluent may actually exceed the fresh water flow of the river into which it is discharged.

In many cases this state of affairs is not only due to an increase in the volume of effluent but also to a decrease in the normal flow of the river as a result of pumping for domestic water supply. The failure or inadequacy of underground supplies for the reason already mentioned has induced urban authorities to rely to an increasing extent upon supplies pumped from rivers. Where, as on the Kennet, the supply is derived near the source the loss to the river may be so great that its upper course dries up completely in a dry season. Where, as on the Essex Stour, the water is pumped from the lower reaches the effect is that the tide flows much further up the depleted river, the salt water ruining once fertile water-meadows and killing bankside trees. Finally, the use of river water for cooling purposes by power stations may have the effect of so raising the water temperature of the river that it can no longer support life of any sort.

The foregoing problems of river control may seem to be somewhat irrelevant to the subject of this book, but it is essential to stress the importance of treating every aspect of river maintenance as part of a whole. The gravity of the position to-day is simply the result of the fact that up to now the diverse functions of our rivers have been dealt with piecemeal, here one interest, there another, predominating. It is to be hoped that the new River Boards constituted under the Act of 1948 will improve the position, although it would appear that navigation and fishery interests are inadequately represented upon them.

Up to the present, river administration has varied so widely both in constitution and policy that it is difficult to generalize. In all too many cases, however, Catchment Boards have concerned themselves almost solely with the task of disposing of flood water in the most expeditious manner. Questions of water extraction and effluent discharge have been left to local authorities, while a potentially valuable water highway has been allowed to become archaic if not impassable. Even in their work of flood prevention the policy of some Catchment Boards has been shortsighted. The bed of the river in its upper reaches and those of tributary streams have been deepened and their banks cleared to prevent flooding and induce a quicker flow. In this way many rich water-meadows whose agricultural value depended on their seasonal flooding are no longer flooded. Moreover, these meadows acted as "washlands" such as those which Vermuyden contrived between the New and Old Bedford rivers, providing a safe outlet for flood waters capable of doing untold damage to property elsewhere. The process of deepening, straightening and bank clearing a stream will certainly prevent flooding for a time in the immediate vicinity. But this end is achieved at a heavy cost and will prove only a temporary palliative, for the rate of bank erosion is increased and this again increases the rate of silting at the river mouth, a circumstance which will ultimately cause worse flooding. Although it may be more costly and laborious there is only one solution of this aspect of river control. This is to apply the principle of controlled flooding and water conservation in suitable ares in the upper reaches, to prevent bank erosion by vegetation or piling, and to deepen outfalls by dredging and the prevention of silting.

It is obvious that no authority can effectually carry such a policy into execution if at the same time other bodies are either removing vast quantities of water from the river or adding an equally large volume of effluent full of organic solids. The amounts of water extracted and effluent discharged must be subject to the control of the river authority. If, as seems highly probable, the demands of urban authorities in both these respects can no longer be met without harmful results, then those authorities must find other sources of water supply and sewage disposal. This is a question which is beyond our terms of reference, but a solution probably lies in the method of converting sewage into organic manure for return to the soil which has been tried at Maidenhead and elsewhere. The consequent reduction of sewage discharge into rivers would reduce silting and would also enable more water to be drawn from the lower reaches where it can more often be spared. Ultimately, however, it may be that the only solution of the water supply problem will be that of a national "water grid" drawing supplies from the mountainous regions of the north and west. Such a scheme might also, as Mr. J. F. Pownall envisages in his Contour Canal scheme, provide an inland navigation network.

In the past, river navigation schemes were often opposed on the ground that the impounding of river reaches by locks would increase flooding, and the idea that the interests of inland navigation and drainage are irreconcilable is still current to-day. That this is so is simply due to the misguided policy of river control already mentioned. The functions of navigation and drainage could and should be complementary if the policy of controlled flooding and water conservation was adopted. Locks of the guillotine type used on the River Nene, or the principle of the moving barrage as employed on Continental rivers would assist rather than hinder control. Moreover, the regular passage of commercial craft both assists and enforces the maintenance of a clear channel. There are only two respects in which such navigation may be harmful, and these should be the subject of strict regulation and supervision by the controlling authority. Firstly, the use of either excessively large or fast craft may cause a wash which will damage the river banks. Secondly, oil carelessly discharged from diesel powered boats can be as damaging as any other form of pollution.

Dredging and the maintenance of locks are tasks which are common to both river navigations and canals, but with these exceptions the canal maintenance engineer has to face a very different set of problems. Although questions of water supply to and pollution from industry do arise on the canals they are of relatively minor importance compared with the maintenance of navigation for which purpose they were constructed. Whereas river maintenance consists of the regulation of a natural flow of water, the first and most important task of the canal maintenance engineer is to keep supplied with water a wholly artificial channel which would otherwise dry out. In this task there can be no conflict of interests, for should the supply fail the waterway would be useless to boatman, industrialist and fisherman alike.

If the canal does not (as is frequently the case) supply water for industrial use, and there is no serious leakage, then the only "flow" or consumption of water will be occasioned by the passage of a boat through the waterway. Assuming that the canal passes over a summit level on its course between two river valleys, then the boat will draw the capacity of two locks of water away from that summit level, one as it ascends and the other as it descends. Adequate water resources must therefore be provided on this summit level to replenish the water so consumed, and the extent of the supplies available will determine the amount of traffic which can pass through the canal. Sometimes the canal summit level is fed directly by streams or by direct pumping from springs or rivers at a lower level, but in most cases such methods are not practicable at the summit altitude. The usual source of summit supply consists of catchment reservoirs which impound the waters of springs and streams over the widest practicable area of the watershed which the canal crosses. The reservoirs on the Naseby Wolds which supply the Leicester section of the Grand Union Canal, those at Foulridge on the Leeds & Liverpool, or the Bittal Reservoirs in the Lickey Hills near Barnt Green which feed the Worcester & Birmingham Canal are good examples of this type of supply. Sometimes, as at Barrowford on the Leeds & Liverpool or at Tardebigge on the last named canal, they are supplemented by storage reservoirs into which the waters of the canal can be released through a sluice whenever heavy rainfall provides a surplus. All these reserves the maintenance engineer considers in terms of locks of water; a certain reservoir has a capacity of 3,000 locks; a certain pump can provide three locks an hour. This unit naturally varies with the particular canal, but on the canal system of the Midlands the average narrow lock consumes 25,000 gallons and the wide lock 56,000 gallons.

The larger or deeper the lock, the greater will be the consumption of water. This is a point which those who advocate enlarging our canals frequently overlook. If locks are widened the canal may pass the same tonnage for water consumed because proportionately larger craft will be accommodated, but if the locks are merely deepened to reduce the number in a flight, working time will be saved only at the expense of increased water consumption.

It is also preferable that the locks in a flight or along one line of canal should not vary greatly in depth, otherwise the water levels in the pounds between them will not equalize unless the canal is constantly "running weir" throughout. Such differences do exist, and the side weirs provided beside the locks allow for them, but from the maintenance engineer's point of view, all water not consumed in lockage is water wasted.

Ideally, given a canal with locks of equivalent depth and assuming no undue leakage, all that the engineer should have to do would be to ensure an adequate water supply at the summit.

But this state of affairs never exists in practice, for many other variable factors are involved. Nearly all canals supply water to industrial or domestic consumers who may draw from intermediate pounds. All traffic on a canal is not necessarily through traffic, and some boats may work to and fro over a short length and never reach the summit level. Long intermediate pounds will be subject to considerable evaporation losses, particularly in summer. A branch canal can create another complication, a good example being that of the Northampton Branch of the Grand Union Canal. This leaves the main London–Birmingham line on the Stoke Bruerne–Long Buckby level and falls away to join the River Nene at Northampton. Northbound main line traffic automatically makes good the water drawn off in locking up at Stoke Bruerne when it ascends the Buckby Locks on to the Braunston Summit level which is supplied by Daventry reservoir. But northbound boats which branch off to Northampton draw two locks of water away from this intermediate level, one at Stoke Bruerne and the other at the top lock of the branch. In other words, where this traffic is concerned, the Stoke Bruerne–Long Buckby pound is a summit level, and as such it must have water resources of its own to compensate for this loss.

For all these reasons an adequate supply at the summit level of a main line of canal is not enough, and additional feeders must be provided for intermediate pounds. In practice this need is met by additional storage or catchment reservoirs, by direct feeders, by pumping from rivers and streams or by pumping back the water consumed in lockage. In the particular case of the Stoke Bruerne–Long Buckby level, losses are made up by pumping back the lockage water at Stoke Bruerne from the pound below which receives independent supplies from the River Tove, augmented in dry seasons by pumping from the River Ouse at Wolverton.

The majority of canal pumping stations date from the period of canal construction, though in most cases their original plant has been replaced by diesel or electrically driven pumps. Original pumping stations do, however, survive, and a monograph could be written on this subject alone. A good example of an original pumping installation is situated at Crofton, a remote place in the Wiltshire Downs near the village of Great Bedwyn. Here two magnificent non-rotative beam pumping engines may be seen at work, supplying the Savernake Summit of the Kennet & Avon Canal with water drawn from the neighbouring Wilton Reservoir. One of these engines is said to be a Boulton & Watt, installed at the time Rennie built the canal. If this is so it means that for nearly a century and a half the massive eight-ton beam has swung tirelessly to and fro in this lofty, lonely engine house, a striking testimonial to the craftsmanship of our early mechanical engineers.

Another interesting pumping engine, though in this case no longer at work, is to be seen on the Coventry Canal at Hawkesbury. This is of the Newcomen type and its precise age is not known. It is thought to date only from the Boulton & Watt period when engines of this type were still being constructed in order to circumvent Watt's patent rights.

It is also interesting to recall at this point that one of the first engines that the firm of Boulton & Watt installed in the Midlands pumped water to the Birmingham Canal and was equally long lived.

Protracted droughts or periods of excessive rainfall are the testing times for the canal maintenance staff. When cloudless day succeeds cloudless day, the engineer eyes his reservoir gauges anxiously and takes stock of his dwindling resources. If they fall to danger level he must take emergency measures. At certain hours water may be run down through a flight of locks from a pound that is better supplied. Emergency pumps may be brought into action to return lockage water or to draw supplies from neighbouring rivers. A branch canal at a higher level may be temporarily closed and its waters drawn off to keep the main line open, or a branch to a lower level closed to avoid the loss of its lockage water. The number of boats allowed to pass over the summit level each day may have to be limited, or boats may be ordered to "wait turns" at locks to ensure that the maximum number of boats pass with the minimum consumption of water. If all these measures fail, boats may have to load light on account of the reduced depth of water, or the canal may have to be closed, though this happens rarely.

In times of excessive or abnormally heavy rainfall, the maintenance staff may have to keep a night and day watch upon the canal. If the catchment reservoirs are full the sluices or "paddles" must be raised to admit the surplus into the storage reservoirs, but if these are full also, or where they do not exist it must be disposed of in other ways. Otherwise the canal may overflow its banks and flood adjoining property, or the banks themselves may burst under the strain. On every canal pound of any length there is one or more run-off weir which conveys surplus water into a stream or drain if the water rises above weir level. But the amount of water with which these can deal is limited, and consequently there are often, in addition, emergency "flood paddles" at suitable points which can be raised on these occasions. Alternatively, or in addition, the lock paddles may be drawn and the surplus water run down the locks into some lower pound where it may be more readily disposed of. If a canal overflows or bursts its banks the consequences may be serious as it may run upon embankments high above thickly populated areas.

When such a breach does occur in an embankment, if the pound is a long one a great deal depends upon how soon it is detected. Under certain over bridges there are "stop grooves" in the masonry side-walls into which "stop planks," kept close at hand, can be fitted to form a temporary dam or stank. On some canals, such as the Birmingham & Liverpool Junction Canal section of the Shropshire Union, which is remarkable for its lofty embankments, stop gates like ordinary lock gates are used instead of planks so that sections of canal can be isolated even more readily. By such means, if a burst bank is quickly detected, the outflow can be confined to a short length of canal only.

In October 1939, 3 inches of rain fell in one night in the Daventry area, and despite every effort to discharge the surplus flood water, a breach occurred in the Weedon embankment of the Grand Union Canal. The local lengthman, who had been on duty all through the night, was aware of this danger-point, discovered the breach almost as soon as it carried away in the early hours of the morning, and dropped the stop planks. Only minor local flooding occurred and damage to property was negligible, but had it not been for this prompt action, fifteen miles of waterway could have poured out through an ever widening gap.

Of all the many never-ending jobs upon which the security and comfort of our lives and property depend, that of the canal lengthman is probably the least known or appreciated. When we sweep to the north in a night Scotch express or awaken from sleep to hear a locomotive whistle and the clash of buffers we do occasionally remember the signalman's vigil in his lonely cabin or the endless work of shunters and train crews on the steel webs of the marshalling yards. We sometimes hear the roar of night lorry traffic on a trunk road, or flick a switch in the small hours and think of those who tend the turbo-alternators and switchgear in some distant power station. But when a great storm lashes rain against the panes and booms in the chimney it merely induces, by contrast, a sharpened sense of comfort and security. Yet a quarter of a mile away there may be a canal whose water level is higher than our roof top, and we do not realize that we are only being saved from a catastrophic flood by the vigilance of one man. He may have forfeited a night's sleep to plod, storm lantern in hand through the blinding rain along the towing path watching his levels, regulating his paddles, looking for danger signs. He is often a solitary taciturn old man, accustomed to keeping his own company, for his little red-brick cottage dating from the day the canal was built is often remote even from the village by-road, accessible by land only along the towing path or by a footway over the fields. Sometimes if you are walking the towpath in the daytime you will meet him, a slow-moving, heavy-booted figure bow-hauling his small punt-shaped boat with a load of hedge trimmings or some clay puddle to stop a small leak in the bank. You may perhaps see his weather-beaten face in the village pub of a night, the beer froth whitening the fringe of his heavy moustache. He may not talk to you about his job, for he is seldom a conversationalist, preferring a contemplative pint, but even in these surroundings you can generally recognize him by the queer little hump between his shoulder-blades. It is caused by the end of the lock windlass which he habitually carries tucked over the shoulder under his coat. He is a countryman just as the canal has become a part of the countryside, and yet in a sense he stands apart from the village being a member of that unique amphibious community of the canals. Probably he gets his winter coal by water, and if he ever moves house he will do so by boat. His job of regulating the water over a wide area calls for considerable local knowledge, a knowledge which he inherited from his father before him, a knowledge of sluices, weirs, culverts and streams of which his mind is often the only chart. The canal is his life and his first thought. When his time comes, and he must make way for a generation whose first thought is the contents of the weekly pay packet, it is probable that much of this inherited knowledge

111

will go with him. So much the greater will be our loss. The welfare of society depends upon those who live for their work. We are already finding out to our bitter cost what happens when their places are taken by those who live for their wages.

After drought and flood, the canal engineer's greatest natural adversary is frost. As a general rule, the canal fares better than the river navigation in dry or wet seasons. There are no reservoir reserves to augment the flow of rivers in a drought, while a flood may make river navigation impossible by reducing headroom under bridges if for no other reason. Frost, however, is the one natural condition which turns the tables and sets the canal at a disadvantage, for its still waters quickly ice over. Three inches of ice have been known to form in one night on the summit level of the Leeds & Liverpool Canal at Foulridge, whereas it is only under most rare circumstances that a river navigation freezes up so seriously as to stop traffic.

Canal traffic may force its way through ice half an inch thick or more, though the planks of wooden boats will be badly scored in the process, but if the frost continues it will soon bring trade to a standstill. It is then that the maintenance department bring out the ice-breakers. The traditional pattern of canal ice-breaker which is still widely used consists of a small boat whose stout timbers are protected from damage by strong metal sheathing or which may be built of iron. It differs from the majority of canal craft in having rounded bilges instead of a flat bottom. It is drawn by a team of anything up to twelve or fifteen horses depending on the thickness of the ice. The shape of the hull enables the boat to be rocked vigorously by the gang who man her and who cling all the while to handrails fixed along the gunwales or on a raised platform along the centre-line of the craft. This rocking motion effectually breaks up the ice upon either side to leave a wide channel for the liberated working boats which follow. If the boat were not so rocked but allowed to "swim" on an even keel it would only break a channel its own width in which it would frequently jam. Either this or, as sometimes happens when the ice is exceptionally thick, it might leave the water, sliding out on to the top of the ice.

In recent years, mechanically propelled ice-breaker boats driven by powerful diesel engines have been widely used, but they suffer from various disadvantages as compared with the traditional horse-drawn breaker which become apparent when the ice is particularly thick. Very often they consist of adapted tug boats whose hull shape is not especially suited to the job. Lacking the considerable sheer of the special ice boat which literally beats down the ice on either side, they tend to cut a narrow channel and leave unbroken ice at the margins no matter how vigorously they may be rocked. As a result they are inclined to ride out or jam, and in the latter case if they come astern to free themselves and "take another run at it," their propellers are prone to damage by sucking in floating ice blocks. Moreover, on sharp turns the channel they break may be so narrow that the longer trading craft following them may be unable to negotiate them and become wedged across the corner. One ingenious device designed to overcome this defect consists of a pair of wheels, mounted like paddle wheels on one shaft across the fore-end of the boat and revolved by a small stationary engine. Weights fixed to swinging links on the periphery of the wheels beat and break the ice with a flail-like action.

Given sufficient power, a level length of canal can be opened up under the most extreme conditions. Long after the arctic weather of January and February 1947 had brought practically all canal traffic to a standstill, ice boats drawn by great teams of horses kept open the 11-mile level of the Coventry Canal between Atherstone and Hawkesbury to enable coal boats to reach Coventry Power Station. Traffic was eventually stopped by the masses of pack ice which formed as a result of this constant breaking in continued severe frost. But such conditions are exceptional in England. The real trouble with frost on the canals occurs at locks, and this is what usually brings traffic to a standstill. Broken ice is drawn down to the locks where it fouls gates and paddles or floats into the lock chambers to jam between the boats and the lock walls. There is no more arduous, tedious and heartbreaking task on the canals than to attempt to work a pair of boats through a flight of locks under such conditions. It is a labour of Hercules which in really severe weather soon becomes impracticable. The substitution of the orthodox swinging gates by drop or "guillotine" gates would doubtless improve matters because the latter would not be so easily fouled and would enable ice to be flushed out of the lock chambers more readily, but because protracted periods of frost are comparatively rare in this country, such a costly changeover would scarcely be warranted.

The canal engineer may hate frost, but from the onlooker's point of view ice-breaking, particularly with horse-drawn craft, is easily the most spectacular feature of canal maintenance. Long before it can be seen the ice-breaker's approach is heralded by the crashing, splintering and rending din of its passage which carries far on the keen air while the unbroken ice ahead reverberates like a drum or creaks like an unoiled hinge at the presage of its coming. Then the straining, steaming team appears round the turn moving at that urgent pace which is almost a trot, and finally the boat itself comes into view, rolling almost gunwale under in a flurry of spray and shattered ice as the red-faced crew swing in unison. It is all very dramatic and thrilling for the small boys who crane precariously over the parapets of the bridges to watch their passing, but the canal maintenance man heaves a sigh of profound relief when the wind veers and blows warm from the south and the ice-breaker can return to that backwater of the depot basin. Here through spring and high summer she will lie forgotten unless some venturesome fisherman comes to settle himself on her sun-warmed timbers to dangle an optimistic line between the water lilies.

This summer season, when iridescent dragonflies which know nothing of ice and snow skim over the surface of the water, is the time when lock repairs are carried out. The holiday periods of Whitsun and August are the occasions most commonly chosen for this work. A small notice posted in the window of a lock cottage will announce the "Whitsun Stoppage"; that Lock No. 12, Fiddler's Green will be closed for repairs from noon on Saturday until 8 a.m. on the following Tuesday. Walking through the meadows you may see, rising unexpectedly above the fresh green of the towpath hedge, the tall triangle of a derrick or "sheer legs" straddling the canal. Perhaps a pair of gates have been lifted for repairs and re-bedding, a new pair installed, or a sill rebuilt. A maintenance boat is moored to the bank above the lock, and the lock sides are littered with tools, planks, packing blocks, ropes and sling chains, ladders, portable pumps and snake-like hose pipes. This is the time to see the construction of a lock, for stop planks have been dropped into the grooves provided for the purpose above and below and the lock chamber has been pumped out so that the water is "off the gates." The culverts of the top ground paddles, the sills against which the soles of the gates fit, the invert of brickwork at the bottom of the lock chamber itself, and the paddles in the bottom gates, all these underwater works are now revealed. Ladders descend to the depth of the chamber which looks much deeper now. Perhaps a new pair of gates has -- been slung into place, and down below a carpenter is wielding his adze with delicate precision, skimming the mitre posts with the accuracy of a plane so that they will bed one against the other to make a snug watertight joint.

Much depends upon the weather. In soaking rain it can be misery. Spirits become as damp as clothing, everything is soon covered in a treacherous, slippery film of mud, and dejected figures squelch to and fro in gum-boots, shoulders shrouded in sacking. But in fine weather no one could wish for a better job. The sun makes everything warm and friendly to the touch, and to the scents of the summer fields is added the satisfying astringent smell of fresh hewn oak. The work goes forward smoothly until the light fails and bats flicker over the water. Then it is time to cycle home down the towpath through a dusk made faintly luminous by the May blossom in the hedgerows and by an after-glow reflected in the still water. Over one pair of handlebars dangles a sizeable eel, caught floundering in the mud when the lock chamber was pumped out.

For the carpenter, the installation of a new pair of lock gates is only the culmination of many weeks of work, for in all proba-bility he made the gates himself. His is an enviable occupation. Only on the occasion of lock gate repairs does he emerge from his workshop to take charge of operations. Last winter, when most of those who have been assisting him at the lock were manning the ice-breaker, he was snugly employed in his workshop fashioning that new pair of gates for Lock No. 12, Fiddler's Green.

But the lock-gate maker earns this privilege, for his is a highly skilled craft. Here in his quiet shop is no ordinary carpentry but wood-working on the grand scale, work that is strange to our sight because it has been growing increasingly rare in England ever since we fed our forests into the iron furnaces in the seven-teenth century. But the shade of the medieval craftsman who hewed the timbers of the tithe barn or the hammer beams of the village church would feel at home in this carpenter's shop. The sight of the massive squared timbers of oak shaped and cut to tenon and mortice would occasion him no surprise, while the tools of the lock-gate maker, shell auger, adze and plough, would come sweetly to his hand.

The shell auger, which dates from a day long before the spiral bit was invented, has almost become a museum bygone. Unlike the latter, it is not self-starting and its use calls for considerable skill. Given this skill, however, it possesses this advantage: it will always bore true, whereas a shake in the timber will cause the spiral bit to run off. Hence in this work where holes have to be bored through eighteen inches of timber to locate accurately with the holes in the metal straps upon either side, the ancient tool still lives.

Lock-gate making is not repetition work. When the Braunston-Birmingham section of the Grand Union Canal route from London to Birmingham was reconstructed in the 1930's, standardization of locks was partially achieved, but this is an exception. Speaking generally, the gates of each lock differ more or less from their neighbours. Locks differ in depth and slightly in width, or, at a certain lock there may be an over bridge placed so close to the lock tail that the balance beams of the bottom gates may have to be either cranked or shortened and weighted in order to clear the parapet when the gates are swung open. Apart from these individual differences there are two types of gate, depending on the method of construction, some canal companies favouring one and some the other. One type is known as the "frame gate." In this, the gate itself consists of stout planking secured to a rectangular framework of oak timbering tenoned and morticed together, the heel post and mitre post forming the two vertical members. The alternative is the "solid gate" which consists entirely of solid timbering of the same thickness as the heel and mitre. There being fewer tenons, the solid gate saves labour in construction and is very strong, but it uses much more timber, while if the gate be large it may be inordinately heavy and so demand a balance beam of massive proportions. For this reason, generally speaking, the solid gate is only practicable for narrow locks. To-day, owing to the acute shortage of hard woods, experiments are being made with lock gates of welded steel which, if they prove successful, may kill the craft of wooden lock-gate making. On the face of it this may seem an obvious innovation, but in practice the wooden gate cannot be so lightly superseded. If a boat damages a wooden gate by collision, the resulting damage

116

is seldom so serious that it cannot be repaired at the expense of a short stoppage. Upon the other hand, once a welded steel gate is sprung out of truth by such means it can seldom be re-aligned but must be replaced. Consequently a steel gate, to be truly satisfactory, must be extremely strong and well-braced in order to minimize this risk. Therefore, unless canal locks themselves could be standardized so that steel gates could be pre-fabricated in quantity, it is doubtful whether any great saving in first cost could be affected. The metal would have to be treated against exposure to water and weather, and their length of life is an unknown quantity. Nevertheless, steel gates might affect a saving in maintenance costs particularly on little used waterways where wooden gates dry out and leak. The life of a wooden gate varies widely according to use and particular local conditions. For example, the brine which enters the Worcester & Birmingham Canal at Stoke Prior near Droitwich eats away the metal bolts and bracing of the gates at Dodderhill. A canal engineer will tell you of lock gates which have been replaced twice in his working life and of others which have never been renewed in living memory, but it is probable that forty-five years is a fair average estimate of the life of a wooden gate.

Bricklayers, of course, play a large part in the work of lock maintenance, for there are times when the chamber walls need repairing or re-pointing. Sometimes the action of severe frost in wet ground behind the walls may force walls and copings inward to such an extent that craft become jammed in the lock. In such cases the defective wall must be cut down and rebuilt.

All the year round there is work for the bricklayer. Bridges, cottages or warehouses must be kept in repair, and sometimes— a job he dislikes most—the brickwork of a tunnel may need attention. On such occasions, peering into the tunnel's mouth, you will see the lights mounted on the staging rigged on the maintenance boat throwing serpentine reflections down the dark water and hear, echoing through the stygian darkness, the hollow murmur of voices or the scrape and clink of trowels. Some tunnels need almost constant attention and others scarcely any. Much depends on the characteristics of the local strata. Thus the upkeep cost of Braunston Tunnel on the Grand Union Canal has been negligible so long as records exist, while Blisworth Tunnel, only 16 miles further south in the same county, has proved a constant source of trouble to generations of maintenance engineers. Sectional drawings of the tunnel which each successive engineer has had occasion to prepare survive to record the "headaches" of long ago, and to show how, time after time, movement of the jointed clay rock and limestone through which the tunnel was driven has produced ominous distortions of roof, walls or invert.

While on the subject of this particular tunnel, one of the most peculiar and unusual features of canal maintenance may be mentioned. During the period when steam tugs operated through the tunnel the deposit of soot on the roof grew so thick that its removal became essential. Thereafter the tunnel was periodically swept out like a great chimney by means of a boat upon which large brushes were mounted and manipulated by men who must have been blacker than the blackest sweep by the time they reached the other end.

Next to the work of water supply and control, the most important task of the maintenance engineer is to ensure that the canal has a navigable depth sufficient to enable craft to travel freely with a full pay load. This means dredging, and our canal system to-day is suffering more from the lack of this essential work than from any other single cause. The condition of the railway owned canals in this respect, and the reason for that condition has already been mentioned, but many independently owned waterways are little better. The explanation is simple. Systematic dredging is a costly process. It involves much capital equipment and the employment of a substantial labour force for a considerable period. Mechanical dredgers are the main, but by no means the only major item of equipment required. There are very few situations where the mud brought up can be dumped by the dredger directly on to the canal bank. As a general rule a suitable canal-side site for a spoil dump must be found. This means a fleet of spoil boats, men to man them, horses or tugs to haul them, and a mechanical grab at the dump to unload them. At a time when the extensive introduction of power-driven craft on our canals has greatly increased the rate of silting owing to the bank erosion which they cause, very few canal companies have been in a financial position to embark upon a systematic dredging programme. The more restricted the cross section of a waterway becomes the more readily will craft set up a damaging wash, and in consequence a vicious circle is created. As a result, on many of our canals to-day the navigable channel consists merely of a narrow furrow carved by the boats themselves between shoals of mud. If traffic were to cease the shoals would soon converge and the canal become impassable. This state of affairs may surprise some people who seem to imagine, to judge by the rubbish they throw into them—anything from motor tyres to perambulators or old bicycles—that our canals are bottomless. How the boatmen wish they were! Instead, these appalling conditions slow up traffic, reduce pay loads and lose time and money until, if nothing is done, navigation is no longer an economic proposition and traffic ceases.

Many canals lack both adequate dredging equipment and labour to handle it. Some possess no mechanical dredgers but depend solely on manual "spoon" dredgers which, by dint of a great deal of laborious effort slowly and literally spoon out the mud half a hundredweight at a time. Such equipment can only postpone the day when the canal will become impassable to boats carrying a paying load, and consequently if our canal system is to play the valuable part in our economy which it is capable of doing and should do, additional equipment must be provided and a systematic dredging policy embarked upon. Experiments have already been made with dragline dredgers as opposed to the orthodox bucket type, and though these have not so far proved very successful they should be pursued as there is no reason why improved methods of canal dredging should not be evolved. Lack of capital and enterprise has hitherto hindered such development. The process of dumping spoil might be speeded up. It has been found that once the spoil banks of dredged mud from canals have become consolidated they possess a high fertility. The possibility of discharging the dredger directly into muck spreaders for distribution over the neighbouring fields should not therefore be ignored.

On any canal over which it is proposed to pass a considerable traffic of screw-propelled craft, the banks should be protected by piling wherever necessary; otherwise the most thorough dredging will be so much labour in vain because the erosion trouble will inevitably recur. The greater part of our canal mileage remains substantially as it was when constructed for horse-drawn traffic and is quite unsuitable for motor boats. While the "inside," or towpath side, may be reinforced to a limited extent by dry-bonded masonry, the outside bank is seldom protected in any way.

Where piling was used in the old days it generally consisted of light wooden piles driven home by hand by means of a heavy "beetle" with two helves. This was operated by three men, one gripping each helve while a third stood between them to assist in raising the beetle by grasping the metal cross brace between the helves. This method of piling can still be seen to-day when a temporary dam or "stank" has to be made in connection with underwater repairs. For the permanent purpose of bank protection, pre-cast concrete or interlocking steel piles are now generally used and are driven home by mechanical means. A great deal of bank protection work with concrete piling has been done on the Grand Union Canal, a continuous concrete coping being added, but nowadays steel piling is more generally favoured. A permanent job depends not only on driving the piles to a sufficient depth, but also upon adequately consolidating the bank behind the piling. All too often a length of otherwise sound piling has been left in such a way that the wash from the boats can get behind it. In this way the process of erosion continues and the piles will eventually be loosened.

The operations of bank protection and dredging are both laborious and costly, but when efficiently carried out they convert a semi-derelict waterway into a commercial highway which will retain its efficiency for years at a maintenance cost for tonnage carried which is far less than either road or rail.

The operation of dredging may appear to the layman to be a happy-go-lucky affair. In fact this is far from the case. The true bed of the canal consists of a waterproof layer of puddled clay. The art of dredging consists of cleaning out the channel down to this layer, which marks the full depth at which it was constructed, but no further. For if the puddle is dredged up the canal will start to leak, and this, on elevated levels or sideling ground may have serious consequences which can only be remedied by re-puddling.

In the spring of 1762, when the Duke of Bridgewater's Bill to extend his canal to Runcorn was before Parliament, his engineer gave a practical demonstration of the properties of clay puddle before an astonished Committee of the House of Commons. ". . . Brindley," writes Samuel Smiles, "caused a mass of clay to be brought into the committee room, and, moulding it in its raw untempered state into the form of a trough, he poured into it some water, which speedily ran through and disappeared. He then worked the clay up with water to imitate the process of puddling, and again forming it into a trough, filled it with water, which was now held in without a particle of leakage." What the eighteenth-century cleaners of the House of Commons must have thought of "that Mr. Brindley and his goings on" when they came to clear up the aftermath of this experiment, history does not relate. The fact remains that to-day, after the lapse of nearly two centuries, the water in our canals is still held in its bed by this simple principle which Brindley demonstrated. Furthermore, if any leaks occur fresh puddle is prepared in the same time-honoured way. The introduction of fresh puddle is not an haphazard affair. It is useless merely to throw it down; it must be kneaded and con-solidated. There is a tradition that when the canals were built and puddled, but before the water was let in, herds of cattle were driven along the bed, the "skew tread" of their cloven hooves effectually performing this work of consolidation. While this is only hearsay, the legend is worthy of permanent record before, in company with many other little-known features of canal history, life and work, the recollection dies in some lonely cottage with an old lengthman, and the winds of this age of dissolution blow away the slender threads of folk-memory.

CHAPTER V

BOATS AND BOATBUILDING

THE earliest known types of craft to float upon the waters of our English rivers were the dug-out canoe and the coracle. One of these canoes, hollowed out of a single trunk of oak, was discovered miraculously preserved in the peat of the Shropshire mosses and may be seen in Shrewsbury Museum. The shape of these canoes, though not their method of construction, is thought by some to be perpetuated by the narrow and curiously raked Severn punts which are still used by fishermen on the Severn, especially in the neighbourhood of Deerhurst and Apperley. There is certainly a striking similarity between them.

The Celtic coracle consisted of a frame of woven withies over which a hide was stretched. The result was a small boat of approximately oval plan which was extremely light, buoyant and manœuvrable. The coracle was used principally for net fishing, and the stone net weight rings of these earliest navigators have been dredged up from the bed of the Severn. Two men, each in a coracle, worked a net, one arm, crooked round the loom of the paddle, being sufficient to propel the boat, leaving the other hand free to manipulate the net.

When the Celt retreated towards the west before the advance of the Saxon, the coracle disappeared from the waterways of eastern and southern England and became confined to the rivers of Wales and of the Marches, to Teifi and Towy, to Usk, Wye, Severn and Dee. Here they continued in use for generations, only to be stamped out in modern times by the restrictions imposed upon net fishing for salmon. A few coracle men still work their nets on the Teifi and the Towy, but on the Severn coracles are only rarely used for rod fishing or ferrying, while on Usk, Wye and Dee they are no longer seen at all. The argument used to justify the destruction of the ancient craft of the coracle fishermen was that they were depleting the salmon population, but, as these dispossessed men pointed out, their ancestors had been netting

122

the rivers for a thousand years without having exhausted the stocks. In fact, it was not in their own interest so to do, and with their intimate local knowledge they made far more effective guardians against the depredations of the poacher than the bailiffs of a remote Fishery Board. On the contrary, the enemies of the salmon are industrial and domestic pollution and the cooling water from power stations which, in summer, raises the temperature of the river to a degree fatal to the salmon. If authority had applied itself to combating these evils instead of depriving the coracle men of their ancient calling, salmon would not have become a rare luxury on our dinner tables.

Although its shape and method of use has remained the same, the form of construction of the latter-day coracle has changed. Instead of the withy frame and hide covering of the prehistoric prototype, tarred calico is stretched over a frame of interlacing laths of sawn ash or cleft oak. As late as the nineteenth century, however, hide coverings were still being used at Bewdley on the Severn, the reason being that defective hides could be obtained cheaply from the local tannery.

The Celts were masters of the craft of wattle work, as is apparent from the plaited motif so characteristic of their decorative work whether in bronze ornament or Romano-Celtic architecture. The "hafods" or summer houses situated on the uplands to which this pastoral people resorted with their flocks during the summer months were of wattle construction, and it is reasonable to assume that they applied the same technique to build boats much larger than the diminutive coracle. The Irish curraghs of Achill or Aran bear witness to this and were once thought to have been evolved from the coracle. But it is now generally believed that the ancestors of both coracle and curragh existed side by side in Celtic Britain, the larger and more seaworthy curragh being adopted for use along the coast or in tidal estuaries. According to Irish historians, seagoing and cargo-carrying sailing vessels of curragh construction were used in Ireland from ancient times down to the medieval period, and the boat in which St. Brendan made his first voyage in search of the Isles of the Blest is believed to have been of this type. Thus it may well be that in this ship of Brendan's we have the prototype of the first cargo-carrying craft to navigate our inland waterways. Although fragile, the extreme lightness of this form of construction would have been a great asset in working upstream and in negotiating fords and shallows.

Precisely when these Celtic craft were superseded by heavier timber-built vessels recognizable as the forerunners of the river barge with which we are familiar is uncertain. The Saxon was no great navigator, and the Danish long-boat would seem to be a more likely ancestor than the Roman galley. The Norsemen brought with them to England a knowledge of ship-building and of navigation that was already long established and highly developed. It may be that by so doing they founded a tradition of craftsmanship which has survived down to our own day and which continued to reign supreme and unchallenged until 1788 when, defying a sceptical world, John Wilkinson successfully launched an iron vessel of 40 tons burden on to the Severn at Coalbrookdale.

In the course of centuries of river navigation, a number of regional types of craft, adapted to suit local conditions and needs, were evolved and perpetuated in the boatyards of many a riverside town or village; at Framilode and Tewkesbury on the Severn; at Oxford and Thames Ditton on the Thames; at Newark, East and West Stockwith, Misterton and Butterwick on the Trent, and at Selby, Wistow, Stillingfleet, Naburn, Fulford and Cawood on the Yorkshire Ouse, to mention only a few.

In the seventeenth and early eighteenth centuries the largest craft in regular use on inland waters were the "western barges" of the Thames and the Severn trows. In 1720, according to Defoe, barges of 50 tons burden were able to trade to Lechlade and of 90 tons to Oxford. In the summer season, however, they had to make use of "lightening boats" into which they discharged part of their cargo before they could pass through weirs and over shoals. The Severn trows were of from 40 to 80 tons burden, though there was also a smaller type of 20 to 40 tons called variously a barge, frigate or up-river trow. On the other hand, probably the smallest commercial craft in use during this period were the flat-bottomed boats loading 4 tons on a draught of 1 ft. 4 in. which could navigate the Wye to Hereford. The above-mentioned types represent the two extremes, the average craft in use on our rivers at this time probably having a burden of from 20 to 40 tons. It is difficult, however, to generalize with any accuracy since the size of boat used on a particular river at any given time tended to vary according to the state of that river.

Thus in the time of Charles II vessels carrying 100 tons could trade to York, but by the eighteenth century this maximum had fallen to 70 tons owing to the decay of the Yorkshire Ouse. Conversely, the navigation of the Great Ouse improved during this period with the result that the size of the lighters used on this river increased from 40 tons in the seventeenth century to no less than 130 tons in 1749.

Almost invariably, these early river craft were sailing vessels carrying a square rig, fore-and-aft rig not being widely introduced until a much later date. The larger Severn trows, however, were exceptional in carrying a combination of both forms of rig. They were two-masted, carrying square-rigged main and topsails on an 80 ft. mainmast and a lateen sail on the mizzen. The power of sail was assisted by drifting with the tide or stream and by hauling by gangs of men. Non-sailing vessels did not appear in great numbers until the widespread introduction of horse-towing paths in the canal era and the later appearance of steam tugs for towage. Probably the earliest non-sailing craft were the rafts, "flottes" or drags on which heavy loads were floated down rivers on the current.

All the regional types of river craft and their modern successors can be broadly classified as barges, the term signifying a vessel having a beam of not less than 14 ft. and capable of entering tidal waters though not necessarily suitable for open sea or even coastal navigation. Also, as a general though not invariable rule, barges are flush-decked, that is to say the cargo is stowed in a covered hold or under hatches, while living accommodation, if provided, is also below deck.

During the period of canal construction a number of waterways were built to dimensions suitable for the particular type of craft already in use on the rivers with which they connected. Such waterways are often termed "barge canals." The greater proportion of canal mileage in this country, however, was built to dimensions which excluded river barges, and this led to the introduction of specialized types of canal craft. These are properly referred to collectively as boats. Their beam is less than 14 ft. and they rarely enter tidal waters to which they are unsuited, the majority being quite unseaworthy. Their cargo is carried in open holds, and if living accommodation is provided the cabin usually consists of a superstructure.

A century of steam and diesel power combined with the supercession of wood by iron or steel for boatbuilding has resulted in the rapid disappearance of many beautiful regional types of river barge. Though their numbers are rapidly diminishing, the most numerous surviving class are the sailing barges of the Thames and Medway whose range extends to the ports and estuaries of the south and east coasts and even to the Continent. The extinct west-country barges already referred to which traded up river to Oxford and beyond were presumably so-called to distinguish them from these seagoing down-river craft. Unlike the Severn Trow which long retained her square-rigged main and topsails, the Thames barge of modern times is fore-and-aft rigged in so ingenious a manner that she can be handled by a crew of two. No other vessel in the world carries so great a cargo or so large a sail area for so small a crew. A Thames barge coming down London River on the evening tide with all her brown canvas set is a beautiful sight which, alas, the next generation may never see.

The term "barge" also applies in the particular as well as the general sense to the non-sailing craft which navigate the Thames, the Medway, the Wey, the lower portion of the Grand Union Canal, and the Lee, as well as to the smaller vessels used on the Chelmer & Blackwater Navigation. The latter measure 58 ft. 6 in. by 16 ft. and load 25 tons on a draught of only 2 ft., for the Chelmer & Blackwater has the distinction of being the shallowest navigation in the country upon which trade is regularly conducted, the maximum permissible draught being 2 ft.

The other type of craft in use on the Thames as on most of our larger navigable rivers and docks is the lighter. Lighters vary in build from district to district, but they may generally be distinguished from barges by the fact that they carry no cabin accommodation, being used only for short-distance journeys usually in connection with the discharge of seagoing vessels. Thames lighters are sometimes referred to as "punts" because, like a punt, they have flat, sloping "swim ends." Some Thames barges were "swim-headed" in this fashion, but the type is extinct. Unlike those elsewhere, the majority of Thames lighters are rudderless, the lightermen controlling them by means of a long sweep with a skill which seems miraculous to the casual onlooker. A lighter drifting swiftly on the tide down London River will appear to be about to crash broadside into a bridge when, just at the moment when disaster seems inevitable, an unhurried, almost careless thrust of the sweep will send the clumsy craft skimming fairly beneath the arch. Some of these lighters do, however, carry a helm, in which case they are known as "rudder punts."

Trade on the Norfolk Broads group of waterways was once carried on exclusively by the sailing wherry, there being no horse towing paths on the Rivers Bure, Yare and Waveney. The Norfolk wherry varied greatly in size from small craft 35 ft. long by 9 ft. beam loading twelve tons, to the *Wonder* of Norwich which measured 65 ft. by 19 ft. and carried 83 tons on a draught of 7 ft. But an average wherry would be 55 ft. long with a beam of 11 ft. loading from 20 to 25 tons on a draught of 2 ft. 6 in. They carried no standing rigging, the mainmast being stepped in a tabernacle right forward, counterbalanced by lead weights at the foot and raised by a windlass. No boom was used, the single fore-and-aft mainsail being loose-footed and rigged on an enormous gaff. The wherry was reputed to be able to sail closer to the wind than any craft afloat, but where wind power failed the wherrymen resorted to their quants—20 ft. shafts with forked steel ends, not unlike the Severn shafts of the trowmen. Not many years ago it was still a common and splendid sight to see the great tanned canvas mainsail of a wherry moving majestically over the Fens, but to-day the commercial craft most commonly encountered on these waterways is the small diesel coaster carrying sugar-beet. Of the handful of wherries left, only one still carries sail, the rest having been engined. Unlike the majority of river men, the Norfolk wherryman and the Yorkshire keelman sometimes carried their families aboard.

The sailing Yorkshire or Humber keel with its great square-rigged mainsail had at one time almost a monopoly of trade over the network of rivers and broad canals of Yorkshire. The average keel measures 57 ft. 6 in. by 14 ft. 3 in. and loads from 80 to 100 tons on a draught of 6 ft. to 6 ft. 9 in. Here, bow-hauling rather than horse haulage or shafting was the rule when the wind did not serve, but early in the present century a number of keels were dismasted and fitted up as steamers. To-day the traditional keel is being rapidly superseded by larger craft wherever the locks will permit. They are still to be seen, however, on the upper portion of the Calder & Hebble Navigation and the Huddersfield Broad Canal where the locks exclude any vessel exceeding the dimensions of the keel. Though they are all diesel engined or, in a few cases, horse hauled, and carry no sailing gear, stern rails, curious wooden stove chimneys and carved and painted ornamental work (usually a flower or grape pattern) render the keel unmistakable. Moreover, some of the older boatmen who work them can recall the days of sailing and bow-hauling.

A much larger type of sailing craft was the Lower Trent boat, now either engined or drawn by tug. They were so called to distinguish them from the Upper Trent boats, smaller dumb craft, unsuitable for working the tidal river below Keadby, which navigate the upper reaches including the River Soar and the Trent & Mersey Canal to Shardlow. This is a rare case where river craft of the barge type are locally known as "boats."

Craft trading on the Rivers Mersey and Weaver are generally called flats, the Weaver flat, 90 ft. long and 21 ft. beam with a draught of 10 ft. 6 in. when loaded with 250 tons, being the largest type. Some of these Weaver flats once carried sail in which case they were known as No. 1 or black flats.

The open hold barges trading on the Bridgewater Canal are known as lighters. They are approximately the same size as the Mersey flats, but unlike the latter they do not work out into the tidal waters of the Mersey.

The term lighter is also applied to the small craft built for working over the drainage navigations of the Bedford Level of the Fens. The average Fen lighter measured 42 ft. by 10 ft. beam and loaded 25 tons on a draught of 3 ft. 6 in. It was usual to work them in gangs of five, close coupled by "seizing chains." The crew of the leading lighter controlled the rest of the gang by manipulating a long "steering pole" attached like a bowsprit to the second lighter, and by working two "fest ropes" passing from the fore-end of the pole to each side of the lighter. Shorter "jambing poles" attached to the lighter next ahead by ropes called "quarter bits" enabled the last three lighters in the gang to follow. As a rule, only one lighter in the gang carried a living cabin and was called the house lighter. Only one gang of Fen lighters remains in commission at the time of writing.

The fully-rigged Severn trow has only become extinct in the last few years. In the early years of the present century she was still a familiar sight, not only on the Severn but in the South Wales ports and all the little harbours of the West Country to which the trows brought coal from Wales or from Dean Forest, loading

PLATE XXV.—BURST EMBANKMENT AT WEEDON, GRAND UNION CANAL, OCTOBER 1939

(*a*) Water pouring through the breach

(*b*) The breach closed with temporary piling tied to opposite bank and leaving a passage for traffic

PLATE XXVI.—ICE-BREAKING WITH STEAM AND HORSE-DRAWN CRAFT,
MARTON POOL AND GARGRAVE, LEEDS AND LIVERPOOL CANAL

PLATE XXVII.—LOCK REPAIRS
ON THE WORCESTER AND
BIRMINGHAM CANAL

(*a*) Making a new top gate at Tardebigge depot

(*b*) A bottom gate on the Tardebigge flight about to be lifted. Note the brick invert, and the bottom gate sill

(a)

PLATE XXVIII.—A SECTION OF THE GRAND UNION CANAL BEFORE AND AFTER
BANK PROTECTION WORK WITH CONCRETE PILING AND CONTINUOUS COPING

PLATE XXIX

(*a*) A steam dredger at work on the Grand Union Canal

(*b*) An old photograph of the brushing boat once used in Blisworth Tunnel, Grand Union Canal

PLATE XXX.—TYPES OF CRAFT

(*a*) A Weaver Flat on the Weaver at Northwich

(*b*) A Yorkshire or Humber Keel on the Calder & Hebble Navigation

PLATE XXXI.—SEVERN TROWS, PAST AND PRESENT

(a) Severn Trows ("The Wich Barges") on the Droitwich Barge Canal at Droitwich, *circa* 1904
(b) The last of the old "Wich Barges" on dry dock at Saul, 1948. Now working as a dumb barge in the Bristol coal trade

PLATE XXXII.—
TYPES OF CRAFT

(*a*) Coal container boats of the type evolved by Brindley on the Bridgewater Canal, 1948

(*b*) A Bridgewater lighter on Worsley Turn, Bridgewater Canal

at Lydney or Bullo Pill. The smaller trows also went up the Stroudwater Canal to load bales of cloth from the Stroud Mills and up the Droitwich Canal for salt. The last named were generally referred to as the "Wich Barges." But to-day the trows are gone, and the eye looks in vain across the wide levels of the Severn Hams by Tewkesbury or Upton for a glimpse of the once familiar masts and sails. Instead the characteristic portent of river traffic on Severn side is now one of sound, not sight; it is the deep-noted throb of a diesel engine as the steel barges, low laden and invisible beneath the high red banks, forge upstream with their cargoes for Worcester or Stourport. A few trows survive as dumb barges and may be seen in train behind a tug on the Gloucester & Berkeley Canal. Until recently, one of these survivors still carried her sailing gear. One or two more trows which still trade to the little harbour of Lydney to load coal have been fitted with petrol/paraffin engines, but rig a small steadying sail in rough weather.

With the rapid disappearance of these ancient regional types of river craft, the wooden canal "narrow boat" dating from the beginning of the canal era seems destined soon to become the oldest surviving type in use on our inland waterways. These boats are built to pass the locks of the narrow canal system of the Midlands or to work in pairs through the wide locks of broad or barge canals. Although river navigations such as the Weaver, the Severn and the broad waterways of the North, notably the Aire & Calder or the Sheffield & South Yorkshire, may handle a greater annual tonnage, the narrow boat is undoubtedly the most numerous and most widely distributed class of vessel in use on the English canal system. Its practicable working range extends from London to Stockwith on the Trent in the East, and from Sharpness on the Severn to Ellesmere Port, Manchester, Liverpool and Wigan in the West. "Narrow Boat" is the usual term for these boats throughout the Midlands, but in the London area they are often called "Monkey Boats" and in the Severn district "Long Boats." Their dimensions vary slightly from district to district, the average being: length 70 ft., beam 7 ft., draught unladen 8 in., and loading approximately one inch to the ton to a maximum of 30 tons. Beside the Boatage Depot at Stourport-on-Severn may sometimes be seen one of the narrow boats which now work between Stourport and the Black Country, but which were originally built for handling general cargo on the Welsh section of the Shropshire Union Canal. These measure 70 ft. by 6 ft. 10 in., are built fine and with rounded bilges to load 20–25 tons. In the same basin there may be a typical Severn "long boat," virtually a floating box 72 ft. by 7 ft. 2 in., and loading up to a maximum of 40 tons. These two types illustrate the extreme limits of narrow boats still in use. Also to Stourport come the "day boats" or "open boats" carrying coal to the power station. These might be called the lighters of the canals. They are extensively used for "short-length" hauls in the Birmingham and Wolverhampton area. Of the same dimensions as the long distance-narrow boat, they are of cruder construction and carry no living accommodation, the cabin being either non-existent or a mere shelter for meals.

The "gas boats," as they are popularly called, operated by Messrs. Thomas Clayton of Oldbury are frequently to be seen on the narrow canals of the Midlands, particularly in the Birmingham area and on the main line of the Shropshire Union Canal. These boats are most commonly employed in carrying crude tar or "gas oil" from gas works to tar distilleries. Flush-decked, they are virtually unsinkable, their liquid cargo being poured directly into the hold so that they become floating tanks.

With the exception of these gas boats, the narrow boat's cargo is stowed in an open hold and never under hatches as in the case of a barge operating in tidal waters.

The traditional pattern of the narrow canal boat was horse drawn, and although horse haulage is rapidly dying out, very many of these once horse-drawn boats survive unaltered as trailers or "butties" to the modern diesel boats.

In addition to the canal system, narrow boats work over the non-tidal portions of many rivers such as the Severn, Thames, Trent, Soar, Weaver and Nene, either under their own power or in charge of a tug, as is usually the case on the Severn, where they are underpowered for travelling fully loaded upstream when there is much "fresh" in the river. Owing to its extreme length in proportion to its beam, the structure of the narrow boat is fundamentally weak and quite unsuitable for a seaway. Narrow boats have occasionally worked out on to London River as far down as Greenwich, while under favourable conditions they have been known to make the passage of the Severn estuary between

Avonmouth and Sharpness, but as a general rule their use may safely be said to be confined to non-tidal waters.

The term "wide boat" applies to a type of craft working on the Grand Union Canal between the London area and Berkhamsted. They are the same length as a narrow boat and have similar living cabins but have a beam of 10 ft. to 11 ft. and load approximately 50 tons. When the Grand Union Company was formed by amalgamation and the new wide locks were opened between Napton and Birmingham it was originally proposed to operate wide boats on the through route. To this end the diesel wide boat *Pioneer* was built and worked experimentally between London and Birmingham. But locks are by no means the only factor which determines the size of craft best suited to a waterway. *Pioneer* did not travel so well in restricted sections of the canal as a pair of narrow boats carrying the same load. Moreover, the introduction of a fleet of such boats would have led to passing difficulties in many places and the introduction of a one-way traffic system in Braunston and Blisworth Tunnels. To-day, the wide boat is almost extinct and its use confined to the section south of Berkhamsted though they may work as far north as Leighton Buzzard.

Another type of craft known as a wide boat works on the Yorkshire Canal system. It is of similar dimensions to the Yorkshire keel, but unlike the latter it was never rigged for sail and never enters tidal waters.

Barges, lighters or flats can use the main line of the Leeds & Liverpool Canal from Liverpool to the tail of the twenty-first lock at Wigan, including the Leigh Branch, but from Wigan to Leeds the locks are 10 feet shorter and traffic is handled by Leeds & Liverpool "short boats." These measure 62 ft. by 14 ft. 3 in. and load 45 tons on a draught of 3 ft. 9 in.

The tub boats of the old Shrewsbury and Coalport Canals which once handled coal and ore traffic in the strange industrial backwater of Shropshire have passed into history. They were simply floating boxes, 19 ft. 9 in. by 6 ft. 2 in. and loading 5 tons on a draught of 2 ft. They were towed by horses in trains of as many as twenty at a time, a man walking the towpath keeping the leading boat in mid channel by means of a long shaft. The locks on the Old Shropshire Canal between Trench and Wappenshall and between Wappenshall and Shrewsbury were 71 ft. and

81 ft. long respectively, locking through three and four tub boats at a time. They were only 6 ft. 4 in. wide, and at one time a special type of narrow boat was built to work through them.

The nearest equivalent to these tub boats still in use is the compartment boat or "Tom Pudding" used for the heavy coal traffic handled on the Aire & Calder Navigation. The compartment boat is an oblong iron box 20 ft. long by 16 ft. beam and loading 35 tons on a draught of 6 ft. When first introduced they were pushed ahead of a tug and steered by steel ropes passing along the sides of the boats from winches on the tug. They are now towed in the normal way in trains of as many as thirty-two boats. A short wedge-shaped boat called the "Dummy Bows" is attached to the fore-end of the leading compartment. The locks on the main line of the Navigation from Leeds and Wakefield through Castleford to Goole can pass six compartment boats at a time, and the result is the cheapest method of handling heavy mineral traffic in the world.

The locks on the canals of South Wales were built to different gauges, none of which correspond to that of the English canal system. Thus the Glamorgan, Aberdare, Monmouthshire and Brecon & Abergavenny Canal boats measure 60 ft. by 8 ft. 6 in. Neath and Tennant Canal boats 60 ft. by 9 ft. and Swansea Canal boats 65 ft. by 7 ft. 6 in. They are thus a striking example of the variations of gauge from which the canal system as a whole has suffered so much. Many of these old South Wales coal boats are to be found sunken and rotting in the reedy waters they once travelled. A few Monmouthshire boats migrated across the Bristol Channel to the Kennet & Avon Canal where they serve as maintenance boats. They were the equivalent of the "day boats" of the Birmingham Canals, few carrying cabins and many being "double ended," that is to say the rudder could be hung at either end so that turning was avoided.

Barges, many of which were built at Honeystreet near Pewsey, navigated the Kennet & Avon Canal. They were steered from a platform for'ard of the stern cabin, the long tiller passing over the cabin roof. They continued to carry timber between Avonmouth or Bristol and Honeystreet until 1929 when the trade had to be finally abandoned owing to the bad state of the navigation under railway ownership.

When steam drove sail from the sea and the "wooden walls of

England" became walls of iron and steel, the little boatyards of the rivers and canals became the last custodians of the great traditions of the ancient craft of timber ship building. The clatter of caulking mallets, the pungent aroma of hot tar, pitch and fresh oakum; these immemorial characteristics of the boatbuilder's yard lost their association with the scents and sounds of the sea to live on in such a pastoral setting of willows and water-meadows as Constable portrayed in his picture "Boatbuilding on the Stour," or among the Georgian warehouses of a canal wharf in some quiet country town. Yet even here metal is rapidly superseding wood. Because we have failed to husband our resources of hardwoods, supplies of oak suitable for boatbuilding become increasingly scarce, costly, and of poor quality. Soon they will be non-existent. Moreover, there will soon be no craftsman left to build in oak even if material is available. The deafening clangour of pneumatic riveters is the characteristic of the modern barge-builders' yard, while the sailmakers' loft and the ropewalk have been replaced by the mechanic and the fitting shop. Woodwork is confined to the repair of existing barges. Even cement has been used as a building material and a number of concrete lighters, built during the first World War, are still in use on the Thames and on the Gloucester & Berkeley Canal.

The same process of change is occurring on the canals, the smaller yards devoting themselves increasingly to repairs while the larger adopt metal construction. The first departure from traditional construction on the narrow canals was the "composite" boat, iron-sided but with an elm bottom. And here it is of interest to note that "composite" is an inherited term originally used to describe the hulls of wood planking over an iron frame which were built in the last days of sail. The great clipper ship *Sir Lancelot*, built by Steele of Greenock in 1865, was such a one. A number of composite narrow boats are in use on the canals to-day, and represent the transitional stage between the traditional wooden boat and the latest all steel type.

For the wooden canal boat, oak is used for the planking, which is alternately wet and dry as the boat is loaded or empty, and elm for the flat bottom which is constantly submerged. Whereas the oak timbers are tarred, the elm bottoms are not treated in any way but are allowed to absorb water like a sponge. Constantly saturated in this way, elm will last for years. When elm boat bottoms have to be renewed it is usually because they have worn thin through rubbing the canal bed when loaded. An old bottom removed for this reason will be as hard and sound as the day it was fitted, yet if it is allowed to dry out thoroughly it will soon crumble to powder.

In the early canal boats the elm bottoms ran longitudinally from stem to stern and were spiked up to the bottom strakes and to transverse oak ribs scarphed to the oak "knees," as the angle brackets between bottom and sides are called. There was no keelson. They were known to boatbuilders as "long-bottom boats" but no examples of this type of construction survive. In the present form the elm bottoms are transverse, bolted to iron or steel "knees," and spiked up to the bottom strakes and to a three-inch keelson of oak or pitch-pine. In building a new wooden canal boat the bottoms are first laid out on a wooden frame, 6 ft. wide, high enough to allow them to be spiked up to the keelson and to the first plank from below, the spikes usually being subsequently riveted over washers on the upper surface of the keelson. The iron knees are then bolted in position on the bottoms, and the stem and stern posts fixed in place. Next comes the two-inch oak side planking, the bottom planks being fixed first, spiked up through the bottoms and bolted to the iron knees. The boatbuilder must ensure that the scarph joints between these planks are "staggered" as much as possible, otherwise the hull will be weakened. At bow and stern the planks must curve to meet the stem and stern posts to which they are fastened. In the finer types of long-distance narrow boats this is a graceful inward and upward sweep which is secured partly by steaming and partly by selecting timber having a suitable curvature in the grain. The plank is steamed in a wooden steam chest, withdrawn, quickly secured in position at one end by means of a cramp or props and wedges, and then pulled round while still hot and pliant. This is one of the trickiest operations in boatbuilding. "Pull while the plank is hot" would be the boatbuilder's appropriate variant of a hackneyed phrase, for if he does not secure one end of the plank in position with well-rehearsed speed it may stiffen. In this case either it will refuse to come round or, if enough force is applied, it will split.

When the main timbering of the hull is completed, hot "chalico," a mixture of Stockholm tar, horse dung and cow-hair is plastered over the inside of the planking, sheets of brown paper smoothed over it, and finally the thin vertical oak planks called "shearing" are nailed on. This not only seals the hull, it also provides a backing for the seams. Without the shearing, the oakum might be driven right through the seams by the caulking tool.

The oakum for caulking is bought loose in sacks, and the boatbuilder's first job is to roll it out into rope-like lengths. This he does by drawing it out with one hand while with the palm of the other he rolls it over a sack laid across his thigh. Caulking is a long job, for every seam in the bottom and sides must be sealed, including the diagonal scarph joints between the planks. If a seam is too close to allow the oakum to be forced in, it is wedged apart with a chisel-like "opening iron." The caulking tool also resembles a chisel, but instead of a sharp edge it has a blunt face about an eighth of an inch wide bearing a longitudinal groove which holds and packs the oakum. The long head of the caulking mallet is of metal-banded boxwood. If the wooden blocks or "bostocks" on which the boat rests in the dry dock or on the slip are not high enough, the boat must be tipped with jacks first on one side and then on the other, to enable the bottom seams to be caulked. When caulking is completed the seams are pitched and then the sides of the hull are ready for a coat of tar applied hot with a long-handled brush.

The hull is now ready for the cabinwork and fittings. If the boatman has a large family requiring extra accommodation, a small cabin is built for'ard in addition to the usual stern cabin. Most of the "Gas boats" operated by Messrs. Thomas Clayton are so equipped, but more usually the fore-end is flush-decked and forms a locker for spare tackle and, in the case of a horse boat, for fodder. The hull is strengthened by means of detachable cross-planks called "stretchers" which fit into wooden brackets on the "lining pieces" which stiffen the gunwales, and thus occupy the position of the thwarts in a rowing boat. The stands which support the gang plank pass through slots in the stretchers and rest in mortices on the keelson. The gang-plank running fore and aft is lashed down to these stands, to a block known as the "cabin block" on the deck of the aft cabin, and to a triangular board called the "deck cratch"[1] for'ard. A square telescopic towing

[1] The front surface of the deck cratch is usually decorated, but sometimes it is padded out by means of wooden formers and hay covered with canvas to produce a graceful deep curve at the fore-end. This arrangement is wholly decorative and is known as a "bulk."

mast, still fitted to motor as well as horse boats, a false floor in
the hold fitting flush with the top of the keelson, and, in the case
of horse or butty boats, the great wooden rudder with its post
or "ram's head" and curving wooden tiller bar, complete the
new narrow boat.

It is not many months since I saw such a boat finished on the
slipway of a small boatyard in the Midlands, a sight to gladden
the eye of anyone who can appreciate fine wood-craftsmanship.
She had not yet been tarred, so her sides had still that pristine
honey colour of the fresh cut oak that scented the air. Yet it was
sad to reflect that I might never see her like again; that this small
canal boat, to be launched without stir or ceremony into the still
waters of the canal, might well be the last of a line of oak ships
stretching back to the days of the Armada, to *The Great Harry*, or
further still to that remote past of the long boats of the Dane.

Even though there may be few more wooden boats built, it
will be many years before the last wooden craft disappears from
the waterways, for they are long lived. In fact, if they are docked
regularly every two to three years, they will last almost in-
definitely although, in the case of very old boats that have seen
fifty or more years of service it may be unlikely that any of the
original timbers remain. It is one of the advantages of a wooden
boat that its planking can always be renewed fairly readily. Up
to a point, an iron or steel hull can be patched up by riveting or
welding on new plates, but there comes a time when wear and
wastage have between them so reduced the strength of the hull
that it is only fit for scrap. Perhaps the greatest constructional
fault of the wooden boat is the method of iron fastening. The
action of the iron spikes and knee bolts tends to set up rot in the
planking at these points, a fault which the Shropshire Union
Company overcame to some extent by galvanizing all iron work.

When the boatbuilder's work is done there are still fenders
and sheets or "cloths" to be provided. Each boat must be equipped
with a bow fender woven out of rope to soften the impact when
nosing up to lock gates. In addition, motor boats carry a fender
or series of fenders called "tip-cats" on the counter which protect
the rudder from the butty or from lock gates. Side cloths and top
cloths are fitted to protect the cargo from the weather. The
former are permanently secured to the gunwale and furled when
not in use. When unfurled they are held up by strings strained

over the gang planks. These side cloths serve the dual purpose of preventing water from coming inboard in locks, for there is little freeboard when the boat is fully loaded, and of preventing a load of small coal from running overboard. When a cargo must be completely protected from the weather the top cloths are laid over the gang planks. These overlap the side cloths and are secured by strings to small rings along the gunwales. A boat is then said to be fully sheeted up. When loading bulky cargo such as long steel bars the stretchers and stands must all be removed, but otherwise it is only necessary to shift the gang planks.

Before a new boat, or even a boat which has been extensively overhauled or re-planked, can be put into commission it must be gauged so that the weight of cargo carried can readily be estimated for toll-charging purposes. This "first gauging" as it may be called is carried out at a weigh dock. Here the draught of the boat when empty is first carefully measured and then she is loaded with one-ton weights by means of a crane up to full capacity, the draught being measured at each ton of loading. It was the practice of the Shropshire Union Canal Carrying Company to fix graduated scales to the sides of their boats from which the tonnage carried could then be read off by the toll clerk at any time. The more usual practice, however, is to enter the tonnage displacement figures in a register, a copy of which is kept at each toll office on the waterways over which the boat is to work. Under this system, in order to assess the tonnage the toll clerk gauges the boat by measuring the freeboard or "dry inches" at four points, at each side near the bow and at each side near the stern. Sometimes these points are marked by small metal plates. The tonnage carried is then determined by calculating the average draught and comparing the result with the register. The instrument used to carry out this gauging consists of a float moving in a graduated tube which is fitted with a bracket mounted at right angles. This bracket is rested on the gunwale of the boat so that the float indicates on the scale the number of inches between the gunwale and water level.

Before finally leaving the subject of boats and boatbuilding a word should be said about boat painting, for in this respect the narrow boat of the Midland Canal system is quite unique. So elaborate is this painting that to decorate a boat in the full traditional style is a work of art, but the owner-boatman never grudged the expense. The cabin inside and out, the bow and stern, the hatches or "slides," the ram's-head and tiller, the mast, stands and cratch, even the mop, water-can and hand-bowl which each boat carries, all are decorated with fabulous "castle" scenes, with garlands of roses or with geometrical patterns of contrasting primary colours until the newly painted boat rivals for brilliance of colour the decorated poop of an Elizabethan galleon. In this drab, machine-dominated England of ours the narrow canal boat is as unique and striking as some vivid tropical bird seen amid a flock of sparrows, but, like the bright bird, it has strayed into an alien world and may soon perish. It is a reminder of those days before the rise of the Puritan and the merchant when man expressed his joy in an unselfconscious richness of colour, colour which once gave to every rib, vault and boss of the grey Gothic cathedral a brilliance which we should find overwhelming. How this unique tradition originated we shall have occasion to consider in a subsequent chapter.

CHAPTER VI

TRAFFIC WORKING AND MOTIVE POWER, PAST AND PRESENT

MENTION has already been made, in the first chapter of this book, of the hazards and delays to which early river navigation was subject. Traffic was liable to frequent interruption owing to drought or flood or to the intransigence of mill owners controlling flash locks. When wind, tide or current did not serve, the heavy craft were hauled by gangs of bow-hauliers, hired by stages, or occasionally propelled by the boat's crew using long shafts. In addition to the risky proceeding of winching through flash locks there were other difficulties such as the negotiation of bridges where there was no hauling path under the arch. When travelling with the stream or tide, boats could drift through such bridges, but when working upstream a special technique had to be employed. The bow-hauliers made their way on to the bridge and hauled the boat up as far as was practicable. The hauling line was then held fast while the free end was dropped over the parapet on the upstream side whence it floated downstream. The boat's crew then retrieved it, made it fast, and at the same time cast off the other end. Thus the towline now passed through the arch and the hauliers were free to continue on their way upstream. Grooves worn by the towlines in the stonework of Eckington Bridge over the Lower (Warwick) Avon remain to reveal the oft-repeated use of this method by the Avon bow-hauliers at this point.

Inland water transport in the seventeenth and early eighteenth centuries was not only subject to natural and physical hazards and delays which made it slow and arduous, it also suffered from monopolistic abuses and exactions. Under their Letters Patent the undertakers of river improvements were often given the sole right to carry goods upon such waterways, and in the seventeenth century traffic on the Rivers Larke, Wey, Wiltshire Avon and Wye was monopolized in this way, although the tonnage rates were regulated by statute. Even where no such exclusive rights obtained on the river itself, a monopoly was sometimes secured by acquiring all the available wharfage facilities. Thus in 1699 Lord Paget obtained an Act empowering him to improve the River Trent between Wilden Ferry and Burton but assigned his powers to a man named Hayne who owned the only wharf at Burton. Under these powers, Hayne was able to prevent the erection of any other wharf or warehouse, and, in partnership with a merchant and boatmaster named Fosbrook who owned a wharf at Wilden, he obtained a complete monopoly of trade on the upper reaches of the Trent. When certain bargemasters from Nottingham sailed up the river in an attempt to break the monopoly they were confronted by a boom of boats, manned by forty or fifty of Fosbrook's men, across the river at Wilden Ferry. This formidable monopoly was only finally broken by an injunction issued by Chancery. A similar monopoly was acquired by the proprietors of the Mersey & Irwell Navigation. Although their tonnage rates were limited by statute, they owned all the wharfage facilities on the Navigation so that by raising wharfage charges to an exorbitant figure they were able to eliminate competition.

On the Thames, trade for a time was almost crippled by the high charges exacted by the owners of the flash and pound locks. Charges for sixteen locks originally fixed at £2 19s. were raised to £8 19s., a figure which forced a number of bargemasters out of business. This abuse was eventually remedied by an Act of regulation passed in 1751. In this respect, however, the Thames was unique, for as a general rule river transport in England never suffered the burden of heavy toll charges which beset so many Continental waterways at this period.

Despite all these natural and imposed handicaps there can be no doubt whatever that water transport in the seventeenth and eighteenth centuries was infinitely cheaper and more advantageous than land carriage, particularly over long distances. Except on the smaller rivers or on the upper reaches of the larger rivers where navigation was either particularly difficult or made practicable only by costly works, water transport costs averaged one penny per ton per mile, a figure which land carriage could not approach.

Then, as now, the most important traffic and the greatest in volume was coal, agricultural produce occupying second place. Passenger "wherries" and barges plied on the Thames and Avon in the vicinity of London and Bristol, but strangely enough in view of the bad state of the roads, there appears to have been little long-distance passenger traffic despite the fact that passenger carriage is mentioned in a number of river navigation Acts and Patents.

River traffic was operated by carriers and owner-bargemasters, by merchants, millers or manufacturers, and by navigation proprietors, three classes of operator which have survived down to the present time.

In view of the increasingly heavy demands which a growing trade placed upon transport, it is a surprising fact that the practice of hauling barges by men on our rivers continued throughout the eighteenth century and on some, notably the Severn and the Warwick Avon, until well into the nineteenth century. The Severn horse towing path was only completed in 1811, while on the Avon such a path was never constructed and bow-hauling by men persisted to the last. The reason for this was the argument that the supersession of men by horses would cause unemployment and hardship. An exception to this rule was the Great Ouse where horse haulage was introduced at a very early date.

The horse towing paths of canals are generally isolated from adjoining property by a hedge, but on rivers this is seldom or never the case and consequently the path must be enclosed at each field boundary to prevent stock from straying. A self-closing gate, opening in either direction, which the towing horse learnt to push open, was the usual solution to this problem, but on the waterways in the Bedford Level of the Fens there were a series of stiles which the unfortunate horse was forced to jump. To-day, except on the Rivers Calder, Lee, Stort and Wey, horse haulage on rivers has practically ceased so that such problems no longer arise.

On the canals a "turnover bridge" carries the towpath from one side of the canal to the other and a "roving bridge" takes it across the mouth of a branch canal or basin, but on rivers this facility frequently does not exist. In the Fen district a special "horse boat" was towed behind a gang of lighters, and this was used for ferrying the horse at such points. In other districts a special ferry boat was provided. Until the last war such a boat was still kept at Trent Junction and occasionally used for ferrying boat horses across the Trent from the mouth of the Soar Navigation to the junction of the Erewash Canal on the north bank. Many river ferries originated for the purpose of conveying first bow-hauliers and later horses across the river.

On rivers, where the towpath ceased owing to bridges or buildings at the water's edge, the horse-boatman was faced with the same problem which had confronted the bow-hauliers. The usual procedure adopted when travelling upstream was to tie up the boat, walk the horse round the obstruction and then float the towline down to the boat. A retired Oxford Canal boatman has described to me how he used to do this on the Thames and on the Kennet river section of the Kennet & Avon between Blake's Lock and High Bridge, Reading. The latter obstruction was particularly awkward, the waterway being built up to the water's edge for some distance and the current swift. He carried with him a very long line for use at this point, and this was floated down to the boat by means of a special wooden float which was kept there for the purpose. A similar float was kept at Newbury Lock for the use of craft negotiating Newbury Bridge. The same boatman also gave me a graphic description of his passage through the old navigation weirs of the paddle and rimer type on the Upper Thames, and it was a fascinating experience to hear a first-hand account of so ancient a practice.

The introduction of horse haulage did little to diminish the hazards of river navigation. When travelling downstream the maintenance of steerage way depended entirely on the horse keeping up a speed faster than the current. When the river was in flood this was not easily achieved. The most dangerous points at such times were those where a weir channel diverged from the navigation on the towing path side. Here the horse had to cross the roving bridge over the weir channel and yet be in a position to take up the resulting slack in the towline before the boat could be carried by the current on to the weir. There have been many cases where, owing to the horse failing to respond or shying at the bridge, boats have been swept over weirs and smashed to pieces below. Sometimes their occupants have been drowned, but more often they have been able to cling to the bridge above as the boat went over. In such respects the introduction of powered craft has undoubtedly spelt increased safety, although similar catastrophes have been known to occur as a result of engine failure or error of judgment, and it is not many years since a motor narrow-boat and butty were swept over Redhill Weir on the Trent and their crews drowned.

Horse towage on the still water canals was not beset by such perils, and with the exception of the earlier canal tunnels, and certain bridges, the tow paths are generally continuous. The methods of propelling the horse boats through tunnels have already been described.

Hauling a loaded canal boat is a very different proposition from drawing a cart or wagon, and a boat horse must be trained to "hang in the collar" in order to get the boat under way. A simple but ingenious device is adopted on most narrow canals to assist the horse to move the boat out of the lock chambers. A single pulley block is attached to the stud on the towing mast and the towline is provided with a wooden stop and a loop at the boat end. When he is ready to leave the lock, the boatman runs the slack line over the pulley and hangs the loop over a stud, provided for the purpose, which is set in the masonry of the abutment wall at the head and tail of the lock. By this means the horse obtains a two-to-one purchase on the boat, but when the towing-mast draws level with the stud on the wall, the line slips off the stud automatically and runs through the pulley until it is checked by the wooden stop. The normal direct pull is then resumed. A less orthodox method of getting a loaded boat moving out of an empty lock is to draw the top paddles and flush her out, but because this wastes water it is a crime in the eyes of canal authorities who often post notices threatening to fine any boatman caught "flushing."

When two horse boats meet, one of them must give way by stopping his horse and allowing the towline to fall slack in the water so that the other boat and horse can pass over it. It is the custom for empty boats to give way to loaded, but when loaded boats meet the question of who is to give way is either settled by local ruling or becomes the subject of heated dispute. Sometimes one towline is detached from the boat or passed over the other craft instead of under.

Another potential source of dispute, and one not peculiar to horse-drawn craft, is the question of precedence at locks. A boatman who seeks to pass another just before a flight of locks with the intention of stealing "the road" from his fellow is obviously asking for trouble and the aggrieved one will do his utmost not to let the other pass. Usually such contests end with the bows of both boats firmly wedged together in the mouth of the lock, both crews determined not to give way. Not infrequently, a canal may be blocked for hours in this way until the matter is finally settled by the delicate diplomacy of some third party, generally a distracted canal engineer. Similar disputes may arise between the "lock wheelers" of craft approaching a lock from opposite directions. If the lock should be full, the boat coming downhill has the road, and woe betide the lock wheeler from the ascending boat if he draws off the lock within sight of the other. In the attempt to obviate these disputes on some canals, notably on the Grand Union, posts are set by the towpath at a fixed distance from the head and tail of the lock and the rule was made that the first boat to pass either post took the lock.

The great majority of the old horse boatmen owned their horses, their tackle resplendent with brass ornaments, painted feeding-bowl and brightly coloured wooden "bobbins" on the traces to prevent the latter from chafing. Some preferred to keep a well-trained horse which would "go of hisself" along the towpath while others, despite the labour involved in training, had the gypsy's love of horse-dealing and were forever changing horses. Some firms made a practice of hiring out boats, and sometimes horses as well, on a weekly basis, and many young boatmen would leave their parents and start in this way until they had earned enough to acquire a boat of their own.

Some canal companies provided horses, a practice which survives to this day on the Worcester & Birmingham Canal, although it is one which tends to lead to neglect and ill-treatment. Horses are also provided to-day either by the canal authorities or by individuals for a small charge to haul the "butty" boats of pairs through certain flights of narrow locks such as those at Wolverhampton and Audlem.

Many boatmen of the old school preferred mules to horses for the same reason that led "the Canal Duke" to breed and use them exclusively on his Bridgewater Canal. Though more difficult to train, mules possess great staying power, work harder and longer, need less attention and are remarkable for longevity. A few mules are still to be found on the canals. For similar reasons donkeys were favoured on the waterways of the West Midlands. Until the time of the first world war many donkeys, or "animals" as they were called, could be seen working in pairs on the Stroudwater, Worcester & Birmingham, Droitwich, and Stafford-shire & Worcestershire Canals, and more rarely on the Shropshire Union. If the boats passed on to the Severn in charge of a tug, the "animals" were frequently carried on board.

Because, unlike their predecessors the river navigation under-takers, the canal proprietors were at first forbidden by law to act as carriers, traffic during the heyday of the canals was handled either by independent carriers, the majority of whom were small owner boatmen, or by merchants or manufacturers who made use of water transport for their own trade. This traffic was classified in three broad groups. Firstly, the slow-moving, heavy goods—the boats handling coal, stone, manure and other bulk cargoes; secondly, the smaller and lighter built boats which carried general merchandise and parcels of every sort. Owing to their lighter build and the fact that they seldom carried more than twenty tons, these boats travelled faster than the heavy traffic which gave way to them. Sometimes they used relays of horses and travelled night and day, in which case they were known as "fly boats." Thirdly, there were the passenger "passage" or "packet" boats which, like the express trains of a later day, took precedence over all other traffic. Sometimes the second and third classes of traffic might be combined in a boat carrying both passengers and light cargo. Such a boat was the equivalent of the "stage wagon" of the roads whereas the true "packet boat" was the stage coach of the canals.

Before the coming of the railways, these canal passenger boats were widely operated and well patronized, but perhaps because of their subsequent rapid eclipse and disappearance very little is generally known about them, while the average history of transport barely mentions their existence. The average packet boat was drawn by two horses which were changed at intervals of from four to six miles. By this means an average of from eight to ten miles per hour inclusive of lockage was sometimes achieved. One, and sometimes both horses carried postillions who assisted in working the locks and who were adept at flattening themselves down to their saddles as the horses dashed under the low bridges. Unlike the goods boats which were towed from a central mast, the towlines of the passage boats were attached to "timber-heads" at the bow and stern. If there was only one postillion, he rode the second horse which was attached to the stern timber-head. The same length as goods craft (70 to 72 ft. on the narrow canal system), the passenger boats were very finely built with bilges considerably rounded and were of a beam which seldom exceeded 6 ft. and might be no more than 5 ft. It was by thus reducing the cross section to the absolute minimum that a relatively high speed in a restricted channel was made practicable.

Two cabins were usually provided giving first and second class accommodation, the first class cabin being generally at the fore-end. These appear to have been comfortably appointed, the proprietors of the "Swift Packets" plying between Wolver-hampton and Birmingham even boasting of the fact that their cabins were "heated by pipes of hot water" in winter. After the discomforts of stage coach travel, such luxury combined with smooth motion must indeed have seemed delightful. This is certainly the view expressed by John Fox in the following extract from his diary for the year 1839 which was sent to me by his grandson, Sir John Fox.

Sept. 21st, 1839. Rose at six—breakfasted—came outside 3-horse coach to Manchester. . . . Streets of good red brick houses within three miles of Manchester; many building in a place to be called Victoria Park. . . . From here to Preston saw many new factories building. What is it to come to? . . . Heard of a passage boat (at Preston) by Lancaster Canal to Kendal. . . . And now I made the most delightful journey that ever I made in my life, starting at about half past one in the afternoon. The day was most beautiful. The boat was 72 feet long and just wide enough for two persons to sit opposite each other. It will hold about 70. Unladen it draws, I think, 3 inches of water. The head comes to the sharpest point from which 10 feet downwards, open, covered with tarpaulin, is the luggage; then 8 feet open for a boatman and about 6 passengers can sit in the open air. From this point the boat is covered with a hoop-shaped covering, watertight, and divided into three compartments—the first, fare 6s.—the middle a small sort of steward's room—the aft cabin fare 4s. The thing looked like a canoe. It ran into a covered dock. The passengers from the north disembarked and we entered. I took a seat in the open air at the head . . . The canal along which we went was beautiful as a stream, winding in and out constantly—the first 8 miles pretty but not striking—then sometimes a wide prospect, sometimes between green fields, wooded, then under little groves, and we passed beneath 160 grey stone bridges nor came to a lock till we had gone 40 miles; then there were several together for half a mile and then no more. Lancaster was rather more than half way, being 30 miles. . . . As the sun set the full moon rose opposite above a wood. It was beautiful, and the manner in which we went along the water was for beauty of motion unequalled. Our boat rushed along at the rate of 9 miles an hour with a smoothness incredible. From the bow not the least wave arose but the water, unbroken, swelled gently against the bank. Two horses, one before the other, towed us in an unceasing canter. They were changed every four miles, not half a minute being taken to change. We had but two postilions for the whole way—one a boy of 19, to Lancaster from which he had but just returned so that he rode 60 miles post without stopping. I never did enjoy a journey as I did this. It was like a journey in a dream or in an Eastern tale—water, weather, scenery, motion—all was most beautiful. We were at Kendal before 9 o'clock.

The boat in which John Fox travelled made a round trip each day and was booked to cover the 57 miles between Preston and Kendal in seven hours. This time included working through the eight locks at Tewitfield and the passage of Hincaster Tunnel where there was no towing path.

On the neighbouring Leeds & Liverpool Canal, the Union Company operated a daily service of "Packets" between Liverpool and Wigan. These boats left Liverpool at 8 a.m. and arrived at Wigan at 4 p.m., the arrival and departure times in the reverse direction being 7 a.m. and 3 p.m. respectively. The distance covered was 35 miles with five locks and there were four booked stopping-places en route at Maghull, Halsall, Burscough and Appley. Fares for the through journey were 3s. "Front Room" and 2s. "Back Room." Each passenger was allowed 28 lb. of luggage free, but had to pay 1s. extra for each hundredweight over this amount.

One of my correspondents, an elderly lady, recently sent me details of a horrific experience on a packet boat. She recalled how, when a very small girl, she travelled with her nurse on a packet boat on the Montgomeryshire Canal section of the Shropshire Union system between Newtown and Welshpool. All went well until they met another packet boat travelling in the opposite direction. A boy was then detailed to pass over the towing line of the oncoming boat, but in doing so he got his head fouled between the two lines with the result that it was pulled off like an apple from its stalk and fell upon the deck. This incident, she concludes, left an indelible impression in her memory, as indeed it might. This anecdote is of interest quite apart from its tragic quality since there must be very few people still alive to-day who have actually travelled by passage boat. Obviously in this case the service must have continued for some years after the opening of the railway between Newtown and Welshpool in 1861.

Even after the railways were firmly established, canal passenger transport did not lack advocates who pointed out the superior smoothness, comfort and silence of the packet boat. No doubt the boats did compare very favourably with rail travel in the first crude coaching stock, but as railway standards improved the old packet boats were soon relegated to backwaters where they lay rotting among the reeds, destined, like the stage coaches, soon to be forgotten.

Organized outings for parties on canals using either special craft or commercial boats temporarily adapted for the purpose have been run in some areas down to the present day. Services of river steamers continue to operate, some of them to a set timetable as do Messrs. Salter's steamers on the Thames during the summer months. But all these services were provided for holiday-makers during the season and cannot therefore be said to perpetuate the tradition of the old "packet boats." Probably the last regular all-the-year-round utilitarian passenger service to operate on any canal in this country was provided by the boats working between Sharpness and Gloucester over the Gloucester & Berkeley Canal and calling at intermediate points en route. For the villages along the eastern shores of the Severn estuary, isolated down winding lanes far from the railway, the broad and lock-free waters of the ship canal were the quickest and shortest route to Gloucester. Only the death of the owner of the boats brought the service to an end about 1930, and now the motor-bus has taken its place. Yet even to-day an efficient canal service would not be substantially outpaced, for the buses have to follow a slow and devious route.

The Gloucester & Berkeley service was operated by small steamers bearing no resemblance to the old horse-drawn "packet boats." The latter have now vanished beyond the range of living memory, and but for one fortunate chance we should have no record of their appearance other than that of a few small contemporary steel engravings and one model in Lancaster Museum. That chance was the miraculous preservation by sinking of the Bridgewater Canal passage boat *Duchess Countess* (a name recalling the titles of the Bridgewater family). This old boat was eventually raised and, still in substantially original condition even to her cabinwork, began a new lease of life as a houseboat. She was moved on to the Welsh section of the Shropshire Union Canal near Frankton Junction where she is still occupied at the time of writing although, owing to the deterioration of her hull, she has now been drawn out of the water. The *Duchess Countess* was the last packet boat in regular service. In the heyday of her career as a packet boat she proudly mounted a great curved knife-blade on her bow. This was of much more than symbolic significance, for it was so contrived that it would sever the towline of any boatman who failed to give way to her. Now the knife has gone, but she still carries her "timber-heads" at bow and stern, their stout oak deeply worn by the towlines of the post horses that once set her skimming through the water. I have tried, so far unsuccessfully, to ensure that detailed measurements are taken of this old boat which would enable a scale model of her to be constructed. For very soon the *Duchess Countess* must inevitably disintegrate, and with her passing the last tangible link with these once extensive but little known canal passenger services will be irretrievably lost.

Though they are not true heirs of the old "packet boats" and are of a different form of construction, their nearest equivalent on the canals to-day are the "Committee Boats" which some canal companies maintain. These are the canal version of the "Directors Saloons" of the Railway, for in them the directors and officials of the company make a dignified annual progress over their waterway. Most stately of all these vessels, perhaps, is the horse-drawn *Lady Hatherton* of the Staffordshire & Worcestershire Canal Company with her 70 ft. of gleaming white hull and cabinwork, her heavy plate-glass windows, mahogany and red-plush interior, and capacious wine bins. Even though she may provide no direct link with the packet boats, at least the *Lady Hatherton* recalls most vividly the vanished opulence of the Victorian age.

Long after the last packet boat service had ceased, horse-drawn "fly boats" continued to trade over the greater part of the canal system. Moreover the term has continued to be applied officially as well as colloquially to latter-day steam and diesel craft handling "priority" traffic. In fact, until just before the last war certain motor boats on the Leeds & Liverpool Canal bore the words "Fly Boat" above the name on bow and stern.

Until the present century the Shropshire Union Canal Carrying Company, operated by the London & North Western Railway, worked horse-drawn fly boats widely over the system they controlled, and the service was only discontinued as a result of a dispute with the National Union of Railwaymen over the hours worked by the boatmen. Though they do not work "fly," the L.M.S. boats carrying general merchandise to and from the company's "Boatage Depots" at Wolverhampton, Kidderminster and Stourport may be said to be a last relic of these once extensive services. These boats, like the majority of the earlier fly boats, are worked by male crews. The family boat worked by a boatman with his wife and family was generally confined to the slower bulk traffic. George Smith, in his *Our Canal Population* (1878), enumerated three classes of canal boatmen, the "fly-boatmen" whose family lived ashore and who worked three men to a boat, travelling night and day, "the old-fashioned family boatman and his family whose father and grandfather were boaters," and lastly the "Rodney boatmen," who, according to Smith, consisted of casuals and ne-er-do-wells "spending their days in drunkenness and wretchedness." Representatives of all three types can still be found to-day.

With the coming of the mechanical age various alternative methods of boat haulage were tried. Cable haulage was introduced on the Bridgewater Canal and on a short section of the Regent's Canal in 1837. The L. & N.W.R. laid a narrow gauge railway along a section of the Shropshire Union Canal towpath and tried hauling the boats with diminutive steam locomotives. The experiment was not a success, and the track and locomotives were removed to Crewe locomotive works where they formed a system of internal transport which continued in use for many years. Electrical haulage, drawing power from overhead cables, was tried on a part of the Staffordshire & Worcestershire Canal but was soon abandoned. The only example of electrical canal haulage which has endured in this country is the electric tug, already referred to, which works through Harecastle New Tunnel on the Trent & Mersey Canal. Such systems of mechanical haulage, whether applied from the towing path or from tugs on the canal itself are not a practical proposition unless the waterway is comparatively free from locks or if the locks are sufficiently large to accommodate a train of boats at one lockage, and unless a heavy and regular traffic can be depended upon. Where these conditions are fulfilled, as on the Gloucester & Berkeley Canal and the Severn, on the River Trent where the new locks can hold four Humber-going barges at one time, on the Aire & Calder, Bridgewater and Weaver Navigations, or on the London end of the Grand Union Canal, then haulage by tugs is extensively used. But over the greater part of the Midlands canal system locks are small and frequent and traffic irregular. In these circumstances the only practical application of mechanical power is to the cargo-carrying craft itself.

The idea of propelling boats by mechanical power can be traced back to the dawn of the steam age, and it is not widely realized that our inland waterways were the cradle of marine steam propulsion. The spread of inland navigation and the development of the steam engine were coincident, and the new still waterways were an ideal field for testing the capabilities of the new power. As is so often the case, however, the first pioneers reaped neither reward nor renown.

Strangely enough the earliest of these luckless inventors, Jonathan Hulls (born 1699), was a native of Chipping Campden, a small Gloucestershire town which could scarcely be further removed from any maritime association. As a result of his experiments Hulls took out a patent in 1736 for a stern-wheel paddle boat powered by a Newcomen atmospheric engine. His idea was that this boat should be a harbour tug, bringing sailing vessels from the roads to the quays and so avoiding the long delays occasioned by contrary winds. In the following year Hulls constructed a small experimental boat and launched it on the Avon at Evesham, but the trials proved a failure and the wretched inventor was subjected to merciless ridicule. Poor Hulls' only memorial was a scurrilous little rhyme which was still remembered in Chipping Campden a century after his death:

Jonathan Hull
With his paper skull,
Tried hard to make a machine
That should go against wind and tide:
But he, like an ass,
Couldn't bring it to pass,
So at last was ashamed to be seen.

Jonathan Hulls was many years ahead of his time, and it was

not until the canal age that the possibility of steam propulsion was again seriously considered. In 1769 when Watt's steam engine was still in its protracted experimental stage and his historic partnership with Matthew Boulton had not yet begun, the Birmingham Canal had just brought the convenience of water transport to Boulton's Soho works. In that year Dr. Small wrote to Watt as follows:

"What Mr. Boulton and I are very desirous of is to move canal boats by this [Watt's] engine; so we have made this model of a size sufficient for that purpose. We propose first to operate without any condenser, because coals are here exceedingly cheap, and because you can, more commodiously than we, make experiments on condensers, having several already by you. Above 150 boats are now engaged on these new waveless canals, so if we can succeed, the field is not narrow."

Watt's reply to this letter anticipated by many years the invention of the screw propeller. "Have you ever," he asked, "considered a *spiral oar* for that purpose or are you for two wheels?" His query was accompanied by a rough sketch of the suggested propeller. These promising speculations never took shape, however, for Boulton and Watt soon became so deeply involved in other enterprises that although they received a number of enquiries for marine engines from other speculators, the partners decided to concentrate upon the development of the stationary engines which made them famous.

Thus it came about that the credit for having constructed the first successful steamboat goes to Scotland—to William Symington of Wanlockhead. In conjunction with a Mr. Miller of Dalswinton, Symington constructed two experimental boats which were tried out on Dalswinton Loch in the years 1788 and 1799. These craft were of the type then known as "twin boats." Two hulls were coupled abreast, the engine being mounted in one, the boiler in the other and the two paddle wheels working in the tunnel between them. Though both boats ran successfully, the first at five and the second at seven miles per hour, serious defects developed in the engines, while the method of deriving rotary motion by means of chains, ratchet wheels and pawls proved, as one may imagine, somewhat unreliable. Miller, who had financed the enterprise, thereupon retired disheartened and Symington had no further opportunity to try his skill until 1801 when Lord

Dundas, Governor of the Forth & Clyde Canal, commissioned a third vessel. For this Symington designed a vastly improved double-acting engine and used a connecting rod and crank to drive the paddle wheel which was mounted in the stern. The result was the famous *Charlotte Dundas*, a model of which may be seen in the South Kensington Science Museum. After her successful trials, the *Charlotte Dundas* was for some time used for towing traffic on the Forth & Clyde Canal and in the Firth of Forth, duties which she performed most efficiently. Lord Dundas informed the Duke of Bridgewater of the success of the boat, and after seeing a model of her the latter was so impressed that he placed an order for eight steamers for use on the Bridgewater Canal. After all his struggles, this order seemed to spell success for poor Symington, but he was destined to be bitterly disappointed. Before the order could be executed the Duke of Bridgewater died and his executors countermanded his instructions. On the very same day that this news reached Symington the proprietors of the Forth & Clyde made an order prohibiting the further use of the *Charlotte Dundas* on the grounds that her wash would undermine the banks of their canal. She was laid up in a backwater of the canal at Bainsford and never moved again.

Among those who examined the *Charlotte Dundas* were the American Fulton and Andrew Bell of Glasgow. As a result, Fulton launched the *Clermont* in America in 1807 while a few years later Bell constructed the *Comet* at Port Glasgow and in so doing laid the foundation of the great Clyde shipbuilding industry. While Fulton and Bell reaped the rewards of the success to which they certainly contributed, Symington the originator died impoverished while his little *Charlotte Dundas* rotted and rusted away in the reeds of the Forth & Clyde, forgotten like her inventor in the headlong progress of the Industrial Revolution. Like so many before and after him, William Symington's achievement was only honoured after his death.

However unjust it may have appeared to Symington, the decision of the Forth & Clyde proprietors to ban the use of his boat was by no means actuated solely by hidebound prejudice. On the contrary the damage caused to canal and river banks by the wash from powered craft moving in a restricted channel can be very considerable and presents a problem which has exercised the minds of engineers ever since. It was for this reason that little more was accomplished in the way of applying steam power to canal boats until the new threat of railway competition induced the canal proprietors to change their minds even though it entailed the risk of damage.

In 1829 and 1830 it was this threat which induced the Forth & Clyde and Union Canal proprietors to re-open the whole question and to embark upon an exhaustive series of experiments to study the wash created by different types of vessel moving in a restricted channel at varying speeds. The results of these tests were summed up by William Fairbairn in his *Remarks on Canal Navigation* (1831). Nowadays, when it is generally held that the only solution of the erosion problem is to protect the banks by piling, this little book makes interesting reading. One series of experiments was conducted with a lightly loaded twin-hulled "passage boat" 68 ft. long with a beam of 11 ft. 6 in. which was horse drawn, and another similar boat propelled by a central manually operated paddle wheel. In the case of the horse-drawn boat both the wash created and the tractive effort required were found to increase with the speed until just under eight m.p.h. At this speed the water washed over the towing path, but thereafter it was found that both the wash and the pull required decreased as the speed increased until, with the horses at full gallop at fourteen m.p.h. the observers reported "no surge." Similar results were obtained with the paddle boat, but in this case the wash made by the paddle wheel at the higher speeds was described as "like a mill-race" down the centre of the channel, leaving the water at the margins scarcely disturbed.

These experiments, and others conducted with a stern-wheeled iron steamer, the *Cyclops*, induced Fairbairn to recommend two types of steamer for canal use; a light twin-hulled steamer with central paddle for the rapid carriage of passengers and parcels on narrow canals, and a larger single-hulled vessel with two stern wheels for heavier duty on voyages which included tidal waters. As a result of the experiments the Forth & Clyde Canal proprietors commissioned the firm of Fairbairn & Lillie of Manchester to build the steam twin-hulled passenger boat *Lord Dundas*.

Fairbairn recommended the widespread introduction of steam power on the canals and included in his book a long list of waterways which he considered suitable for steamers. Nevertheless, despite his advocacy, the introduction of steam was by no means rapid or widespread. For this the collapse of the canals in the face of railway competition was partly responsible, though it was also due to the fact that, when applied to the actual carrying craft itself, the advantage of steam power over horse haulage was not great. In a restricted channel there was little difference in speed, while the machinery occupied valuable cargo space and called for skilled engine men. Thus it came about that most of the early canal steamers were tugs, used where long levels and density of traffic made their use most advantageous.

In 1852 a steam boat fitted with a variable pitch propeller was tried out on the Kennet & Avon Canal, while two years later the Regent's Canal Company initiated a prize competition for the best tug. This was won by the twin screw boat *Birmingham* entered by a Mr. Inshaw of that city. The *Birmingham* worked on the canal for ten years, but the use of a similar boat on the Ashby Canal was prohibited by the Midland Railway Company who had acquired that waterway. This led to legal action and an enquiry into the damage caused by steamers, Doctor Pole, who conducted the enquiry, recommending that speed be restricted to three miles per hour.

An epidemic on the Bridgewater Canal which resulted in the death of two hundred boat horses led Sir E. Leader Williams to introduce tugs on that waterway, but in this case considerable bank protection work was carried out.

In 1874 Messrs. Thornycroft built a steam tug with a tunnel screw but it did not prove popular. Later, both this firm and Messrs. Crossley were to equip narrow boats with suction gas power units.

One of the last and most interesting of these experimental craft was the steam narrow boat *Thistle* which was built by the firm of Savery & Company. *Thistle* was fitted with a high-pressure water-tube boiler and a high-speed engine. As a narrow boat she was unique in posessing wheel steering, the wheel being mounted on a raised "bridge" forward of the cabin.

When cargo carrying steamers began to appear, their use was mainly confined to "fly" traffic, sail and horse haulage continuing to hold their own for the heavier bulk cargoes until the appearance of the diesel engine. Perhaps the two most notable fleets of steam cargo boats on the canals were those operated by the carrying firm of Messrs. Fellows Morton & Clayton and by the Leeds &

Liverpool Canal Company. The Fellows Morton steamers were narrow boats of composite construction. The machinery occupied ten tons of cargo space and consisted of a horizontal return tube boiler of the Scotch type supplying steam to a tandem compound condensing engine built by A. H. Beasley & Sons of Uxbridge. Like their diesel successors, each steamer worked in conjunction with a towed butty boat. These steamers ranged widely over the narrow canal system of the Midlands, but their principal field of operation consisted of those waterways which later amalgamated to form the Grand Union system. Here they worked "fly" with a full complement of six men to a pair of boats. The boats ran with clockwork regularity, the crews taking duty turns at certain fixed points. There were three regular workings: Brentford to Braunston, City Road Basin (Regent's Canal) to Birmingham, and Brentford or City Road to Leicester, Nottingham and Derby. Owing to the number of narrow locks then existing between Braunston and Birmingham, a transhipment depot and stables were established at Braunston which may still be seen. Here the Brentford-Braunston steamers discharged their cargoes, reloaded, and exchanged loaded butties, the traffic being worked between Birmingham and Braunston by horses. The City Road–Birmingham steamers, on the other hand, worked straight through, either man-handling the butties through the narrow locks or more usually working the butty with a Braunston horse as far as Hatton top lock.

The coming of these steamers must have seemed revolutionary and not altogether welcome to the old school of horse boatmen accustomed to a more sober method of progress. They affected a certain contempt for the new boats, christening the crews of the Regent Dock–Birmingham steamers "greasy wheelers" or "greasy ockers." This term referred to the cargoes of soap which they usually carried and to the fact that the office of the company was at Ocker Hill, Birmingham, at that time. The crews of the Leicester and Nottingham boats, on the other hand, were nicknamed the "woolly backed 'uns," a soubriquet more obscure but presumably connected with the Leicestershire woollen trade.

Before the first world war, Messrs. Fellows Morton & Clayton began to change over from steam to motor boats using the Swedish single cylinder Bolinder semi-diesel engine. This effected a saving of five tons of cargo space and dispensed with the need for an engine man. Many of the old steamers were converted. Others passed into the hands of small traders who continued to operate them for a few more years. The last steam narrow boat made her final trip over the Grand Junction Canal in 1931 and found a final resting-place on a backwater of the Oxford Canal at Hillmorton where, like Symington's *Charlotte Dundas*, she rotted and rusted away.

The Leeds & Liverpool Canal steamers were of a very different design. They were 62 ft. by 14 ft. "short boats" of the standard type evolved for working traffic on this canal above the twenty-first lock at Wigan. As in the case of the narrow boats, the conversion entailed a considerable sacrifice of cargo space. The steam machinery was designed and built by the company at Wigan. Vertical boilers with thimble tubes in the firebox supplied an unusual type of tandem compound four cylinder "Vee" engine. This means to say that the cylinders were inclined in pairs, the high pressure being mounted above the low pressure cylinder, and each pair sharing a common piston rod and connecting rod. Curiously enough, condensers were never fitted, the engines running as "puffers" exhausting up the funnel like a locomotive. When the carrying side of the company's business was entrusted to a subsidiary known as the Canal Carrying Company, the steamer fleet was gradually converted to or replaced by diesel craft, in this case the locally built single cylinder Widdop engine being selected. Here again, some of the old steamers passed into the hands of small traders, but in this case a few are still hard at work at the present time. Their owners swear by the reliability and low maintenance costs of the steamers, and in one case, at least, the original machinery was installed in 1936 into a new steel hull. So far as I am aware, these Leeds & Liverpool boats are the only examples of steam cargo carrying boats (as distinct from tugs) still at work on the canals.

It has been the advent of the diesel rather than the steam engine that has resulted in the eclipse of the horse boat, for unlike the latter, the diesel engine was readily applicable to family boat working as well as to the "fly boat" with its male crew. Many horse boats were converted to motor boats, while others became "butties." Conversion involved substantial alterations which included a counter stern, and one conversion unit was evolved with the idea of obviating all this work. The engine was mounted on the cabin top and propelled the boat on the principle of the outboard motor via a fearsome arrangement of shafts, universal couplings and bevel gears. It is hardly necessary to add that this idea did not become popular on the canals. One boatman I know who was rash enough to try it has told me that steering called for the muscles of a Sandow.

Until the 1930's, direct reversing single cylinder semi-diesel engines of the Bolinder type virtually held a monopoly of canal transport, and there are still a great number in use to-day. Their advantages are great simplicity, reliability and long life because they run at slow speed and have a minimum of moving parts. Their disadvantages are noise, vibration and the necessity for pre-heating with a blowlamp before starting. Latterly the two cylinder full diesel has come into extensive use, a number of makes now being represented. Engines of this type start from cold and are much more silent and smooth running. On the other hand they are much more complex, must be equipped with reverse-reduction gear-boxes, and run at a higher speed. Consequently their trouble-free life is shorter and they are more liable to suffer from maltreatment in unskilled hands.

It seems probable that before many more years have passed horse haulage on the canals will become a thing of the past with the possible exception of short distance hauls by open boats in the Black Country area. Even ten years ago there were still a number of owner-boatmen or "Number Ones" working their own family horse boats on long-distance turns, but to-day the "Number One" is almost extinct. The current of our time, the innumerable restrictions, regulations and difficulties tell against the master-man in every trade and particularly against the owner-boatman who, frequently illiterate and knowing little of the world beyond the canal bank, finds himself unable to cope with the forms, orders and officials of our servile state. Consequently he has either retired or sold his labour and his boats to one of the carrying companies whose fleets of motor boats now handle the traffic. Already, horse-drawn boats have disappeared from the Grand Union Canal except near its terminals, and the towing path, where it is not used by "lock wheelers" going ahead to set locks, has become impassable for horses in many places. Horse boats are still to be seen on the Coventry and Ashby Canals and, though increasingly rarely, on the Oxford Canal to Oxford,

158

bringing coal from the Warwickshire coal-field. The firm of Thomas Clayton still operate a few horse-drawn "gas" boats over the Shropshire Union Canal between Wolverhampton and Ellesmere Port. There is also horse-drawn traffic on the Trent & Mersey Canal between the Potteries and the Anderton Lift or Preston Brook. Four horse boats still trade over the Worcester & Birmingham Canal, being hauled by a tug through the summit tunnels. There is very heavy horse-drawn trade in coal on the Staffordshire & Worcestershire Canal from collieries on Cannock Chase to Stourport Power Station. This traffic, however, is worked by the "open boats" of the Birmingham Canal net-work on the section system, one group of men working the boats from the pits to Stewponey Wharf, and another taking them on from Stewponey to Stourport. This concludes the catalogue of long-distance "turns" which are still performed by horse boats. For the rest, the use of horses is now confined to short hauls in industrial areas, most notably in the Black Country where many horse-drawn "open" or "day" boats trade over the whole district and seem likely to continue to do so for many years to come.

Yet while the advantages of powered barges for river traffic are overwhelming the superiority of the diesel-engined canal boat over its horse-drawn predecessor is by no means so great as might be imagined. There is little difference in speed between the two, or if there is it is achieved only at the expense of bank erosion caused by the resulting wash which is set up. Speed in a restricted channel is governed, as Fairbairn discovered, not by the power applied but by the ability of the water to pass the moving hull, or in other words by the ratio between the cross section of the waterway and that of the hull. Under these conditions a slight increase in speed may be dearly bought at the price of increased canal maintenance costs. Unlike the horse, however, the diesel engine does not tire, even though the boatman may, and this, in our world, is its decisive advantage. The diesel engine requires no food when the boat is not travelling, while the passage of tunnels no longer calls for the aid of "leggers" or tugs. Consequently the steady throbbing of the diesel engine, reverberating in the dark depths of the tunnel, or carrying far over the fields on some still evening, has now become inextricably associated with the life of the canals. But though we have become accustomed to it, diesel power seems to have brought with it that sense of urgency and unrest which besets modern life but which seems alien to the quiet of the waterways. When, pausing to lean over the parapet of a canal bridge, we chance to watch the passage of the rarer horse boat, how quiet, leisurely and effortless does its progress seem by contrast. There is the measured clip-clop of hooves, reverberating more loudly for a moment as the horse passes under the bridge. Polished brasses and the brightly painted "bobbins" make a brave showing on the horse's tackle which creaks with a small, comfortable sound as he moves. Perhaps, too, he is munching a feed of corn from a flower decorated nose-bowl. Behind him the taut cotton line swings and sways, hissing as it runs through the deep groove which, in the passage of a hundred and fifty years, innumerable similar lines have worn in the cast-iron rubbing plate that protects the spring of the bridge arch. Then comes the boat, moving with only the faintest rippling sound as the water, parted by her bluff bows, fans away towards the banks where the rushes bend and sway to the gentle swell. A glimpse of the resplendent cabinside, dazzling by contrast with the sombre cargo of coal, and she is moving away, the water eddying in little whirlpools under her stern as the boatman swings over the tiller for the next turn. Soon she has disappeared behind the high hedge that screens the towpath, and all we can see is the wisp of smoke that drifts away from the cabin chimney. All these things seem to have become as naturally a part of the life of the waterways as the birds which have made their home upon them. Small wonder, then, that in this distracted age the life of the old horse boatman seems idyllic, a leisurely and nomadic existence of the kind which features in romantic picaresque fiction. But it is only in fine sunny weather that we are tempted to linger by the parapets of canal bridges. When the snow falls or the blinding rain, or when a biting east wind whips over the water we are not there to watch the boats pass by. Though few of the older boatmen would say that working conditions on the modern diesel-engined boats were better, or even as good, as they were in the old days when they were master-men, the job was never an easy one. Like his mechanized successor the old horse boatman was paid by the trip whether he worked for himself or for another, and tonnage rates were often so low that he had to work very long hours and lose no time on the journey in order to earn a bare livelihood.

PLATE XXXIII.—
TYPES OF CRAFT

(*a*) A train of compartment boats on the Aire & Calder Navigation

(*b*) A modern steel tanker barge on the Gloucester & Berkeley Canal

PLATE XXXIV.—TYPES OF CRAFT

(a) A Leeds & Liverpool Canal motor driven "Short Boat"

(b) Narrow boats at Banbury, Oxford Canal

PLATE XXXV

(*a*) Gauging narrow boats on the Grand Union Canal

(*b*) Canal boat maintenance: caulking and fitting new bottoms to a narrow boat, Banbury Dock

PLATE XXXVI.—CANAL BOAT
MAINTENANCE, BRAUNSTON
DOCK

(*a*) Decorating a narrow boat

(*b*) Making new side cloths

PLATE XXXVII

(*a*) A horse-drawn narrow boat, Oxford Canal

(*b*) Last of the passenger "Packet" boats, the *Duchess Countess* on the canal bank at Frankton, Salop

PLATE XXXVIII.—CANAL STEAMERS

(*a*) An early photograph of a Fellows Morton steamer

(*b*) A steamer of the Leeds & Liverpool type still at work, 1948

PLATE XXXIX.—
WATERWAY TRAFFIC

(*a*) A steam tug and train passes Saul Junction, Gloucester & Berkeley Canal

(*b*) Diesel narrow boats and butties passing on the Grand Union Canal, Berkhamsted

PLATE XL.—
WATERWAY TRAFFIC

(*a*) Transhipping copper ingots to narrow boats, Regents Canal Dock, Limehouse

(*b*) A coasting steamer unloads in Gloucester Docks, Gloucester & Berkeley Canal

The popular illusion that because the canal boat travels slowly boating must be a leisurely form of employment is quickly dispelled by a trip on a working boat. Apart from the work of the locks, steering demands constant attention and is heavy work. The task of the motor steerer is made easier if the boat is fitted with a balanced rudder, but no such provision can lighten the arduous job of steering a loaded butty. Here there is no propeller slip-stream to impinge on the rudder and assist steering; hence the fact that despite its great size the heavy rudder must be swung this way and that like a sweep, and because the boat's course is apt to be affected by the wash from the motor boat ahead, the rudder is in almost constant movement. In order to minimize this in the case of a loaded pair, the butty is towed, whenever conditions allow, on a long line. This generally consists of a coarse and thick manilla rope called, rather misleadingly, a "snubber." If the motor steerer eases down for any reason, he must coil in the slack on the snubber, otherwise it may foul his propeller. Getting the "snubber" caught in the "blades" is an ignominious mishap of the type H. M. Bateman delights to portray, and by the time it is disentangled, tempers are apt to be as frayed as the "snubber."

Where wide locks are frequent, the butty is towed on a short strap or "snatcher." This saves repeatedly coiling the snubber and has other practical advantages. As the motor steerer eases up on entering a lock and the fore-end of the butty draws level with the motor counter, he casts off the strap from his boat and lays it over the side-cloths of the butty in such a way that he can pick it up easily as he leaves the lock. When he does so he takes a short running hitch round the stud or hook on his counter before finally making it fast. This not only relieves the initial strain on the rope as it starts the other boat moving, it also pulls the butty over into the wake of the motor, and in this way both boats can pass out through one gate.

Meanwhile it is the duty of the butty steerer to check or "strap" the butty as it comes into the lock beside the motor, jumping ashore with an "uphill" or "downhill strap" as the case may be, and using the "strapping posts" provided beside the lock. When locking downhill, in addition to strapping, the butty must be prevented from moving forward by a light line passed round either the gate paddlegear support or a special pin on the beam in such a way that it can be released from the boat as soon as the motor steerer has picked up the "snatcher." This is necessary because otherwise the butty tends to drift out of the empty lock beside the motor, making it difficult or impossible for the latter to get ahead and pick up the tow.

Sometimes a pair of boats will pass through a continuous flight of wide locks "breasted up," that is to say, secured side by side. This saves labour, particularly for the butty crew, but it takes longer because breasted up boats move sluggishly.

When a pair of boats is travelling empty on a long level the butty is towed close-hauled, a line from the fore-end stud on the butty being secured to the two hooks or studs on each side of the motor's counter. Secured in this fashion, which is impracticable when loaded, the two boats behave as a unit rather like an articulated six-wheeled motor vehicle. It is when travelling in this manner that the boatman's wife (who is usually the butty steerer) has an opportunity to get on with her cooking and household chores, for the butty tiller needs little attention.

When a pair of boats is worked through a canal having narrow locks, it is usual to tow with a long cotton line attached either to the fore-end stud or sometimes to the mast stud on the butty. On approaching a lock, the tow is cast off. When the motor has locked through and the lock has been re-set, the butty is either bow-hauled into the chamber by the crew or drawn in by the motor. In the latter case, when locking up, the line is attached to the butty mast because the motor will be pulling from the head of the lock on the higher level.

Yet another alternative towing method used in working a pair through wide locks is to carry the towline through a pulley on the side of the mast and wooden "running blocks" to a stud mounted on the butty cabin top within reach of the steerer. The butty steerer can thus control the towline, taking up slack or strain, but the method demands skilled promptitude and nice co-operation on the part of both steerers otherwise it can be dangerous, especially for the fingers of the butty steerer.

The foregoing account of working methods applies especially to the Grand Union Canal and to the narrow canals connecting with it. But different canals with their differing lock details require different tricks of technique to ensure the most expeditious working, tricks which become second nature to those who have worked over a particular route all their lives. Consequently, in some respects even the most expert boatman becomes an amateur on a strange waterway. He may travel without mishap, but he will not pass through the locks with the speed of the expert. The expert, too, will know that he can pass through the narrow channel under one bridge with a loaded boat without slowing down, but that another must be taken slowly or the water, pushed forward by the bows, will land the stern on the bottom. The stranger must either "chance his arm" or slow down at every bridge.

Working a "short boat" through the Leeds & Liverpool Canal is a totally different, and in many ways simpler job than handling a pair of narrow boats. The former usually work singly, and often one man only will be in charge of a motor short boat. Here again there are special tricks of the trade. Many of the locks on the Leeds & Liverpool are so deep that when locking downhill the boatman working alone would have great difficulty in boarding his boat after opening the bottom gates. When he jumps ashore to work the lock he carries a light cord attached to the gear lever which, on these boats, is on the cabin top. When the lock is empty he pulls the cord to engage ahead gear, the boat moves out, and he steps aboard easily at the lock tail.

Few jobs in England are more exacting than that of working a pair of loaded narrow boats on such a heavily locked turn as that between London and Birmingham. And whereas three should be the minimum working crew on a pair, one on each boat and one to lock-wheel ahead, low rates have induced many boaters to work two-handed. Unless they are lucky enough to get a "good road" right through, which is unlikely, this means a slower journey. Nevertheless the speed with which a two-handed pair will bring their boats neatly into the locks and work through them in far less time than it would take a crew of four amateurs to lock through a small launch seems little short of miraculous. Yet to work a pair of boats two-handed involves taking risks which sometimes result in damaged boats and personal injury or even death. On more than one occasion a boater has slipped into a lock with the motor running astern and has been drawn into "the blades" with fatal results. Nevertheless the canals can fairly claim to be the safest form of inland transport, for accidents comparable with road crashes or railway disasters are extremely rare and seldom hold up traffic or involve loss of life.

One of these rare accidents occurred some years ago on the Leeds & Liverpool Canal. A steel boat locking down the Wigan flight entered one of the locks too fast. One of the crew of two jumped ashore to check her but the check strap parted. The boat struck the lower gates with such force that it burst them outwards. Falling as the water rushed out, the boat became so inextricably wedged between the reversed lock gates that it had to be partly cut up with oxy-acetylene flame cutters before it could be removed and repairs to the gates begun.

While on this subject of accidents it is worth recording that the Regent's Canal was the scene of what was surely the most spectacular and probably the most serious disaster in canal history. A boat load of gunpowder exploded just as it was passing under Macclesfield Bridge in Regent's Park, killing the crew and completely destroying the boat and the bridge. Evidence of the tragedy can be seen to this day, for when the massive cast-iron columns from Coalbrookdale which support the bridge were re-erected they were placed "back-to-front." Consequently the grooves worn in them by the towlines prior to the explosion may be seen in an otherwise inexplicable position on the side of the columns away from the tow path and facing the abutments. The explosion resulted in legislation controlling the carriage of explosives, and to this day the bridge in question is known to the boaters as "Blow-up Bridge."

Another popular illusion, fostered perhaps by the term "water gypsy," is that the boatman is a nomad, wandering about the canals of England and picking up a cargo here or there. Although the boatman may be "always moving on" he is by no means nomadic in the haphazard sense of the word. Though the narrow canal boat can range over a much greater mileage of inland waterways than any other type of commercial craft, very few even of the old master-men ever covered more than half that mileage. Usually their movements were confined to regular turns which never extended beyond a particular canal or group of canals. Some, it is true, may have "followed the trade" about the country, but as a rule the average "Number One" acted as carrier for some canal-side country town, bringing to its wharves coal from a particular colliery and only occasionally travelling elsewhere, perhaps to fetch a load of moulding sand for the local agricultural foundry.

To-day, a boatman employed by Messrs. Fellows Morton & Clayton may travel more widely than did the great majority of "Number Ones," for this firm's fleet trade over the whole of the Midlands system of narrow canals with the exception of the waterways connecting with the Severn. For the rest, the Carrying Companies' boats operate on more circumscribed routes with the result that a cross country journey by waterway to-day is reminiscent of a long railway journey in the days before the 1923 grouping when the liveries and build of locomotives and rolling stock had an intimate regional significance.

Until 1939, night and day "fly" working was still carried on on the main line of the Grand Union Canal from London to Birmingham. But when the war broke out a rule was made that stop-planks must be put down at certain points as a precaution against the flooding which might result from bomb damage. This put an end to "fly" working, and it has never been resumed. Boats do, however, continue to work long after darkness falls where they are not prevented from doing so by the closing of a lock at a certain hour. When this night travelling was carried on by the dim light of an oil lantern some companies made a practice of whitewashing lock-sides and the arches of bridges. Nowadays, however, when powerful electric head-lights are rapidly superseding the oil lantern, this helpful aid to navigation is seldom seen. An exception is the Leeds & Liverpool Canal, where the bridge arches are still outlined in this way, a vertical line being added to indicate the centre of the channel. This is apparent in the illustration of the ice-breaker at work on this canal.

The Grand Union Canal Carrying Company were responsible for introducing a system of "boat control." Under this arrangement a central control office is kept informed of the movement and progress of the boats from a number of checking points on the canal system. The position of the boats is then indicated by markers on a large map from which it is thus possible to see at a glance the exact disposition of the fleet at any time, and so to arrange the movement of boats according to loading demands. Under present-day conditions these demands are subject to frequent variation, particularly where shipments of imported cargoes from docks are concerned. Consequently the "boat control" scheme is preferable to the regular operation of a given number of boats over a given route.

The aim of any system of canal traffic control should be to eliminate as far as possible the mileage worked by empty boats, this being an uneconomical proceeding for all concerned, including the boatman who is paid a tonnage rate when loaded but only a flat rate when travelling empty. It is an unfortunate fact that at the present time empty boat mileage is indeed very considerable. The bulk of the traffic between the Midlands and the London area, for example, consists of coal from the Coventry coal-field. The "back loading" of these coal boats is almost wholly dependent on the carriage to the Midlands of imported goods, chiefly metal, such as copper ingots, from London docks. Because the volume of this traffic is variable, many boats return empty to the coal-field. Even when back loading is secured it is usually consigned to Birmingham, whereupon the boats have then to work empty back to the coal-field. To do so they have to take one of two circuitous routes, proceeding either via the Grand Union, Oxford and Coventry Canals through Warwick, Braunston and Hawkesbury or, more rarely, by what is known as the "bottom road" via the Birmingham & Fazeley Canal to the Coventry Canal at Tamworth. Incidentally, had the "Central Union" project for a canal from Coventry to the then Warwick & Birmingham Canal at Catherine de Barnes materialized, this devious working would have been avoided.

On many other canals the same problem of counter-balancing a regular one-directional haul arises and is by no means easily solved. Other factors are involved. Boats carrying a dirty bulk cargo may not be readily adapted to carry different loads such as foodstuffs or cement which are liable to be spoiled through dirt, contamination or damp. Again, any serious delay in securing the back loading of craft may seriously interrupt the steady flow of traffic in the opposite direction. Nevertheless it is certain that a great deal could be done to reduce empty boat mileage which is undoubtedly very much greater proportionately than it was fifty years ago. The owner-boatman, wholly depending on his single boat for his livelihood, naturally saw to it that it was used to the maximum advantage. In this matter of transport, as in so many other spheres of social and productive activity, the fallacy of the notion that the largest organization is necessarily the most efficient is becoming increasingly apparent despite all the efforts of propagandists and statisticians to prove otherwise. Nevertheless, though we may have misgivings, we must hope that the present co-ordination of our transport services will ultimately result in more economical and efficient working.

In the past, before the internal combustion engine banished the horse from the roads as well as from the waterways the great variety of goods carried by water included quantities of hay. When carrying such a bulky cargo the boatman frequently stood on the cabin top and steered by means of an extended tiller called a "loodel." Nowadays, whereas the river navigations and broad waterways still handle much general merchandise as well as an enormous tonnage of petroleum, paraffin and diesel oil, an increasingly large proportion of the traffic carried over the narrow canal system consists of bulk minerals for the carriage of which they are best suited. These include washed gravel and granite chippings, moulding sand, metals in ingot and bar form, salt, china clay, flints and china stone for the pottery trade, and, above all, coal. The last war proved, however, that these canals were capable of handling efficiently a much wider range of goods. At that time canal-borne Government stores were often delivered days before similar goods which had been loaded simultaneously on rail for the same destination. This was a case of the tortoise and the hare, for although the boats were slower they were not subject to delays in marshalling yards and goods lay-bys.

Even on the narrow canal system which some regard as archaic, one small diesel engine can haul fifty-five tons in a pair of boats provided the waterway is reasonably maintained. For economy in fuel, so important at the present time, no system of land transport can compete with this. Furthermore, both the first cost and maintenance cost of a boat is lower per ton carried than either the motor vehicle or the railway train, while if the canal banks are protected against erosion, wear and tear of "the track" is negligible. Schemes for enlarging the narrow canals to accommodate larger craft may or may not be practicable in the future, but it is certain that the waterway system, even in its present form, could play a very much greater part in the internal transport of this country at the expense of a comparatively small outlay. That they are not doing so at present is due to a number of factors. The majority of waterways are badly maintained owing to lack of labour, capital and modern equipment or, in the case of railway controlled canals, deliberate policy. Carriage rates are chaotic, archaic and unrealistic while there are no co-ordinated facilities for through working. Unlike the railways, the waterways are capable of loading or discharging goods at any point on the system without the necessity of laying down costly sidings with their attendant signalling and other traffic working complications. Therefore they should form a flexible system capable of meeting changing economic, social and industrial conditions. In fact, however, they have never been regarded in this light. On the contrary each canal or navigation has been considered in isolation and its standard of maintenance (or abandonment) determined by the actual traffic carried. Every secondary route or branch canal which becomes unnavigable for this reason robs the main routes of potential traffic and renders the whole system less adaptable to changing requirements. Pursued to its logical conclusion, such a piecemeal policy can only lead to the downfall of the whole system.

Another reason for the failure of the waterways to attract new traffic has been the defeatist, and in the case of railway companies actually hostile, attitude of the canal proprietors. With a few notable exceptions little attempt has been made to publicise the waterways and so make potential traders aware of the facilities which they offer. Moreover, cargo handling and distribution equipment at canal wharves is often either inadequate and archaic or non-existent. Many canal-side coal wharves to-day may be found stacked with coal brought to them exclusively by rail and road. Often the reason for this is that although canal transport may be cheaper, the saving is offset by the cost of the labour of shovelling the coal by hand out of the hold of the boat as opposed to the easier job of unloading a railway wagon which can be left standing unattended in a siding. In such cases simple mechanical handling equipment, or box containers on the principle evolved by Brindley on the Bridgewater Canal, would often tip the scale in favour of water transport.

The railway practice of quoting a special (and often un-economic) rate in exchange for an undertaking that no other form of transport will be used, is another and very potent reason why many firms make no use of water transport even though they may possess waterside premises. That industrialists should agree to such arrangements is understandable, but their cumulative effect upon the transport system is deplorable. The waterways become wasting assets while railway sidings become choked with unremunerative traffic.

Road, rail and canal could each play a useful part in the internal transport of this country because each is best fitted to handle certain classes of traffic. But these special qualifications cannot emerge until transport charges are based on transport costs which include the maintenance of the track. The position until 1948 has been that the road haulier uses a public track, paying a contribution to maintenance by licence fee; the railway operates its own vehicles on its own track, while the water carrier has operated on a track owned by private companies to whom he pays toll. Under these circumstances an accurate assessment of comparative costs for a given haul has been impossible. In the case of the waterways, the system is an archaic survival of the toll road era, and the failure of the industry to set up a canal clearing house to facilitate the quotation of through rates as it was empowered to do by the Act of 1888 is one of the chief causes for the decline of water-borne trade.

CHAPTER VII

THE BOATMAN

THROUGHOUT the history of river navigation there were three classes of men responsible for handling the traffic; the barge-master, who often owned his own barge and sometimes acted as a merchant as well as a carrier; the bargemen who acted as crew and were either paid hands or partners in the ownership of the barge; the bow-hauliers or "halers" who were engaged to tow the barge. More often than not the bargemasters were men of substance, but the position of the bargemen was more variable. Complaints of distress as a result of toll increases or working delays often indicate no more than a "hand to mouth" living, but, to generalize, the wage of the employed bargemen appears to have been high. It was usually commensurate with that of the skilled craftsman as indeed it deserved to be. The bow-hauliers usually consisted of casual labourers of the lowest class who were generally ill paid.

The bargeman seems to have acquired his reputation for strong language at a very early date, while from time to time we find the landsmen in the neighbourhood of navigable rivers complaining bitterly of his violence, his depredations, and his drunkenness. While it is true that the waterman has always been an outspoken, independent character, calling no man master, given to occasional bouts of hard drinking, and to such spare-time occupations as poaching, this reputation for lawlessness is not altogether deserved. More often than not he was held responsible for the sins of the bow-hauliers by persons to whom all river men were "bargees" and who thus failed to distinguish the highly skilled and responsible navigators from the vagrant casual labourers of the haling way.

That river navigation was indeed a highly skilled craft there can be no question. It was also a strictly local one depending as it did upon a thorough knowledge of a particular river, a knowledge handed down from father to son. The deep sea man has always tended to regard the river man with a certain contempt. Certainly in the days of sail the seaman had the harder and more perilous life, but there is little doubt that the river man was the more knowledgeable and highly skilled. For while the bargeman frequently put to sea, making long coastal voyages, river navigation was always an exclusive craft. The successful practice of that craft involved a familiarity with treacherous tidal estuaries so intimate and intuitive that it should be called sympathy rather than knowledge. The bargemen inherited the accumulated experience of generations who had pitted their skill against the river's every mood, and over whom the river exercised so strong a fascination that in the retirement of old age it would still draw them back to gaze hour after hour over its waters, spellbound as a lover enthralled by a fickle mistress. Fickle indeed were those narrow waters, beset by shoals and treacherous shifting sand banks, to men dependent upon the power of sail alone. Its hazards, the tide-rips, the whirlpools and powerful cross currents were not constant factors to be reckoned with but subject to change, not only with every conjunction of wind and tide but also with the amount of "fresh" coming down the river. This last was the most unpredictable element of all. For example, while the Vale of Gloucester lay basking in sunshine a great storm might be raging over the mountains around Plynlimmon to send a roaring spate of flood water down the Severn and her tributary Vyrnwy which might cause the river to rise as much as 18 ft. in five hours at Gloucester and so entirely alter conditions in the estuary below.

Though the danger to life might not be so great, skill and intimate knowledge were equally important in the non-tidal upper reaches of the rivers, particularly in times of winter flood or summer drought. When floods transformed the whole river valley into a great inland sea the bargemen followed the main channel by means of a subtle system of bearings and sights taken upon the conjunction of local landmarks; a church tower, perhaps, sighted at a particular point in relation to a solitary tree. He could judge to a nicety, also, whether the height of the floodwaters would allow him to pass under a particular bridge or to float safely over a weir and so save using a lock. In summer drought the uninterrupted passage of a fully laden boat depended on a knowledge of every yard of the river bed, of every deep pool and shallow most of which became known by names that were never printed on any map. The waterman's memory was his only chart as he swung his heavy craft now to this bank now to that, following the channel of deep water.

To-day, powered craft, new locks and modern dredging equipment have robbed river navigation of many of its hazards and uncertainties, and with these improvements a great deal of the river lore possessed by the old school of watermen has been lost. Nevertheless it would be quite wrong to suppose, as many people doubtless do, that the present-day pilot of a diesel driven river barge is no more than an aquatic lorry driver. Though diesel power has diminished his knowledge of natural forces by reducing his dependence upon them, the road he travels is still subject to continual change. In flood and drought he is often still guided by the knowledge of his forerunners, while the winds and tides of the estuary are as fickle as ever. Under normal conditions some of our rivers may provide safe and simple cruising grounds for the amateur with his shallow draught cruiser, but river navigation at all seasons by craft of commercial burden will always continue to call for considerable skill and local knowledge.

The coming of the canals created entirely new conditions of inland navigation. In some districts the new barge canals were in effect still water extensions of the pre-existing river navigations and so merely increased the range of operation of the local watermen. This is particularly true of Northern, Western and Eastern England. But across the Midlands there spread a network of narrow canals using a newly evolved and specialized type of craft on a number of new water routes, many of which included no river navigation. It was this Midland canal system that bred a new class of boatmen; boatmen who soon acquired tenacious traditions of their own.

At various points on the waterway system the communities of the canal boatmen and of the older river men met and overlapped. Nevertheless, the two have remained to this day quite distinct. It is at once apparent that the river bargeman is first cousin to the seaman. He uses the technical terms of the seaman, and his barge manifests this affinity in numerous ways. In its fittings and layout it generally follows orthodox marine practice in miniature. Decorative or "fancy" work is chiefly remarkable for its absence on the modern barge, while on the older wooden craft it is confined to carved scroll or other ornamental work, gilded or painted, on stem and stern, a tradition inherited from the deep sea sailing ship. Even the older "short boats" of the Leeds & Liverpool Canal with their sterns elaborately and brightly painted in the baroque style of the fair ground may be said to follow this tradition. Finally the river barge is rarely the home of a family. Like the deep sea ship it is usually the exclusive province of a male crew whose cabin, with its built-in bunks, follows orthodox marine practice.

With his exclusive knowledge of the tides and currents of his native waters, the river bargeman was of necessity half a seaman even if he had not, as was frequently the case, actual seagoing experience. The passage of the still and tideless waters of the new narrow canals in the Midlands on the other hand demanded no such qualifications or exclusive knowledge. Instead, the navigation of the long narrow craft along channels equally narrow and through tunnels and flights of locks called for skill of a different order and for new tricks of technique. The canal boatmen quickly became the exclusive masters of this new technique. Proud of this mastery, they soon invested their trade with traditions and with a trade language which owed very little to the older craft of the river bargeman and nothing at all to the sea. For example, to the canal boatman there is no "port" or "starboard" but an "inside" or "outside" depending on the position of the towing path, while his lines are "straps" and not "warps," and his hatches "slides."

If the seaman is apt to regard the river bargeman with a certain disdain, he usually dismisses the canal boatman altogether as a mere "ditch crawler." But when, some years ago, some ex-merchant seamen were engaged to work traffic on the Grand Union Canal they very quickly discovered that "ditch crawling" was by no means such an elementary task as they had supposed. Most of them retired defeated, one crew deserting their boats precipitately as they were about to enter Braunston Tunnel and making off over the fields while the boats proceeded through the tunnel on their own. The consequences in this instance might well have been disastrous, but the crew of an oncoming pair of Fellows Morton boats not only managed to pass the runaways in the depths of the tunnel without accident, but to put a steerer aboard them as they went by.

The narrow canal boatman of the old school is a member of a unique and exclusive community the origin of which is a fascinating mystery. From what source were the boatmen recruited when the narrow canals first came into being? I have found no answer to this question in the literature of the period so that it is only possible to advance very tentative theories. No doubt some came from the ranks of the river men, but all the evidence seems to indicate that many were of gypsy origin.

It is well known that in the eighteenth century the Mosses in the neighbourhood of Manchester, which at that time were Mosses in fact as well as in name, were favourite haunts of the gypsy. It is therefore fairly reasonable to assume that when James Brindley began cutting the Bridgewater Canal across Trafford Moss many of the gypsies were employed as casual labourers on the works. When the construction work was completed the change from the wagon to the narrow-boat cabin would have been an easy one for men in whom the nomadic instinct was strong. The new occupation demanded no knowledge of navigation; on the contrary it involved the management of horses in which the gypsy excelled. Moreover, he could take his wife and children with him as he had always been accustomed, and the limited living space would not trouble him. Evidence that such a migration from gypsy wagon to canal boat in fact took place is certainly not lacking. In the first place, the layout of the narrow boat cabin corresponds exactly with that of the average gypsy wagon. In this correspondence the stern end of the narrow boat is the equivalent of the driving platform of the wagon. On entering the cabin the small coal range is situated on the left. Facing it on the right is a longitudinal bench which serves as a seat by day and a bed by night and which is called by the boatmen a "side-bed." Next to the stove is a crockery cupboard the lid of which is hinged at the base and folds down to form a table for meals. Beyond the table and side-bed, the "cross-bed" lies athwart the boat. On the wagon the extra height often allows for two berths one above the other, but on the narrow boat there is one double berth with a centre portion which folds back when not in use to leave a clear passage through to the cabin door leading into the "back end" of the hold. When folded, this centre section forms the lid of a deep cupboard in which the bedding is stowed. A narrow piece of wood called a "seat-board" can be laid across the space left by the folding portion of the cross-bed to make an extra seat at mealtimes. At night-time, lace curtains, looped back during the day, screen the cross-bed alcove from the rest of the cabin. Cleverly contrived shelves, cupboards and lockers make use of every inch of space and are often decorated with crochet work hangings. This, briefly, is the arrangement of the narrow boat cabin, an arrangement quite unique on the water because it was not derived from any marine tradition but was an adaptation of an ingenious plan for living in the minimum of space originally evolved and perfected by the Romani.

The cabin layout is by no means the only evidence of Romani influence to be found on the narrow boat. Gleaming brass rails, ornamental knobs, stove chimney bands and safety chain all reveal a delight in brightly polished metal inherited from the Romani coppersmith. The cherished ornamental plates with open lacework borders which hang round the alcove containing the cross-bed are traditionally handed down from mother to daughter and so perpetuate the strong matriarchal influence characteristic of gypsy family life. These plates, many of them of great age and highly prized, were generally bought or won from a stall at a fair or on some rare and long-remembered outing to the seaside.

The origin of the paintings, the roses and diamonds and fabulous castles that adorn the cabin inside and out, is more obscure. While they undoubtedly betray the gypsy love of bright primary colours, the canal boatman has made these particular forms of decoration peculiarly his own and you may look in vain for roses or castles in the modern gypsy's wagon. But this may not always have been the case. The nearest equivalent of canal boat decoration is to be found in the carts of the Balkan peasantry which are bright with painted flowers. May it not be that at the time James Brindley cut the Duke's Canal there was encamped on Trafford Moss a tribe of gypsies fresh from the Balkans who had brought with them the first vans, the tradition of the painted flowers, and the recollection of the fairy-tale castles of Eastern Europe which they perpetuated in paint? The possibility may not be too fanciful. The gypsy is traditionally a tent dweller, but it is generally believed that it was in the latter half of the eighteenth century that the gypsy wagon was first introduced to England from Europe where its use had already become established.

To-day the great majority of the canal boaters bear no resemblance to the gypsy either in looks, speech or manners. What is more, they strongly resent any suggestion, such as that implied by the term "water gypsy," that they are in any way connected with the Romani. Yet on the other hand I have met boaters who quite obviously had Romani blood in their veins, while it is surely more than a coincidence that there are Stanleys, Taylors, Lees and Boswells on the canals. Yet however weak the ties of blood may have become, the Romani traditions are still perpetuated. There is the love of step dancing and music; the delight in bright colour and the fondness for metal ornament which often includes ear and finger rings of gold or silver worn by both sexes. Then, too, there is the fact that when two boaters marry the man tends to leave his own family and to associate more closely with his wife's relatives. But the resemblance is more than a matter of ornament and custom. Beneath his courtesy and natural good manners there lies in the heart of the boatman's character a hard core of proud reserve, an instinctive independence which he has inherited, I am sure, from some remote nomadic ancestor, and which our civilization has so far failed to break.

A fact which would seem to upset this theory of the boatman's origin is that in no early canal print that I have seen does any sign of decorative work appear on the boats portrayed. In many of these prints, however, the artist is obviously concerned with landscape, the boats being incidental and portrayed without any attempt at accuracy. In a set of early prints of scenes on the Regent's Canal the boats figure more prominently, but they are all boats operated by Pickfords, first of the large carrying firms who, like their counterparts to-day, may well have eschewed such "unnecessary" embellishment. Again, the cabin interior which appears in a steel engraving illustrating George Smith's *Our Canal Population* (1878), though of traditional arrangement is completely devoid of any decoration, ornament or furnishing of any sort. Because, however, that earnest busybody was concerned to prove that the majority of canal boatmen and their families existed in abject poverty, drunkenness and squalor, he would scarcely have permitted an illustration which would tend to disprove his thesis.

By refusing to accept the evidence of these early prints and illustrations it may appear to the reader that I am merely explaining away awkward facts in order to sustain a tenuous theory. Yet if we do accept them as evidence that the decoration and ornament of the narrow canal boat originated not earlier than the latter part of the nineteenth century, then we must believe that in a period when the heyday of the canals was already long past, when everyday life was becoming increasingly drab and utilitarian, and popular art was already dying under the influence of mass-production, a brand-new popular art form suddenly came into being on the canals. I find this idea incredible. Moreover, it is refuted by the boatmen themselves. I have questioned on this point several old boaters whose memories went back to the 1870's and who assured me that in their recollection the decoration of the boats was at once more lavish and more widespread than it is to-day. The owner-boatmen or "Number Ones" whom they recalled vied with each other in the splendour of their boats, and they have told me that in some cases the whole length of the top plank from stem to stern was decorated, a richness never seen to-day. Such boats were to be seen on the Shropshire Union, Worcester & Birmingham and many other canals from which they have now disappeared. To-day, with the exception of the boats owned by one Manchester firm, the range of the narrow boat decorated in the traditional manner inside and out has virtually shrunk to the Coventry, Oxford, Ashby and Grand Union Canals where it is perpetuated by one or two surviving "Number Ones" and some of the smaller carrying companies. Lavish interior decoration is more widespread, for the boatmen themselves, many of them dispossessed master-men, have brought their traditions into the cabins of even the latest type of all steel diesel craft operated by the big carrying companies.

To sum up, I believe that the gypsy was the first master boatman, and that he followed the network of still waterways as they spread eastwards and southwards across the Midlands from their first small beginning on Trafford Moss, bringing his customs and traditions with him. I believe that the "Number Ones" of later years, whether they were gypsies or English countrymen, perpetuated those traditions which are now passing away with them.

These traditions, and in fact the whole life of the narrow canal boatman, have been built upon the principle of the family boat, and if the family boat is to be banished forever from our waterways, then that life and tradition will perish with them. Such a fate seems probable, in fact it is remarkable that the canal boatman's way of life should have survived so long in an age when education and material amenities are the shibboleths of our ardent social reformers.

The provision of better education and better material standards of living for all is a worthy aim with which no one will quarrel. But like all worthy aims it is of limited value only and should be recognized as such. Education and material comforts *may* enable the individual to lead a happier, fuller and more contented life, but this conclusion does not necessarily follow, in fact they may have precisely the opposite effect. Reforms of this nature are only good so long as they are regarded as means; pursued fanatically as ends in themselves they may all too readily become evil. We are discovering this to-day when, because we are all struggling to be kings, there are many to echo the lament of Henry V: "What infinite heart's-ease must kings neglect that private men enjoy!" The quotation is particularly apt in this context because the canal boatman is a supreme example of the "private man." Proud, independent, resourceful, courteous he is the nearest surviving counterpart of that "bold peasantry" whom Cobbett championed.

The foregoing is not an argument against all reform or progress but a plea for wise reform. The wise man seeks out what is best in existing institutions and ways of life and seeks to encourage them accordingly, while the doctrinaire fanatic seizes upon the worst as an excuse for condemning the whole out of hand. Both will find what they seek on the canals. The one will seek out the family boat of the best type, perceiving that its gleaming paint and metal work are not merely superficial and romantic survivals but the outward and visible symbols of values no less precious for being imponderable. How then, he will ask, can we best preserve the qualities of independence, self-reliance, fellowship and pride in craft that are manifest here, and what are the difficulties which prevent their wider attainment? The zealous reformer, intent as always on minding everybody's business but his own, will see only what his fanatical predecessor George Smith called the "Rodney boatman," the casual born in the slums of an industrial city who has taken to the boats. Pointing to his squalid, bug-infested boat and rickety ill-nourished children he will argue for the abolition of the whole system of the family boat.

It is true that the boater family to-day faces many difficulties, hardships and handicaps. In the days of single horse boats, many cabins were terribly overcrowded, and a result of George Smith's campaign was the Canal Boats Act which laid down a minimum amount of air space per person in boat cabins. Under this Act, each boat must be registered and periodically inspected by the local representative of the Ministry of Health at the place of registration. The boatman with a large family on a single boat usually overcame this difficulty by sending the surplus children into hiding as soon as he heard that the inspector was on the way. To-day when the majority of families work a pair of boats the accommodation is doubled. The butty, perhaps an old horse boat once owned by the family, is still "home" and the centre of domestic life while the motor boat provides extra sleeping space. Nevertheless, living conditions could be further improved if the carrying companies paid serious attention to the problem. A more compact engine-room on the motor boat could be designed which would enable the living space to be proportionately increased, while if the canals were properly maintained so that the boats could be fully loaded, the butty cabin could be enlarged without loss of pay-load. How little attention has been paid to the boatman's comfort is shown by the fact that the motor boat exhaust is carried through the cabin roof so that the steerer inhales diesel exhaust fumes all day long. The fact that the exhaust might be carried astern never seems to have been considered.

On paper the tonnage rates paid to the boatmen seem liberal enough, but in practice he is one of the poorest paid workers in the country. In the first place only the captain of a pair of boats is paid and must distribute his earnings amongst the family, or among the crew if he is not a family man. He is also the only insured person, it having been decided in a test case that his wife, though she works as hard as her husband, is only a domestic help. Consequently she is only insured if he chooses to pay the whole of her contribution out of his earnings, which he can seldom afford to do. When working light he is only paid a low flat rate so that a reasonable income depends on back loading. It also depends on many other variable factors; on prompt loading and unloading and on the state of the canal. In recent years the condition of the canals has deteriorated to such an extent that boats must load light and still take longer over the journey. All this affects a wage based on tonnage carried. It was only during the last war that an agreement was reached that a captain's earnings over a period must equal a minimum of £5 per week and must, if necessary, be made up to this figure. This fact indicates how small is the income which the boat family receives.

Food is another problem under modern conditions. In the old days the boatman's diet, though simple and frugal, was adequate and included quantities of meat. To-day it is very far from adequate. By a most unjust anomaly, the river boatman, working a comparatively short and regular turn and with a wife and house ashore, may draw seaman's rations if his boat enters tidal waters. But the canal boatman, though he works harder and longer hours and though his wife is with him and has no such facilities for buying or preparing food, is not entitled to these extra rations. Unable to scour the shops, to stand in queues or to register with a few regular suppliers, the boatman's wife may miss even the small regular rations which are her family's due and the special allowances to which her small children are entitled. In any case she is often illiterate and so can neither comprehend the rationing system nor read the labels on the tins which now conceal so many of our foodstuffs.

In these days of almost universal literacy, the inability of many boaters to read or write is an increasing handicap which they feel acutely. For this reason alone many families have reluctantly left the boats to educate their children so that they shall not be similarly handicapped. It is hard for us to realize the magnitude of this disability in a world where literacy is now taken for granted. The boater is at home in his own world of the canals, but when he or she goes ashore they are lost. Public notices, railway station name boards, bus route signs, all these are meaningless symbols. On his rare visits to cinema or theatre the boater takes the risk of finding he has seen the show before.

All these difficulties which confront the boat family to-day are capable of solution. The only one that presents any real difficulty is the question of education, and this could be overcome by better educational facilities at turn-round points. The ability to read and write is all that is required; for the rest the life of the boats, teaching independence, self-reliance and resource at an early age, provides a better education than any textbook as the children themselves bear witness. Unfortunately, however, the soulless machine of state bureaucracy which every day grows more un-wieldy and inflexible is constitutionally incapable of dealing fairly or sympathetically with so small and highly individual a sub-section of the community which, because it is so scattered and nomadic, is incapable of speaking with a collective voice even if it had a mind to do so. On the contrary, state bureaucracy can only function by imposing its own standard pattern of life upon the community, and by eliminating all those who cannot or will not conform to this pattern. Under such a dispensation the life of the canals seems unlikely to survive much longer. Some years ago a proposal to disrupt family life on the canals was defeated by an opposition in which G. K. Chesterton played a prominent part, but since that day we have moved much further towards that servile state which Chesterton and Belloc so accurately forecast.

One recent proposal is that the wives and families of the boatmen should be housed in cottages or hostels while the boat-men work the boats on the section system. Under this arrangement a trunk route such as the Grand Union Canal main-line would be divided into sections, each representing a day's journey. So many crews would then be appointed to work the traffic through each section, handing over the boats to the crews on the next section. As has already been mentioned, this system of working has been operated for some years by day-boatmen on the Stafford-shire & Worcestershire Canal, but whether it would prove practicable and economical over longer distances is another matter. It is difficult to envisage how it could be done except at the expense of a substantial increase in the cost of canal carriage. Even though the change might mean better pay and shorter hours, the long-distance boatman does not favour it. It would reduce him to the position of a day-boatman (an occupation which he refers to contemptuously as "Joey-boating"), and with this change would go that pride in his boats which the boats themselves so eloquently reflect. Many, on this score alone, say they would refuse to work any system which involved taking over boats from others. Certainly the boats would suffer and main-tenance costs rise steeply. Certainly the resplendent narrow boat would speedily disappear, along with the way of life and the traditions which it symbolizes. For the present, while such radical schemes are debated, many skilled boatmen are leaving the canals, disheartened by the difficulties which might so readily be alleviated.

If the family boat is destined to vanish from the waterways, then I am certain that the canal boatman will go also, and his job, if it survives at all, will be filled by "workers" supplied by the Labour Exchange and caring for nothing except the weight of the pay packet at the end of the week. If I am fated to see this happen, then at least I can console myself with the thought that I was not born too late; that I have known men to whom the canals and the boats were not just another job but a way of life.

The boatman, not without reason, is suspicious of the landsman and not easy to know and understand. It is only when he is assured that the approach to him is sincere, honest, and without patronage or idle curiosity that the barrier of reserve is dropped to reveal qualities that have become all too rare to-day. I shall not dilate upon those qualities except to say that in no other walk of life have I met such true friends. That I have enjoyed their friendship and their trust is a privilege that I shall value increasingly as the years pass and take them from me. I shall remember then the talks I have had with them, on lock-sides or bridges on still summer evenings, or in the lamplit warmth of the narrow cabins on winter nights when a bitter wind sets the water lapping against the boats. I shall remember, too, how I have sung with them or listened to their music in the canal side pubs which few landsmen know. When the boats tie up no more there will be no boatman to fetch his "music" from the cabin to delight the company, and the inns will fall as silent and deserted as the old "Tunnel House" that stands lost in the fields beside the ruined Thames & Severn at the mouth of Sapperton Tunnel.

Such silent inns mean much more than the mere fact that a particular canal has ceased to carry trade, they are the symbol of a whole world, a very ancient world, which is being submerged by our machine "civilization." Like all ancient things, however, it is stubborn and a long while a-dying. It is a simpler world than ours; it contains more physical hardship, and because its vices, like its pleasures, are simple and overt, the puritan and the reformer have always been its embittered enemies. It is a world

182

which the boatman, when he comes ashore, shares to some extent with other travellers, with the gypsy, and with the people of the fair ground and the circus. Here the capacity for sheer unself-conscious enjoyment has not been lost. Here there is little premeditation, hypocrisy or secret malice. If a man likes you he will shake you by the hand and call you friend and you will believe him. If he does not he may well crown you with his pint pot.

I recall one memorable evening at a canal pub which I shall not name when the assembled company recalled to me the gathering at Little Greece on Kingham Waste which John Buchan described in his book *The Blanket of the Dark*. It consisted mainly of boatmen and gypsies. The gypsies happened to be passing in their wagons, but although the two groups had forgathered by chance they were well known to each other. Though he had not set eyes on him for many years, the boatman whom I was accompanying recalled that he had bought several horses from the leader of the gypsies in the days when he was a "Number One." It was not long before there were calls for "the music," and a melodeon, the instrument which most boatmen favour, was produced. Though none of those present could read a note of music, each of the boatmen took his turn as musician. The repertoire is always the same. Apart from a few lively "stepping tunes" such as "Cock o' the North" it is drawn almost exclusively from the nineteenth century heyday of music hall. The boatman's interest in contemporary popular music, in fact, seems to have ceased with the introduction of jazz. When, as on this occasion, some youngster breaks in with a tuneless attempt to croon some dreary lament heard at "the pictures," the "music" falls silent and the song is still-born. There were songs and there were dances while "the music" was passing from hand to hand. Each of the boatmen, one of them over seventy, performed a step dance, footing it with remarkable agility and sense of rhythm in their heavy hob-nailed boots. The gypsies step-danced also, while two gypsy girls gave a spirited and most energetic rendering of "Knees up Mother Brown." After a foursome had danced themselves almost to exhaustion to the strains of "The Cock o' the North," "the music" was given a rest, and the leader of the gypsies commenced story-telling. By this I mean no furtively obscene have-you-heard-this-one story-telling such as we usually associate with the tap-room.

On the contrary, it was a unique demonstration of the ancient art of story-telling as it was practised throughout the centuries which preceded the written word. And because his stories belonged to that oral tradition it is not possible for me to convey them to you by setting them down in print. For example, one of them described how, when passing through a certain town in his wagon he learnt that a relation had left him twenty thousand pounds. To claim this legacy involved a long journey, and at the end of it he found that the fortune consisted of twenty thousand pounds, not of money but of blackberries. This story sounds simple and feeble enough, but all I have given you is a bare frame upon which such a wealth of extravagant detail was embroidered that the story took at least ten minutes in the telling with the audience hanging upon every word. The gypsy stood up and took the floor amid the assembled company with all the assurance of an actor taking the stage, and like the accomplished actor that in fact he was, he at once held his audience with his gift of perfectly co-ordinated gesture, mimicry and vocal and facial expression. Watching him, I thought how readily this gypsy could take the parts of Autolycus or of the First Player in *Hamlet*, and then I realized that here was the display of an art that had given birth to the first strolling player, and through him to all the greatness of the English dramatic tradition.

Occasions such as this prompt interesting and not altogether optimistic speculations. The music, the singing, dancing and story-telling which I have described are the product of a people who, because they are nomadic and uneducated, must necessarily create their own entertainment. Although it may never reach a high artistic standard itself, all great art has been built upon the foundation of this spontaneous art of the people. Moreover, if the arts are to flourish this humble foundation must exist beneath them as a vital source of renewal, inspiration and enrichment. Had it not existed in Elizabethan England there would have been no Shakespeare. The commoners of England were at once his inspiration and his audience. As the vigour and richness of their speech reveals, the illiterate have a fine ear for word music, and an audience of executants, however humble, will always be more critical and appreciative. Thus while my gypsy story-teller would most certainly appreciate a performance of *A Mid-summer-Night's Dream* and show a better understanding of

Bottom and his crew than most professional critics, the machine-
minder for all his State education prefers the narcotics of the
cinema. Shakespeare and the common man of his day both saw
life as a whole, and the difference between them was one of
degree only. It is arguable that as a civilization advances and
becomes more complex and specialized, individual experience
becomes increasingly fragmentary until, despite all the efforts
of the educationalists and the achievements of the specialists, a
point is reached when that civilization overreaches itself and
relapses into barbarism. It may be that we of this generation are
the witnesses of such a relapse, but it would be out of place here
to pursue the problem further. I am merely concerned to record
a surviving fragment of an older England before it vanishes
utterly; and to point out that for all its faults it possessed certain
precious qualities.

The particular boatmen who were my companions on this
memorable evening had all, until recent years, been master-men
owning their own boats, and they have told me many tales of
the hardships they have suffered. Tonnage rates were sometimes
so low that they had to work far into the night to earn a bare
livelihood. In a hard winter they might be frozen in for weeks
and be forced to live on their precious "docking money" set
aside for the repair of their boats. One of them told me how, one
bitter winter when he was a boy, he was left in charge of a boat
which was frozen in at Kingswood on the Stratford-on-Avon
Canal. The ice held until he found himself without money, food
or fuel and went begging for scraps from door to door in the
village. Finally, privation forced him to give in; he left the boat
and walked from Kingswood to Sutton Stop, near Coventry,
where his father was.

"Ah!" exclaims the reformer, "Those were the bad old days.
Now we are changing all that." How then can he explain why
these men should have clung tenaciously to this way of life until
they were forced out of it? Why should they be moved to music
and dancing in their canal-side inns and to spend their precious
"docking money" on the elaborate decoration of their boats?
These are questions which the reformer cannot answer. Independence is the answer. Human nature is such that a man will suffer
a great deal to be his own master; make him a dependant and he
becomes perpetually dissatisfied. This is the reason why hardship

and misery, comfort and contentment do not necessarily accompany each other.

It is because this fact is not recognized to-day that I may be fated to see the last of the old race of canal-boatmen. Already many of them have retired to small cottages ashore but close to the canals they know at Longford, Braunston, Banbury, Thrupp or Long Buckby. You can tell a boater's cottage as soon as you cross the threshold, for he brings with him the possessions he has treasured all his life and which once adorned his cabin. Here are the lacework plates and the brown Measham teapot ornamented with flowers and the motto "God Bless Our Home" or "A Present from a Friend" which he bought so many years ago on the Ashby Canal—"the Moira Cut" as he will call it. There, over the mantelshelf, are a pair of miniature brass lock windlasses, highly polished, and tucked away in a drawer no doubt is his brightly coloured embroidered "spider-web" belt, or the elaborate black sunbonnet which his wife once wore. On the table is the boat "china" with its characteristic pattern of Chinese figures, while beside the hearth, as like as not, is his old cabin stool, the colours of its flower decoration now somewhat dulled and faded by the heat of the fire and much polishing.

But when once these precious possessions and symbols of the boatman's life leave the boats for the shore they are soon destined to disappear, some to the antique dealer, some to the junk merchant and others to the rubbish heap. How quickly they are vanishing is revealed by the fact that in my first book, *Narrow Boat*, I was able to describe the traditional apparel of the boatman's wife, the long, full-skirted dress, the high-lacing black boots and the black sunbonnet, as I had seen it worn on the Oxford Canal in 1939. To-day such attire is no longer to be seen.

While it is possible that many of the concrete symbols of the boatman's life may be preserved by the folk-museum or the private collector, the traditions, the language and the stories of the boat people must inevitably die with them. Even if they could be fully recorded, the record could be but a pale shadow of the original. How set down, for example, a word which never has been written and whose pronunciation varies slightly between one mouth and another? This was a difficulty which troubled the writers and cartographers of the past and which accounts for most of the earlier variations of spelling. To-day, universal literacy has brought definitive form to the English language so that the difficulty of translating oral into written language is only apparent in the case of literal transcriptions of broad dialect. But in the case of the canal boatman it is more than a question of dialect, in fact there is no such thing as a particular canal dialect. Just as the earlier river bargemen had a name for every pool, bend and shallow of their river, so the canal boatman has christened every lock, every pound and awkward turn on the canals. The late Rodolph de Salis in his monumental *Guide to the Canals and Navigable Rivers of England and Wales* has recorded the majority of the lock names, although in some cases the boatman's nomenclature is different. But names such as "Tunnel Straight" (on the Oxford Canal where there is now no tunnel), "Cabbage Turn," "Braunston Puddle," "Arm End," "Tixall Wide" or "Jackdaw Pound" are recorded by no map or guide and will one day be forgotten. "Tixall Wide," incidentally, applies to the lovely lake-like pound where Izaak Walton learnt to fish on the Staffordshire & Worcestershire Canal near its northern end at Great Haywood.

The traveller by waterway soon finds himself becoming familiar with these terms. What he will find much more confusing is that some canal-side places are sometimes known to the boatmen by names quite different from those recorded on maps and used by landsmen. Thus the village of Marsworth, on the Grand Union Canal near its Chiltern summit level is referred to by the boaters by a name that can best be translated in type as "Maffers." Sometimes, terms and place-names are obvious corruptions, such as "Noble" for "Newbold," but in others of which this is an example, the derivation is by no means obvious.

The continuity of tradition on the canals is such that a boatman will use naturally a word that has become archaic: "I reckon I'm good for a few more years, and the missus is still pretty lissom." Or he will use an expression that spans centuries of boating. Thus the older boatmen on the Oxford Canal habitually refer to the Thames above Oxford as "the West Country." "When I was a-workin' up the West Country by Boblukoi [Bablockhythe] . . ." they will say, and thus unwittingly recall the West Country barges of the seventeenth century.

A highly individual community of boatmen work the Mersey–Weaver and Anderton Companies' boats, a few still horse-drawn, between the Potteries and the Anderton Lift or Preston Brook. While the boats themselves are not especially remarkable they are manned by some of the best examples of the boating family of tradition. Unlike the boatmen elsewhere who show little religious feeling there is a strong chapel-going tradition amongst them. They also took immense pride in their horses and horse tackle, so much so that until recently a parade of boat horses, attended by intense rivalry, was held at Lostock Gralam, near Northwich, every May Day. To boatmen elsewhere, this community is known as "the Cheshire Lock Boatmen" or "the Knobsticks." The origin of the latter term is obscure. It is reputed to refer to the fact that in the early days of the Trent & Mersey a boat marshal was employed to ensure that the boatmen kept moving and did not linger too long in the public houses which are conveniently situated by many of the locks on the Cheshire section of that canal. He is said to have patrolled the tow path on horseback carrying as his badge of office a short baton tipped with silver. This became known as the "knob-stick," a term which attached itself first to its bearer and finally to the boatmen whom it was designed to overawe.

Another possible association with the early days of the canals is the legend of "Spring-heeled Jack."[1] In Cassiobury Park near Watford there is a lock on the Grand Union Canal called Ironbridge. The boatmen will tell you that a lady who then lived nearby was a bitter enemy of the Duke of Bridgewater whose boats at that time traded down the canal to London. She did all she could to hinder the passage of the Duke's boats, and to this end she employed a black servant who lurked in the park woods beside the canal and molested the boatmen as they tried to work the lock, especially after dark. He was a man of great stature and strength and was also so agile that he could leap across the lock-chamber, a feat which earned him his nickname. As fast as the unfortunate boatman could raise the lock paddles, "Spring-heeled Jack" would drop them again or else defeat him by drawing the paddles at the opposite end. His agility and strength made him more than a match for the boatmen until at last one of them succeeded in hitting him over the head with his windlass with the result that he fell into the lock and was not seen again in the

[1] It was after I had recorded this legend that I chanced to read Mr. Turner's delightful book *Boys will be Boys*, and so learnt that "Spring-heeled Jack" was a celebrated character in the Victorian "Penny Dreadful."

flesh. I have had no opportunity to investigate whether there is any factual foundation for this legend. Obviously, if there is it has become magnified, garbled and embroidered in its passage through the years. But the fact remains that many boatmen dislike working through this lock after dark, declaring that unaccountable things happen, that lines are mysteriously cut or cast off, or that paddles drop shut of their own volition. No one, however, claims to have seen the terrifying apparition of "Spring-heeled Jack."

Perhaps the most celebrated, eerie and unpleasant canal ghost is Kit Crew of Harecastle Tunnel. Several old boaters claim seriously to have seen this spectre and that its effect was singularly disturbing. To some it appeared on the horse-path over the tunnel, but more usually it frequented a point known as the Turnrail where Telford's new tunnel intersects Brindley's branch tunnel to the old workings of Golden Hill Colliery.

A related but much more amiable apparition is Kit Crewbucket, an old lady who is said to haunt Crick Tunnel on the Leicester Section of the Grand Union Canal. "If she likes you," one boatman said to me, "she'll come up into the cabin and cook your breakfast for you." But what happens if one fails to please this most obliging and domesticated ghost is not recorded.

A road bridge, spanning Telford's Shropshire Union main line near Gnosall in Staffordshire, is also said to be haunted. I discovered the following account of this haunting in a work on Shropshire folklore.[1]

On the 21st of January 1879 a labouring man was employed to take a cart of luggage from Ranton in Staffordshire to Newport in Shropshire for the use of a party of visitors who were going from one house to the other. He was late in coming back; his horse was tired, and he could only crawl along at a foot's pace, so that it was ten o'clock at night when he arrived at the place where the highroad crosses the Birmingham and Liverpool Canal. Just before he reached the canal bridge, a strange black creature with great white eyes sprang out of the plantation by the roadside and alighted on his horse's back. He tried to push it off with his whip, but to his horror the whip went through the thing, and he dropped it to the ground in his fright. The poor tired horse broke into a canter and rushed onwards at full speed with the ghost still clinging to its back. How the creature at length vanished the man hardly

[1] *Shropshire Folklore* edited by Charlotte Sophia Burne from the collections of Georgina F. Jackson (1883).

knew. He told his tale in the village of Woodseaves a mile further on and so effectually frightened the hearers that one man actually stayed with his friends there all night rather than cross the terrible bridge which lay between him and his home. The ghost-seer reached home at length, still in a state of excessive terror (but, as his master assured me, perfectly sober) and it was some days before he was able to leave his bed, so much was he prostrated by his fright. The whip was searched for next day, and found just at the place where he said he had dropped it.

Now comes the curious part of the story. The adventure, as was natural, was much talked of in the neighbourhood, and of course with all sorts of variations. Some days later the man's master was surprised by a visit from a policeman who came to request him to give information of his having been stopped and robbed on the big bridge on the night of 21st January! Much amused, he denied having been robbed either on the canal bridge or anywhere else and told the policeman the story just related. "Oh is that all, Sir?" said the disappointed policeman. "Oh I know what *that* was. That was the Man-Monkey Sir, as does come again at that bridge ever since the man was drowned in the Cut."

It is remarkable that such tales are not more frequently to be met with, since cases of drowning in the canals are by no means uncommon. Many boatmen have lost small children in this way, but owing to the fact that their depth, except in the case of certain barge canals, seldom exceeds 5 ft. adults rarely drown accidentally except through a fall into a lock-chamber. Suicides, on the other hand, are fairly common and the boatman has acquired a matter-of-fact and practical attitude towards death encountered in this guise. While he may have saved more than one drowning person he will pass a "dead-un" by. He argues that they are beyond his aid and that if he stops to recover the body he may be called upon to appear at an inquest and thus lose much time which to him means precious money. One boatman told me how he once attempted to salvage a smart new pair of boots which he saw floating soles upward in the canal, but relinquished his prize and passed on when he discovered that there were feet inside them.

Corpses excepted, there is little that a boatman will not dredge up from the canal at one time or another. Using a "keb," a type of fork with the prongs set at right-angles to the long handle, he will sometimes spend hours, when waiting to load or discharge, patiently dredging the bottom beside a coal wharf, and in this way he will often recover enough coal to keep the cabin stove going for a week or more. Much less acceptable are the old cycle tyres, ropes, or coils of wire carelessly flung into the canal and which become fouled in his propeller. I have seen a propeller so badly fouled with wire that the boat had to be run on to a dry dock before it could be cleared.

The great majority of the boatmen now working will tell you proudly that they were born in a boat cabin. In their youth when the baby was due the boats tied up, but were often on their way again within a few days of the confinement. Now, however, it has been ruled that in such cases the boats should tie up for twelve weeks. As a result, the wife often goes to the house of some relative ashore for her confinement while her husband may work the boats on with the aid of a temporary hand. As a general rule the boaters are somewhat mistrustful of the medical profession who, through failure to understand their mentality, seem seldom to be able to win their confidence. An exception is the district nurse at a certain canal-side village in Northamptonshire. Not only do the boatmen come to her with all their ills, but she has become their unfailing guide, philosopher and friend. Though there should be more like her, to find her equal would not be easy because her success is due, not so much to medical training as to an understanding of human nature which is rare to-day because it cannot be taught out of a first-aid textbook.

It is exceptional for the boatman to marry "off the land" and so, since the boating community is a small one, everyone appears to be related to everybody else either by blood or by marriage or both. The boatman seems to carry in his head this complex genealogical tree. As he nods to the steerer of a passing boat he will most likely explain: "That's Joe so-and-so as married our Auntie Rose's girl. Uncle Jack, what works for the Limited now, married his Dad's first wife's sister." After receiving such a piece of information, one usually spends the next ten minutes vainly trying to work out the exact relationship and wondering whether it can really be sanctioned by the Tables of Affinity.

Owing to this inter-relationship, practically every member of the considerable company which assembles at a boaters' wedding is in some way related to everyone else. Because in the ordinary course of events meetings are confined to a few minutes shouted conversation as two boats pass each other, a wedding is really a grand family reunion party. Wherever the wedding is to be held, at Tushes Bridge or Braunston perhaps, the boats assemble. All are resplendent for the occasion, but the bridegroom's boat outshines them all, for it is generally docked and repainted especially to receive the bride. After the ceremony, the company adjourn to the canal-side pub, and this is the one occasion when the boatman throws his enforced financial caution to the winds. On this one night he spends royally, for it is an occasion which the married pair will remember for the rest of their lives. Old boatmen have told me in minute detail precisely what the company consumed in food and drink at their wedding although thirty years or more may have passed by. A private room is usually taken at the inn, and here with music, singing and dancing the fun waxes fast and furious until far into the night while glasses are replenished from the painted water-cans filled with beer. And although this is a family affair, drinks are ordered "all round the house" so that any who may chance to visit the inn that night may toast the newly wedded pair. To-day these wedding feasts are perforce less lavish than they were of yore but still, so far as the times will allow, they are kept up with the old liberality.

Even though a boatman may have been born in a cabin, there is usually some canal-side town or village which he regards as his home port. In the old days, if a boatman died when his boat was far away from this "home" he was always brought back. His body was coffined and placed just "back of the mast" on his own boat. The boat was then worked back "fly," every boat on the canal giving way to it. Thus did his fellows pay him their final token of respect by giving him "a good road" on this, his last journey. This practice has now been discontinued, but I know of one old boat still in service which is known to this day as "the coffin boat" because it has chanced to fall to her lot on more than one occasion to act as the boatman's hearse.

The fact that on the funeral boat the coffin was always placed just "back of the mast" reveals how minutely the boatman's life is prescribed by tradition. This extends not only to the decoration and ornament of the boat down to such details as the turk's-head knots or the horse's tail which grace the ram's head of the butty boat, but even to the precise position of movable objects. Thus the water-can is always placed on the cabin top just for'ard of the

192

PLATE XLI.—
CABINSIDE CASTLES

(*a*) Painted at Banbury Dock

(*b*) Painted at Braunston Dock

PLATE XLII.—BOATERS OF THE PAST

(*a*) A christening party below Buckby Locks, 1913

(*b*) Two of the crew of a Fellows Morton steamer

PLATE XLIII.—"NUMBER
ONES"

(a) Mr. John Harwood of the
Searchlight

(b) Mr. Joseph Skinner of the
Friendship in his cabin

PLATE XLIV.—
THE BOATMAN'S WIFE

PLATE XLV.—
THE BOATMAN'S WORLD

(*a*) Narrow boat cabin interior showing stove and folding table

(*b*) Beer and music in the canal-side inn

PLATE XLVI.—BOATMEN'S INNS OF TO-DAY AND YESTERDAY

(*a*) "The Lock," Wolverley, Staffordshire & Worcestershire Canal
(*b*) "Tunnel House," Sapperton, Thames and Severn Canal

PLATE XLVII.—
INDUSTRIAL ENGLAND

(*a*) On the Trent & Mersey
Canal near Burslem, Staffordshire

(*b*) On the Huddersfield
Narrow Canal at Marsden,
Yorkshire

PLATE XLVIII.—
RURAL ENGLAND

(*a*) Winter on the Leeds & Liverpool Canal near Foulridge

(*b*) Summer on the Shropshire Union Canal near Ellesmere

stove chimney with the handle of the mop resting upon it, the head forward. We who scorn tradition to-day argue that it has proved a stumbling-block to progress by inducing men to reject all innovation. This may be true. Man should be the master and not the slave of tradition, but this mastery means understanding and development, not arrogant dismissal. A man who scorns tradition altogether is inevitably the poorer. Not only does he lose a precious sense of continuity with the pride in craft which this brings, but he is the poorer in the practical sense that he rejects methods of living or working which many generations have perfected. This is certainly true in the case of the boatman's tradition. Generations of boatmen have perfected down to the most minute detail the art of living in the confined space of the narrow boat cabin. The "ticket drawer" must be here so that a pass can be instantly produced at a toll office. The brass horn must rest there just below the cabin slide where it comes readily to the steerer's hand when he needs to blow a warning as he approaches a "bridge-hole." Many details about the boats which may appear to the landsman to be purely ornamental in fact combine beauty with utility. The brass chimney chain is there to retain the chimney in case it should be accidentally knocked off when passing under a bridge. The brass knob on the tiller of the motor boat forms the head of a pin which retains the detachable tiller bar and so prevents its possible loss overside. This tiller bar must be detachable, otherwise, when the boat was moored it would either obstruct entry to the cabin or, if free, swing round with the rudder and foul passing craft. The hoop-shaped strip of brass over the vertical exhaust pipe of the motor boat also has its function. This is to deflect the blast of the exhaust and so prevent it from blowing down dust and dirt from the brickwork on to the cabin top when passing under low bridges or through tunnels.

The living cabin of the motor driven narrow boat is of the same size as that on the old horse-drawn or butty boat, and except in a few exceptional cases the cabin is aft of the engine room. Consequently exactly the same layout has been adopted. I do not hesitate to say that the boatman's tradition has carried to perfection the art of living and working in this minute space. Any improvements such as those suggested earlier in this chapter involve structural alteration of one sort or another, and since the boatmen no longer own their own boats, the initiative for these

THE INLAND WATERWAYS OF ENGLAND

improvements can only come from the canal carrying companies. I can only hope that what I have written may do something to hasten these improvements by showing that the life of the canals should be given help and encouragement, not wantonly broken up by misguided zealots. It will be a poor world indeed when those sturdy independent qualities which the canal boatman perpetuates no longer exist.

CHAPTER VIII

TRAVELLING BY WATERWAY

IT is a remarkable fact that with the exception of the Norfolk Broads, the Thames and, to a lesser extent, the Severn, comparatively few people take advantage of the facilities for inland cruising which our waterways provide within easy reach of all the larger centres of population. Non-gregarious mortals like myself who enjoy the waterways for their remoteness from everyday life may feel that this is a good thing. But they should remember that unless traffic of every sort is actively encouraged to use the canals many of them may fall derelict. Some of our most beautiful waterways, precisely because they pass through predominantly rural areas, now carry little or no commercial traffic. These cannot continue to be maintained in navigable order for the benefit of a handful of waterway-minded people. The individualist should console himself with the reflection that the total mileage of the waterway system is so great that however popular they might become no single section is likely to be exactly crowded with pleasure craft even at the height of the holiday season.

The problem of a disused canal is a difficult one. Although it was primarily constructed as a navigation it usually also acts as a channel of water supply and is generally intimately bound up with the drainage system of the river valley through which it passes. Consequently it cannot be abandoned so readily as a road or a branch railway line. When, as in the case of the Welsh section of the Shropshire Union Canal, the waterway must still be maintained as a channel of water supply, the abandonment of navigation rights actually increases the problems of maintenance. The passage of even one boat per week will maintain a clear channel and check weed growth. When traffic ceases altogether weeds will soon choke the waterway, while small streams and field drains entering the canal will build up "scours" of silt across the channel. In this way the canal soon becomes so

195

obstructed that it can only continue to fulfil its function as a conduit at the cost of laborious weed-cutting and dredging. In such circumstances there are only two practicable long-term solutions of the problem; either the resumption of traffic must be encouraged or the waterway must be converted into a pipeline. In the case of a waterway of such beauty and historical engineering interest as the Welsh Canal, everyone must agree that the latter solution would be an act of disastrous vandalism. Although commercial traffic on this canal only ceased as a result of a burst on the Welshpool section in 1936 which the railway owners failed to repair, a resumption of trade could never result in a heavy traffic. The potential value of the waterway for pleasure craft on the other hand is immense, and it remains to consider how such traffic on this and other waterways might be fostered.

In the past, pleasure traffic on inland waterways has never been actively encouraged and in fact in the majority of cases canal officials have positively discouraged it. On many railway owned or controlled canals this discouragement has been part of a policy aimed at the eventual dereliction and abandonment of the waterway, but on the independent canals it has been due to prejudice. The canal official argues that pleasure traffic is liable, owing to ignorance, to interfere with the commercial craft for which the waterway was primarily intended by causing obstructions or by wasting water owing to careless lock working. He also fears damage to the more fragile pleasure craft which may result in a claim for compensation against the canal authority or commearcil boat owner. It must be admitted that there is truth in these arguments. But the official often fails to appreciate that the pleasure boat owner pays for his passage and is thus a source of revenue, and that his prejudice perpetuates the ignorance of which he complains by allowing the public no opportunity to become waterway-minded. There can be no doubt whatever that a more helpful attitude on the part of waterway officials would soon produce a larger and more enlightened cruising public. Commercial traffic must, of course, always have precedence, and on waterways carrying a heavy traffic it might conceivably become necessary to impose a limit upon the number of pleasure craft allowed on the waterway at any one time and to set a reasonable time limit for the through passage. Furthermore, an acute water shortage may make it necessary temporarily to prohibit pleasure boats in order to conserve supplies. Nevertheless, any serious conflict between the two classes of traffic is unlikely because the pleasure cruiser will be attracted to the more rural waterways where commercial traffic is light, and will tend to use the busier routes through industrial areas only as a means of reaching them.

There are other reasons why the canals have not been more widely used for pleasure cruising. One is the limitations of beam, draught and headroom which the canals impose. Undoubtedly the most popular and far-ranging pleasure craft on the waterways at the present time is the canoe, but the canoeist very naturally prefers the swift and, in the context of this book, unnavigable upper reaches of rivers to the still canals. If he uses the latter at all it is usually in order to make a convenient passage between the headwaters of two rivers. The boats in which Temple Thurston and William Black made the canal journeys which they described in *The Flower of Gloster* and *The Strange Adventures of a Houseboat* were horse-drawn, but to-day owing to diesel power many towing paths are no longer passable by horses. Some form of powered craft is therefore the obvious choice for canal cruising, but unfortunately the great majority of small river or seagoing cruisers are dimensionally and practically unsuited for canal work. In this matter of canal dimensions, the figures quoted in textbooks are apt to be misleading. Thus the figure of maximum draught is very seldom less than 3 ft. 6 in., but in fact the state of many narrow canals is such that the trouble-free navigation of a craft drawing 3 ft. 6 in. involves an intimate knowledge born of constant use, and 2 ft. 6 in. should be considered the maximum for a boat in which it is proposed to cruise widely over the narrow canal system. Again, textbook figures for headroom vary from one canal to another but rarely quote less than 8 ft. 6 in. But this is a figure measured from water level to the crown of an arched overbridge and is therefore very misleading. In practice, the height of the craft above water-line should certainly not exceed 6 ft. and even this height should not extend to the full width of a boat of 7 ft. beam. Beam and overall length are determined by the dimensions of the locks which are variable. Thus while the locks of the narrow canal system of the Midlands permit a length of 70 ft. they impose a limit of 7 ft. beam, or slightly less on the Welsh section of the Shropshire Union Canal. Conversely, the locks of eastern and north-eastern England will admit craft of greater beam but impose a more stringent limit on length. The smallest in this respect are the locks on the Middle Level Navigations of the Fens where length is limited to 45 ft. To summarize these figures we can say that the ideal craft capable of cruising with confidence throughout the entire waterway system of this country with an ample safety margin would conform to the following dimensions: draught: 1 ft. 6 in.; beam: 6 ft. 10 in.; length: 45 ft.; maximum height above water-line: 5 ft. 6 in. to a width of 5 ft. 6 in. The boat should be of robust construction since a certain amount of bumping and rubbing in locks is inevitable, and fend-offs are useless in narrow locks unless beam is reduced to allow for them. If little-used waterways are to be navigated a weed-cutting or weed-slipping propeller is a great advantage, while the propeller should be as accessible as possible so that it may be cleared if it does become fouled. Some waterways are stony and shallow near the banks so that the propeller should either be very robust or adequately and strongly guarded. A shearing key or coupling on the propeller shaft is another safeguard. A tiller is preferable to wheel steering for canal work. The boat should be equipped with a good bow fender, a headlight giving a wide rather than a long beam for negotiating tunnels, and a powerful audible warning device. Such a warning is essential on busy waterways when approaching blind turns, especially those masked by narrow bridges. It is also necessary as a warning signal on rivers where the locks are set by resident lock-keepers or on a waterway such as the Gloucester & Berkeley Ship Canal where swing bridges are opened by bridge-keepers. The boat should carry long lines fore and aft, spare lines and a set of rope pulley blocks for emergency use, long and short shafts or boat-hooks, two mooring spikes and lock windlasses of sizes to suit the different paddle spindles of the locks. Three sizes of windlass should suffice for the majority of the locks likely to be encountered. The female square of the largest should measure an inch and a quarter across the flats and be formed parallel throughout its width. This windlass will fit all the paddles on the Kennet & Avon Canal and throughout the Grand Union system with the exception of a few on the River Soar locks which have not yet been standardized. On most of the other canals the squared ends of the paddle spindles are tapered, and the squares of the windlasses to fit them should measure across the flats one inch and one-eighth tapering to inch, and one inch tapering to seven-eighths of an inch. The larger of these will be found to fit the great majority of the paddles, while the smaller is most suitable for use on the Trent & Mersey Canal and for certain paddle spindles which have become worn after long use. The throw of the windlasses should not exceed nine inches for the larger and eight inches for the smaller. A greater throw certainly provides more leverage and makes the effort of drawing paddles easier, but it will be found, perhaps at the cost of skinned knuckles, that when lifting gate paddles the handle of such a windlass comes uncomfortably close to the lock beam or strapping post even if it does not actually foul it and so make it impossible to draw the paddle.

I have sketched the ideal canal cruising craft and its equipment, but ideals are difficult to attain in these days of high prices, material shortages and restrictions. Nevertheless, there can be little doubt that suitable craft could be adapted to meet demands. Ex-army pontoon sections can be converted into small two-berth cruisers suitable for canal work, and a number of these conversions are already to be seen. Perhaps the nearest approach to the ideal craft which could be achieved at the present time would be based on a narrow boat hull reduced in length and cabined over. The standard 70 ft. narrow boat will make a spacious floating home, but for the novice merely requiring a boat for holidays it is too large and unwieldy. It can only be turned at certain points on the narrow canals, while its length debars it from the waterways of the east and north.

In addition to the lack of suitable boats, some people are deterred from canal cruising by the number of locks on the canals and by the fact that these must usually be worked by the crew. While locks may vary in detail, the principle is always the same and once the technique is mastered the passage of the average small canal lock becomes a matter of simple and easy routine. Assuming the boat is entering an empty lock with the lower gates standing open and ready, a member of the crew should jump ashore with a windlass at the steps provided for the purpose at the tail of the lock. Otherwise, if the lock is a deep one, he may find difficulty in clambering ashore. He should close the lower gates behind the boat, ensuring that they close fairly together and are not "fouled" by floating rubbish, also that the lower paddles are fully closed. It sometimes happens that when the locking pawl is released from the rack, the paddle does not drop to its full extent. In doubtful cases the paddle should be tested with the windlass. If the boat is a large one and fits the lock chamber fairly snugly it is sufficient to keep the engine running ahead to hold the bow against the rubbing plate on the upper gate sill. But if the boat is very much smaller than the lock, lines should be put ashore and made fast to keep her against the lock wall and prevent her from being washed to and fro. As the boat rises, these lines will fall slack and must be taken up. The upper end of the lock is often equipped with both ground and gate paddles. In this case the ground paddles should always be drawn first as they cause less "flush" because the water enters through culverts below water level. If the boat is small and the lock large, the ground paddles should be drawn slowly, one at a time. It will often be found that if the ground paddle on the same side of the lock as the boat is drawn first, the wash, recoiling from the opposite wall, will tend to hold the boat steady. The gate paddles admit water through the upper gate itself and should only be fully drawn when the water has risen to the level of their apertures; otherwise the boat may be washed backward or swamped with water if it is near the gate. If the lock is provided with a side-pond, the side-pond paddle should be drawn first. When the flow from the pond to the lock has ceased it should then be dropped and the rest of the water drawn from the upper end of the lock in the usual way. When the lock is full the upper gate or gates can be opened so that the boat may move out into the upper pound. Owing to their greater size, the lower gates of a lock are not so well adapted to hold up the water as the upper ones. Should they appear to be leaking badly it is advisable to close the top gates behind the boat, particularly if the pound above is a short one. On canals where traffic is infrequent it is the usual practice for ascending craft to leave top gates closed. This involves additional trouble, but failure to observe the rule may well mean that some hours later a disgruntled boatman may find himself confronted by an empty pound and be forced to waste precious time and water filling it up again by running water down from the lock above before he can continue his journey.

When ascending a flight of locks which are "against" the boat, the simplest procedure is for a member of the crew to walk ahead and draw off the locks in readiness. Before drawing the bottom paddles to empty the lock he should make certain that the top gate is fairly closed and the paddles shut. Anyone walking ahead to prepare locks in advance should always keep a good look out for boats which may be approaching from the opposite direction and which have therefore "got the road." Unless he judges that there is time for his own boat to pass through the lock before the oncoming craft arrives, he should wait and signal to his boat that another is approaching, for it is bad canal manners to delay oncoming traffic by stealing the road from them.

If a lock is not drawn off in advance, the ascending boat should be kept away from the lower gates until the lock is empty, but when a lock is being filled for a boat her bows may rest against the upper gate, otherwise she may be drawn against it by the suction from the paddles. This suction will also tend to keep the boat against the lower gates when it is descending in the lock. On no account should the boat be allowed to drift back to the upper gates when the lock is being emptied. On some canals, notably on the Grand Union, the upper gate sill projects for some distance into the lock chamber, thus forming a ledge upon which the stern of a boat could settle with disastrous results. It is always advisable to keep an eye on a boat which is ascending or descending in a lock chamber to be sure that she is moving freely with the water. Accidents have often happened through boats becoming lodged or jammed in lock chambers owing to irregularities in the lock walls or projections on the hull. If this occurs, is quickly observed and the paddles promptly shut, little or no damage will result. If the boat is fitted with a long tiller it may be advisable to remove or secure this in a narrow lock, otherwise the flush of the paddles may swing the rudder till the tiller fouls the lock walls. The tiller should also be removed when the boat is moored up, otherwise the wash of passing boats may swing it across the channel. This is the reason why the tillers of canal narrow boats are invariably detachable. In any case, with boats 70 ft. in length, it is sometimes necessary to turn the rudder at right-angles to enable the lower gate to clear as it is swung shut. This is the case on the Farmer's Bridge locks of the Birmingham & Fazeley Canal where single bottom gates are used. Here, the breast of the gate naturally moves through a much wider arc than does the more usual double gate.

Staircase locks, with or without side-ponds, and duplicate locks are naturally more complicated in their working than the simple lock with its single chamber. It would be tedious to attempt to explain in detail the method of working every special type of lock which the traveller might encounter. The principle is always the same, and, once this is mastered, an intelligent examination of the layout of the different paddles will soon reveal their function. The golden rule in every case is to make quite certain before leaving any lock that all the paddles are fully closed. To do this it is better to see that there is no flow of water into or out of the lock chamber rather than trust to the appearance of the paddle gear.

Besides the technique of working locks there are other important rules which the canal traveller should observe in order to earn the respect of canal officials and working boatmen. The latter should be considered especially, and the canal traveller who never forgets that to the working boatman time means money will reap the reward of their friendship and co-operation. He should on no account "take the road" from a working boat by passing or striving to keep ahead of it when approaching a flight of locks. If, when working through a flight he finds himself being overhauled by a working boat he should let it past, for the boatman can work the locks much faster than a novice. The passing rule on the canals is usually "keep right" or, in nautical parlance "port to port." This rule is not invariable, however, and the traveller should ask the rule when he passes on to a strange canal. In any case, the rule is not rigid. A horse drawn boat, for an obvious reason, should always be given the tow-path side or "inside" as the boatmen call it. When meeting loaded boats the cruiser should look out for a signal from the steerer. Loaded boats must keep to the deep water, and the boatman may signal his wish to pass on the wrong side.

When approaching a narrow bridge where the view ahead is obscured it is not enough merely to sound a warning. The crew should listen for an answering warning, the sound of a horn or of a diesel engine or the crack of a whip. If any of these sounds are heard it is wiser to slow down and wait till the oncoming craft have cleared the bridge. With a lightly built cruiser, "race you to the bridge" is a dangerous game to play.

Moorings should be chosen with care and forethought. Obviously it is wrong to moor on a blind turn or in such a way that a narrow fairway is obstructed. Where there is commercial traffic it is unwise to moor in very shallow water where the boat cannot approach the bank. Passing traffic will either wash the boat aground or, as it passes and temporarily draws the water away, it will cause the boat to heel over at an angle which may transfer the evening meal to the cabin floor. The tow-path side should be avoided where practicable on canals which are still used by horse-drawn boats but it is quite in order to moor by the path on canals which are no longer so used. But in this case mooring lines should be kept clear of the towing path where they would obstruct lengthmen or lock-wheelers with results which, after dark, might conceivably prove fatal. For this reason, where rings are not available, mooring spikes should be driven into the bank between the path and the canal. It is not advisable to moor within fifty yards of a lock as this may interfere with traffic waiting to enter the lock. Except when lying at recognized moorings it is wise to exhibit a riding light on canals where traffic moves after dark, but such a light should not be so bright or so placed as to dazzle or confuse steerers.

The channel of deep water is usually in the centre of the canal on the straight and on the outside on the turns. Any attempt to "cut" corners will therefore almost invariably land the boat on the mud. If the stern of the boat is in soft mud it may continue to move forwards but will refuse to answer to the helm. If the boat does become "stemmed up" on a mud bank it can often be pushed off most readily by shafting from the bank rather than from the boat itself, assuming that a member of the crew is able to jump ashore. The best plan is to free the bow and push it well out into deep water, then to push the stern off in a direction as nearly as possible parallel to the centre line of the boat. If this fails, the bow should be swung in and out again and then another attempt made. If all direct efforts fail (a rare occurrence) the rope pulley blocks should be brought into action using a mooring spike or a convenient tree as a fixed purchase. It is quite useless to try to get off a mud bank by using engine power. This may not only make matters worse, it may result in a broken propeller. Not all waterways have mud bottoms. There are often submerged stones or broken piles near the margins which should therefore only be approached under power with extreme caution. For this reason, when coming in to a strange mooring, it is always wiser to stop in mid-channel and shaft into the side. It may look much more efficient to manœuvre the boat neatly up to the bank under power and nine times out of ten this may be carried out with satisfying success. The tenth occasion, however, may result in the disaster of a broken propeller blade. Sometimes a high cross wind may make it impossible for a shallow draught boat to keep to the deep-water channel. In these circumstances it is wiser to tie up until evening when the wind usually moderates, for there is little pleasure and much risk in attempting to carry on under these conditions. It is equally unwise to travel when the waterway is ice-bound, for even a thin layer of ice insufficient to hinder progress will cut the planking at the water-line like a sharp knife.

Finally, the boat should never be propelled at such a speed that a breaking wave is created which follows behind the stern of the boat. This is the most heinous offence from the canal engineer's point of view as it is the chief cause of bank erosion. The fact that such a wave may be seen following many empty working boats is no excuse. They at least have an excuse for travelling fast. In fact, this stern wave means that the boat is pushing the water in front of her and by so doing expending a lot of power and fuel for very little return in extra speed. Most canals impose a speed limit with the idea of checking this damaging wash, but the speed at which it is set up naturally varies with the size of the boat and the design of the hull. Maximum speed is therefore a matter for the judgement of the steerer rather than for a hard-and-fast ruling. It is good manners to slacken speed when passing moored boats.

The most efficient and expeditious working of a boat through a canal calls for many finer points of skill and judgement which it would be tedious to describe here but which are soon acquired by experience once the principles of lock working and the general rules of the waterway are understood. With this basic knowledge clearly in mind the canal traveller can set out confidently for a cruise of six days or six months, for he has a wide cruising ground set in every variety of English landscape before him. In a few cases he must obtain navigation permission beforehand, but usually advance permission is not required, and he may obtain from a canal-side toll office a pass which will cover whatever journey he wishes to make over a particular canal. The river system of lock by lock payments is never employed on the canals. Pleasure traffic tolls vary very widely between one canal and another, and more uniform rates and facilities for through booking are reforms which are long overdue.

The traveller will soon discover that the labour of lockage is amply rewarded, for by means of these locks which lift the waterways over the watersheds he enjoys a variety of scenery unknown to those who confine themselves to river or sea. River and sea create their own landscape, and the most beautiful river scenery is to be found in the upper reaches which are accessible only to the canoeist. The canal, on the other hand, presents the water traveller with an almost infinite choice of countryside and a prospect which changes at every turn. Often these changes are sudden and dramatic, as on the Staffordshire & Worcestershire Canal where, after winding across flat fields just north of Kidderminster, the canal suddenly dives into the narrow valley of the Stour and is soon clinging to a narrow shelf above the river overhung by high sandstone cliffs. Or there is Tardebigge where the Worcester & Birmingham Canal emerges from a tunnel to run along a hillside overlooking a great expanse of the Severn plain backed by the Clee hills of Shropshire. For all its straightness, the main line of the Shropshire Union Canal (Telford's Birmingham & Liverpool) presents some striking contrasts as it leaves a deep and thickly wooded cutting for a lofty embankment from which the traveller can look out across the rolling fields of Shropshire to the high cone of the Wrekin and the more distant border hills of Briedden and Caer Caradoc.

Very different in character but no less fascinating are the scenes which confront the traveller on the Leeds & Liverpool Canal. These vary from the prospects of the Yorkshire moors and dales between Bingley and Gargrave or the lonely levels of Marton Pool from Banknewton to the summit lock at Greenberfield, to the impressive panorama of industrial Burnley, a forest of fuming mill chimneys in the valley below, which suddenly unfolds round a bend in the canal near Brierfield.

In the south, Rennie's Kennet & Avon follows a course of great beauty, particularly westwards from its summit tunnel at Savernake. From the little thatch roofed village of Wootton Rivers which lies almost within the shadow of the great downland camp on Martinsell winds a level of fifteen miles through the rich vale of Pewsey to Devizes with the smooth green folds of the chalk downs marching always on the right hand. Then follows the great descent into the valley of the Bristol Avon where the canal clings to the wooded slopes high above the river and where Rennie's lovely stone bridges and aqueducts fittingly announce the approach to Bath.

Perhaps the most beautiful waterway of all is the Welsh section of the Shropshire Union Canal from its junction with the main line at Hurleston to Llangollen. In clear weather from the top lock at Hurleston the traveller can look back over the levels of the great Cheshire plain to the long ridge of the Pennines. This prospect is soon lost to sight as the narrow waterway winds on its lonely way through fields and woodlands by Wrenbury, Marbury and Grindley Brook to the hamlet of Platt Lane. Here the landscape changes in the most striking fashion. The canal cuts straight and wide over Whixall Moss a wild expanse of peat bog which, backed by the distant mountains of Wales, presents a scene more reminiscent of Ireland than of any English county. Between Whixall Moss and the little town of Ellesmere the canal traverses one of the most remote, lovely and unspoiled districts in England, a countryside of small fields, stretches of heath and woodland which are sanctuaries for an abundant wild life, and of isolated hamlets populated by a sturdy, kindly race of small farmers. As it approaches Ellesmere the canal passes through the heart of the lake district of Shropshire, skirting the wooded shores of Cole Mere and Blake Mere which in winter teem with wild duck. The level lands of the Marches west of Ellesmere make a quiet prelude to the climax of the voyage as the canal enters Wales, crossing the valleys of the Ceiriog and Dee on Telford's great aqueducts and turning westwards from the airy height of Pont Cysyllte, to follow the mountain slopes of the Vale of Llangollen beneath Glendower's fortress of Dinas Bran.

The canals which cross the Midland shires, the Grand Union, the Oxford, or the Trent & Mersey may not compare scenically with the Welsh Canal, but they share the same quality of remoteness, and it is this quality which distinguishes the canal system as a whole. Sometimes it is very real as on the summit levels of the Oxford Canal and of the Leicester section of the Grand Union where it is possible to travel for hours across the wolds of North Oxfordshire and Northamptonshire without meeting a soul save a passing boatman. But sometimes it is an illusion which is shattered so soon as the traveller leaves the waterway. In this respect the canal is the opposite of the road, for whereas the latter brings the town into the country, the canal seems to bring the country into the heart of the town. This is particularly noticeable in the approach to Birmingham. The city extends interminable tentacles of ribbon development along the main roads to Bristol and London while the equivalent water routes, the Worcester & Birmingham and the Grand Union Canals thrust thin probing fingers of green almost to the heart of the city. There is a good reason for this. The three transport systems, canal, rail and road, each initiated a separate belt of urban development, which are often as clearly defined as the rings of growth on the sawn butt of a tree. Each belt naturally tended to concentrate about the lines of communication which initiated it; consequently the canal only becomes truly "built up" when it reaches the older core of the city which belongs to the canal era and pre-dates the railway age. Even here, where the narrow ribbon of blackened water runs through a gloomy and often malodorous canyon formed by old warehouses and factories, the feeling of remoteness persists. The trains, the buses, trams and cars which rumble and thunder overhead belong to a newer and different world, and for this reason the canal traveller still feels himself withdrawn from the ages of steam and petrol. To pass through a large city by waterway is a remarkable experience, and even those who are intimately acquainted with the city's streets often find it difficult to locate their precise position. For years they may regularly have used some busy thoroughfare without realizing that beneath them, through some dark invisible culvert, there ran a waterway linking coast to coast.

Quite apart from the varied scenery through which it passes and the quiet of its still waters, one purpose of this book has been to show that the canal itself is a great source of interest. It provides the observant traveller with a unique opportunity for studying the development of civil engineering and architectural technique over the period from 1760 to 1830. As he passes, for example, from the Staffordshire & Worcestershire Canal to the Shropshire Union main line between Autherley Junction and Nantwich he will appreciate in a way that the landsman cannot do how canal construction developed during this period and by so

doing paved the way for the railway age. These two canals mark
the beginning and the end of the period of canal construction in
England and the difference between them is very striking. Yet
every waterway exhibits individual features; in the details of the
construction of locks and weirs, in the design of overbridges or
in the architecture of lock-houses and other buildings.

The whole history of inland transport has been characterized
by man's rapidly increasing mastery over the obstacles imposed
by the configuration of the landscape. While the material advantages of modern transport are undoubtedly very great, the
arrogant conquest of natural barriers has imposed a bleak uniformity in place of regional diversity. Until the eighteenth
century the watersheds were, as they had been for centuries, the
true boundaries dividing region from region rather than the
arbitrary boundaries of counties shown on a political map. Within
the catchment areas which these watersheds enclose there
flourished a number of highly individual regional cultures,
regional in the most eloquent and intimate sense of the word
because their agriculture and their industries were based upon
the resources of the particular region. It is for this reason that
the regional architecture of the past appears so inevitably "right."
It has grown out of the ground upon which it stands.

To-day, swift transport and the uniformity imposed by industrial mass production have blurred the outlines of the old
regional map of England to such an extent that an unobservant
traveller could cross the country by rail or main road and remain
unaware of their existence. The traveller by canal, on the other
hand, not only cannot fail to be made aware of their existence,
but he will also discover that the veneer of uniformity imposed
by the internal combustion engine is very much thinner than he
had supposed. In the first place he cannot ignore the old physical
boundaries as he climbs slowly lock by lock out of a river valley,
and crosses the watershed, following the canal summit level as it
burrows through or winds over the highlands until it seeks out
the narrow valley of some small brook which, as the canal descends
beside it, proves to be the headwaters of another great river
system. Tributaries, from some of which the canal may draw
supplies, swell the stream until it becomes a wide and slow
flowing river with which the canal may eventually unite. And as
the traveller makes his way from one valley to the other he will

notice not only differences in local building, agriculture and industry, but more subtle distinctions; different wild plants and trees, a difference of climate, a different local speech and manner. He will also find to his surprise that, despite a century of swift transport, the topographical knowledge of the great majority of country people does not extend with any exactitude beyond the confines of their own region.

Travel, for example, up the Grand Union Canal through Blisworth and Weedon where in winter the bitter east winds whip unimpeded across the great levels of the Ouse and Nene, and then turn west and south again by the Oxford Canal into the milder valley of the Cherwell. To do so is to realize that the high watershed of the North Oxfordshire wolds is still a very real boundary. Equally obvious is the transition from the Midland plateau to the vale of Severn by the Worcester & Birmingham or the Staffordshire & Worcestershire Canals. Sometimes, however, regional boundaries are by no means so clearly defined physically and may become first apparent only by a change in local speech. On the Welsh section of the Shropshire Union Canal, for instance, the broad north country dialect of the Cheshire plain suddenly gives place, west of Whitchurch, to the softer speech of Shropshire, a speech with a lilt which informs the discerning ear that the Welsh border is not far distant.

All these things contribute to the unique fascination of canal travel. By attempting to analyse this appeal I may seem to have accorded the river little praise and to have been guilty of special pleading. In fact both river and canal have their particular attractions, and the most interesting water journey is that which is planned to include both. The contrast between the narrow winding canal with its unique brightly painted boats and the broad stream of a great river with its barge traffic enhances the interest of each. But if I have stressed the appeal of the canals it is because, whereas there has never been any lack of writers and poets to sing the praises of our English rivers, there have been very few with any word to say for our canals. Temple Thurston and William Bliss are the only writers fully to appreciate the canals and to express that appreciation eloquently. It is to be hoped that this book as a whole and this chapter in particular may inspire some other writer to follow their excellent example by discovering, as they did, that the canal is the way to the heart of England.

BIBLIOGRAPHY

THE principal works of reference used in preparing the historical sections of this book are as follows:

River Navigation in England, 1600–1750, by T. S. Willan (Oxford, 1938).

The Navigation of the Great Ouse in the 17th Century, by T. S. Willan (Bedfordshire Arch. Soc.).

A Historical Account of the Navigable Rivers, Canals and Railways of Great Britain, by Joseph Priestley (Longman, Rees, Orme, Brown & Green, 1831).

Lives of the Engineers, Vols. I and II, by Samuel Smiles (Murray, 1862).

A Chronology of Inland Navigation, by H. R. de Salis (Spon, 1897).

Bradshaw's Guide to the Canals and Navigable Rivers of England and Wales, by H. R. de Salis (Blacklock, 1918).

Severn Tide, by Brian Waters (Dent, 1947).

INDEX

Aberdare, 132
Abingdon, 54
Accidents, 163–4
Achill, 123
Administration, river, 101 ff.
Ailesbury, *see* Bruce
Aire, river, 20, 33, 34
Aire & Calder Navigation, 47, 49, 67, 129, 132, 151
Aldersley, 44, 57, 81
Alfardisworthy, 83
Alresford, 31
Anderton, 81, 84, 159, 187
Andover Canal, 54, 60
Andover & Redbridge Railway, 60
Apperley, 122
Appledore, 60
Aqueducts, 84 ff.
Aran islands, 123
Armitage Tunnel, 92
Arun, river and Navigation, 59
Ashby Canal, 52, 155, 158, 177
Ashley, Henry, 30
Ashley, Henry, jun., 30
Ashton Canal, 48, 50
Ashton-under-Lyne, 48
Asperton Tunnel, 61, 90
Asphyxiation, 94
Astley, 33
Atherstone, 43, 52
Audlem, 144
Auger, Shell, 116
Autherley, 57, 81, 207
Avon (Bristol), river, 31, 35, 36, 37, 53, 79, 206
  (Hants.), river, 31, 32
  (Lower) Navigation, 71
  (Warwick), river, 16, 31, 71, 139, 141
  (Wilts.), river, 139, 141
  weirs, 72, 75
Avonmouth, 130, 132
Aylesbury, 52, 54
Aylesford, 31

Back loading, 166
Balance beam, 74
Banbury, 43
Bank protection, 119–20
Barbridge, 58
Barford, Great, 30
Barge canals, 125
Bargemasters, 170
Bargemen, 170 ff.
Barges, 125 ff.

Barges, " Wich," 129
Barnes, Mr., 52
Barnsley Canal, 49
Barnt Green, 107
Barnton Tunnel, 88, 92, 93, 94
Barrage, moving, 106
Barrowford, 107
Barton, 39, 40, 43, 87
Barton Swing Aqueduct, 87
Basingstoke Canal, 54, 89
Bateman, H. M., 161
Bath, 35, 53
Bawtry, 34
Beasley (A. H.) & Sons, 156
Bedford, Francis, Earl of, 25
Bedford, William, Earl of, 26
Bedford, 15, 28, 30, 32
Bedford Level, 26, 128, 141
Bedford Level Corporation, 27, 102
Beeston, 72
Bell, Andrew, 153
Belloc, H., 181
Bellows, water, 40
Belvoir, Vale of, 52
Bennet, Sir Humphrey, 31
Berkeley, 53
Berkeley Pill, 53, 54
Berkhamsted, 131
Bevan, 55, 86
Bevill's Leam, 26
Bewdley, 17–18, 19, 23, 37, 42, 123
Bingley Five Rise, 78
Birmingham (boat), 155
Birmingham, 44, 51, 57, 67, 130, 131, 156, 207
Birmingham Canal, 44, 51, 57, 64, 66, 80, 81, 89, 90, 152, 159
Birmingham & Fazeley Canal, 43, 51, 98, 166, 201
Birmingham & Liverpool Junction Canal, 57, 58, 110, 205
Births, 191
Bishop's Stortford, 61
Bittal Reservoirs, 107
Black, William, 197
Blackburn, 47
Black Country, 23, 44, 51, 61, 129, 158, 159
Black Delph, 51
Blackstone, 19
Blackstone Edge, 48
Blagdonmoor, 83
Blake Mere, 206
Blake's Lock, 142
Bliss, William, 209
Blisworth, 209

Blisworth Tunnel, 52, 90, 92, 93, 94, 117, 131
Blow-up Bridge, 164
Boatbuilding, 132 ff.
Boat control, 165
Boats, canal, 125
    , Lower and Upper Trent, 128
Bolinder engine, 156, 158
Boston, 20, 21, 22
Botterham, 78
Bottoms, boat, 133–4
Boulton, Matthew, 66, 152
Boulton and Watt, 20, 109
Bow-hauliers, 139, 170 ff.
Bradshaw, 59
Branch canals, 108
Brandbridges, 60
Brandon, T., 32
Bratch, 78
Braunston, 108, 156, 166
    Tunnel, 52, 92, 93, 94, 117, 131, 173
Breasts, 73
Brecon, 61
Brecon & Abergavenny Canal, 61, 95, 132
Brendan, St., 123
Brentford, 52, 156
Brewood, 98
Briare, Canal de, 68
Bricklaying, 117
Bridge, Thomas, 35
Bridges, 95 ff.
    , towpath, 141
Bridgewater, Francis Egerton, Third Duke
    of, 36, 38 ff., 120, 144, 153, 188
Bridgewater Canal, 41–2, 47, 48, 63, 87,
    128, 150, 151, 153, 155
Bridgnorth, 15, 19
Bridgwater (Somerset), 31
    Bay, 60
Bridgwater & Taunton Canal, 60
Brindley, James, 34, 36, 38 ff., 44, 47, 49,
    53, 72, 78, 79, 85, 87, 91, 120–1, 168,
    174
Bristol, 17, 46, 53, 132
    Channel, 17
Bristol & Taunton Canal, 60
Brown, "Capability," 97
Bruce, Charles Lord, 91
Bruce, Thomas, Earl of Ailesbury, 91
Buchan, John, 183
Buckby Locks, 108
Buckingham, 52
Bude Canal, 83
Bugsworth, 50
Bullo Pill, 128
Bure, river, 34, 127
Burne, Charlotte S., 189 n.
Burnley, 47

Burton-on-Trent, 20, 85, 140
Bury St. Edmunds, 30
Butterley Tunnel, 89
Butterwick, 124
Butty, 161–2

Cabin, layout, 174, 193
Calder, river, 33, 34, 47, 48, 141
Calder & Hebble Navigation, 34, 48, 49,
    75, 127
Calne, 54
Cam, river, 27, 34, 61
Cambridge, 28, 34
Cambrian Railway, 66
Canal Boats Act, 179
Canal Carrying Co., 157
Canal maintenance, 106 ff.
Canals, Royal Commission on, 67
Candle Bridge, 92
Cannock Chase, 51, 159
Canoes, dug-out, 122
Carr Dyke, 24
Carreghofa, 50
Carriers, 63
    canal, 145
Cassiobury Park, 188
Castlefield, 48
Castleford, 132
Catchment Boards, 102, 104
Catherine de Barnes, 166
Caulking, 135
Cawood, 124
Ceiriog, river, 50, 85, 206
Celts, 122–3
Chalico, 134
Charges, lock, 140
Charles I, 26, 31
Charles II, 21, 29, 125
Charlotte Dundas, 153, 157
Chelmer & Blackwater Navigation, 126
Chepstow, 31
Cherry, Mr., 86
Cherry Ground lock, 71
Cherwell, river, 209
Cheshire Lock boatmen, 188
Cheshire locks, 78
Chester, 34, 51
Chester Canal, 50, 51, 57, 58, 72
Chesterfield Canal, 44, 89
Chesterton, G. K., 181
Chillington Park, 98
Chilterns, 52
Chippenham, 54
Chipping Campden, 151
Chirk, 50, 85
Christchurch, 32

City Road, 156
  Basin, 56
Civil War, 26, 30, 31
Claydon, 45
Clayhithe Ferry, 34
  Sluice, 61
Clayton, Messrs. Thomas, 130, 135, 159
Clearing-house, canal, 66, 169
Cleeve Lock, 71
Clermont, 153
Cliff End, 60
Cloths, top and side, 136–7
Cloughs, 74, 75
Clow, 26
Coalbrookdale, 19, 20, 124
Coalport Canal, 82–3, 131
Cobbett, William, 178
Cofton, 108
Cole Mere, 206
Collyweston, 22
Colne, river, 16
Colyton, 60
Comet, 153
Committee boats, 149
Compartment boats, 132
Composite boats, 133
Compton, 42
  Top Lock, 78
Concrete lighters, 133
Congleton, 57
Constable, John, 133
Container boats, 41
Contour Canal Scheme, 105
Cookley, 42
Cooper Bridge, 48
Coracle, 122–3
Costs, water carriage, 140
Cotswolds, 53
Cottages, lock and bridge, 99–100
Coven Heath bridge, 95
Coventry, 43, 52
Coventry Canal, 42, 43, 51, 52, 56, 109, 113,
  158, 166, 177
Cratch, deck, 135
Crick Tunnel, 55, 93, 189
Cromford Canal, 50, 52, 89
Cromford & High Peak Railway, 50
Cromwell, Oliver, 20, 26, 31
Cropthorne, 71
Crossley, Messrs., 155
Crowland, 25
Croydon Canal, 60–1
Cruising craft, specifications, 197–9
Culham, 70
Cumberland Market, 55
Curragh, 123
"Cut and fill," 45, 57

Cyclops, 154

Dalswinton Loch, 152
Daneway Wharf, 89
Danish invasions, 15–16
Dashwood, J. B., 59
Daventry, 92, 110
  reservoir, 108
Day boats, 130
Dean, Forest of, 18, 128
Dearne & Dove Canal, 49
Dee, river, 17, 34, 50, 85, 122, 206
Deerhurst, 122
Defoe, Daniel, 124
Denver Sluice, 27, 102
  Commissioners, 102
Derby Canal, 52
Derwent, river, 20, 33, 34
de Salis, Rodolph, 187
Devizes, 46, 53, 79, 206
Dick Brook, 33
Diesel engines, 157 ff.
Diet, of boatmen, 180
Diggle Summit, 75
Dimensions, 197–8
Dinas Bran, 206
Disused canals, 195–6
Dodderhill, 117
Don, river, 33, 34, 55
Don Navigation, 49
Doncaster, 34
Donkeys, 145
Donnington, 50
Dorset & Somerset Canal, 60
Douglas Navigation, 34
Dove, river, 85
Dragline dredgers, 119
Drags, 20, 125
Drawbridges, 95–6
Dredging, 106, 118–20
Droitwich, 32
Droitwich Canal, 44, 61, 129, 145
Droughts, 109
Drowning, 190
Druxton, 83
Duchess Countess, 148–9
Duckett's (Sir George) Canal, 56, 74
Dudley Canal, 51
Dudley Tunnel, 51, 90
Dukinfield, 50
Dummy Bows, 132
Dunbar, Battle of, 26
Dundas, Lord, 153
Dunhampstead Tunnel, 90
Dunn, river, 20

Earith, 26, 27

Eastcot, 54
East Retford, 34
Eckington Bridge, 139
Edgbaston Tunnel, 90
Education, 180–1
Edward IV, 18, 20
Effluents, sewage, 103–5
Electrical haulage, 150
Elizabeth, Queen, 22, 25
Ellesmere, 50, 206
    Canal, 50, 57, 58, 85
    Port, 50, 129, 159
Ely, 25, 26
Embankments, breached, 110
Empty mileage, 166–7
Enfield, 47
English & Bristol Channels Ship Canal, 60
Erewash Canal, 52, 67, 142
Evenlode, river, 16
Evesham, Vale of, 31
Exeter, 22
    Canal, 22, 68
Eye, John, 38

Fairbairn, William, 154, 159
Fairbairn and Lillie, 154
Farmer's Bridge locks, 201
Fazeley, 43
Fellows Morton and Clayton, 155, 156, 165
Feltwell, 26
Fenders, 136
Fenny Compton, 45, 91
Fenny Stratford, 87
Fens, 23 ff., 80, 128
Fen-slodgers, 28
Ferries, 141–2
Fidler's Ferry, 38
Fishery Boards, 102
Fladbury, 71
Flash lock, 69
Flats, 128
Flood locks, 79
    prevention, 104–5
Flotes, 18, 20, 125
Flyboats, 145, 149–50
Forth & Clyde Canal, 75 n., 153, 154
Forty-foot Drain, 27
Fosbrook, 140
Fossdyke, 20–1
Foster Bros., 66
Foulridge, 47, 107, 112
    Tunnel, 47, 93, 94
Fox, John, 146
Foxton, 55, 78, 82
Fradley, 42, 43
Framilode, 34, 124

Frankton Junction, 149
Frith Common, 61
Frodsham Bridge, 34
Frost, 112
Fulford, 124
Fulton, 83, 153
Funerals, 192
Fussell's Balanced Lock, 60

Gailey, 42
Gain's Cross, 60
Gannow Tunnel, 47, 93
Gardening, landscape, 97
Gargrave, 76
Gas boats, 130, 135
Gates, frame, 116
    , lock, making, 115–16
    , solid, 116
    , steel, 116–17
Gauging, 137
Gaut, R. C., 33
Gilbert, Thomas & John, 39
Gisburn, 98
Glamorgan Canal, 132
Glasson Dock Branch, 50
Glen, river, 24
Gloucester, 17, 18, 19, 46, 53, 61, 148
Gloucester & Berkeley Canal, 96, 99, 129,
    133, 148, 151, 198
Gnosall, 189
Godalming, 31
Godmanchester, 30
Golden Hill collieries, 43, 189
Golden Valley, 53
Goole, 34, 132
Gower, Earl, 39, 41
Grand Junction Canal, 52, 54, 55, 56, 62,
    67, 77, 86, 157
Grand Trunk Canal, 42–3
Grand Union Canal, 55, 78, 80, 90, 92, 93,
    95, 98, 107, 108, 110, 116, 117, 120,
    126, 131, 151, 158, 162, 165, 166, 173,
    177, 188, 198, 206, 209
Grand Union Canal Co., 67, 75
Grand Union Canal Carrying Co., 165
Grand Western Canal, 60, 83
Grantham Canal, 52
Gravesend & Rochester Railway & Canal
    Co., 59
Great Level, 24, 25, 26, 27
Great Western Railway, 62, 66
Greenberfield, 205
Greenwich, 130
Greywell Tunnel, 89
Grindley Brook, 206
Guildford, 31

Guillotine gates, 74, 113
  lock, 26, 106
Gunning, Elizabeth, 38
Guyhirne, 25, 26
Gypsies, 174-7, 183-4

Hadfield Chase, 23, 25
Hadley, 74
Hafods, 123
Halesowen, 51
Halifax, 33
Ham Mills, 30
Hand-spike, 75
Hanham, 53
  Mills, 35, 36
Hardingswood, 57
Harecastle, 42, 78
  Tunnel, 43, 57, 88, 91, 93, 150, 189
Hassell, J., 86
Haulage methods, 150-1
Hawkesbury, 57, 109, 166
Hay, 31, 61
  Railroad, 61
Hayne, 140
Haywood, Great, 42, 187
Hedley, 38
Heel post, 74
Helebridge, 83
Hempstones, 41
Henry I, 20
Henry VI, 18, 22
Henry VII, 25
Henry VIII, 19, 22
Henshall, Hugh, 43, 44, 46
Hereford, 124
Hereford & Gloucester Canal, 61, 90
Hermitage Sluice, 27
Hertford, 15
  Union Canal, 56
Higham, 59
Hillmorton, 52, 78, 157
Hincaster Tunnel, 147
Holland, South, 24
Hollin Ferry, 39, 40
Holmbridge, 47
Holywell, 30
Honeystreet, 132
Hore, John, 70
Horse haulage, 142-3
Horses, 144, 158-9
Horseshoe, the, 26
Huddersfield, 33, 79, 96
  Broad Canal, 96, 127
  Canal, 48, 49, 64
  Narrow Canal, 75, 79, 85, 88
Huddlesford Junction, 51
Hulls, Jonathan, 151

Humber, river, 20, 33
Hunston Bridge, 59
Huntingdon, 28
Hurleston, 51, 206
Husbands Bosworth Tunnel, 55, 93
Hythe, 60

Ice-breakers, 112-14
Idle Navigation, 34
Iffley, 70
Illiteracy, 180
Industrial Revolution, 23, 44, 59
Inglesham, 53, 62
Inns, canal-side, 182
Inshaw, Mr., 155
Ireland, 123
Irlam lock, 76
Ironbridge Lock, 188
Ironworks, 32-3
Irwell, river, 39, 87
Isis, river, 31
  Navigation, 37
Islington Tunnel, 55, 93
Itchen, river, 31
Ivel, river, 71

Jackson, Georgina F., 189 n.
James I, 25
Jessop, William, 46, 49, 50, 52
Johnson's Hillock, 47
Junctions, 80

Keadby, 128
Keb, 190
Keels, 127
Kegworth and Pilling's Flood Locks, 79
Kemble, 98
Kemmett, 35
Kendal, 50
Kennet, river, 72, 104
  and Avon Canal, 36, 46, 53, 54, 60, 64,
    76, 79, 91, 95, 109, 132, 142, 155,
    198, 205
Kennet Navigation, 35, 36, 37; 53, 70
Ketley Brook Ironworks, 87
Ketton, 22
Kidderminster, 32, 150, 205
King's Dyke, 26
King's Lynn, 25, 28
  Conservators, 102
King's Norton, 51
  Stop Lock, 74
Kingswood, 51, 80, 185
Kington & Leominster Canal, 61, 90
Kit Crew, 189
Kit Crewbucket, 189
Knees, 134

Knobsticks, 188

Labelye, 27
Lacock Abbey, 54
Lady Hatherton, 149
Lancashire & Yorkshire Railway, 65, 98
Lancaster, 50, 85
Lancaster Canal, 47, 49, 50, 76
   Museum, 148
Land Drainage Act (1930), 102
Land's End, 60
Language, of boatmen, 186–7
Lappal Tunnel, 51, 89
Lark, river, 27, 30, 139
   Navigation, 71, 74
Latimer, John, 46
Lea, river, 15, 22, 126, 141
   Navigation, 56
Lechlade, 124
Ledbury, 61
Leeds, 33, 47, 132
Leeds & Liverpool Canal, 34, 41, 44, 47,
   48, 49, 50, 62, 65, 75, 76, 78, 87, 93,
   95, 107, 112, 131, 147, 149, 156, 157,
   163, 164, 165, 173, 205
Legging, 92
Leicester, 52
   Navigation, 52, 61, 67
Leicestershire & Northamptonshire Union
   Canal, 52, 55
Leicester & Swannington tramroad, 45
Leigh, 41, 47
Leighton Buzzard, 131
Lengthmen, 110–11
Letters patent, 28–9
Lichfield, 51
Lickey Hills, 107
Lifts, mechanical, 81
Lightening boats, 124
Lighters, 126–7, 128
Limpley Stoke, 85
Lincoln, 20, 21, 22
Littleborough, 48
Littleport, 25
Liverpool, 47, 129, 131
Liverpool & Manchester Railway, 56
Llangollen, 50, 206
   Vale of, 85, 206
Llantisilio, 50
Lockgate Bridge, 50
Lock gates, *see* Gates
   houses, 99
   repairs, 114–15
Locks, 68 ff.
Locks, and water consumption, 107
Locks, how worked, 199–200
London & Birmingham Railway, 52

London & Cambridge Junction Canal, 61
London & North Western Railway, 65,
   66, 150
Londoners' Lode, 25
Long boats, 129–30
Longbotham, 47
Long-bottom boats, 134
Longcot, 54
Longdon Marsh, 15
Longdon-on-Tern, 85
Longford Bridge, 40, 41
Long Moll's Bridge, 95
Loodel, 167
Lord Dundas, 154
Lostock, Gralam, 188
Loudwell, 83
Loughborough, 79
   Navigation, 52, 56, 64, 67
Luddington Upper Lock, 71
Lugg, river, 31
Lune Aqueduct, 50, 85
Lydney, 128, 129

Macclesfield, 57
   Bridge, 164
   Canal, 57, 64
Maida Hill Tunnel, 55, 93
Maidenhead, 105
Maidstone, 31
Malet, John, 30
Malton, New, 33
Malvern Chase, 15, 25
   Straits of, 15
Mamble pits, 61
Manchester, 34, 38, 39, 40, 41, 47, 48, 57
   79, 129
   Ship Canal, 61, 76, 87
Maps, Canal, 59
Marbury, 206
March, 28
Market Harborough, 52
Marple, 57
   Aqueduct, 50
Marriage, 191–2
Marshal, Boat, 188
Marshland, 24
Marston, 52
   Doles, 45
Marsworth, 187
Martinsell, 205
Mathew, Francis, 31
Medlock, river, 41
Medway, river, 31, 60, 126
   Navigation, 32
   weirs, 69
Melksham, 54
Mells, 60

Melton Mowbray, 61
Mersey, river, 38, 41, 42, 50, 128
  & Irwell Navigation, 34, 41, 140
Middle Level, 27
  Navigations, 198
Middlewich, 58, 78
Midland Railway, 65, 155
Mildenhall, 30
Miller, 152
Misterton, 124
Mitre posts, 73
Moira, 52
Monkey boats, 129
Monmouth weir, 69
Monmouthshire Canal, 132
Montgomeryshire Canal, 50, 51, 147
Moorings, 202-3
Mortimer family, 17
Morton, John, Bishop of Ely, 25
Morton's Leam, 25, 26
Mosses, Manchester, 174
Mudbanks, 203
"Mug House," the, 19
Mules, 144
Murray, Matthew, 38
Music, 183

Naburn, 124
Nafford, 71
Nantwich, 50, 57, 207
Napton, 43, 51, 57, 63, 73, 131
Narrow boats, 129-30
Naseby Wolds, 107
Navigators, 28-9
Neath & Tennant Canal, 132
Nene, river, 24, 25, 26, 27, 28, 34, 52, 72,
  74, 106, 108, 130
Nene Catchment Board, 102
Netherpool, 50, 51
Netherton Tunnel, 90
Nettlebridge, 60
Newark, 62, 124
New Bedford River, 27
Newbold-on-Avon Tunnel, 91
Newbridge, 59
Newburgh, 47
Newbury, 35, 53, 142
  Lock, 76
Newcomen, 36, 38
"New Cut," 58
Newport (Salop), 58, 64
Newport Pagnell, 52
New South Eau, 26
Newtown, 51
Night travelling, 165
Norbury, 58
Norfolk Broads, 127

Northampton, 34, 52, 108
North Level, 25, 27
Northwich bridge, 97
North Wilts Canal, 54
Norton, 55
Norwood Tunnel, 44, 89
Nottingham, 62, 67, 140
  Canal, 52
Number Ones, 158, 177
Nutbrook Canal, 52

Oakham Canal, 61
Oakum, 135
Odiham, 89
Oil discharge, 106
Old Bedford River, 26, 27
Oldbury, 130
Old Ford, 56
Oldknow, Samuel, 50
Old Shropshire Canal, 74
Old Union, 52, 55
Open boats, 130
Ouse, Great, 15, 24, 25, 26, 27, 28, 29, 30,
  31, 32, 71, 72, 101-2, 108, 125, 141
Ouse, Little, 25, 27
Ouse, Yorkshire, 20, 34, 124, 125
Ouse Aqueduct, 86, 87
  Banks Commissioners, 102
  Drainage Board, 30
  (Lower) Drainage Board, 102
  Haling-ways Commissioners, 102
  Outfall, Conservators of, 102
Outram, 46, 49, 50
Owner-boatmen, 158
Oxenhall Tunnel, 61, 90
Oxford, 42, 62, 124, 126
  Canal, 42, 43, 45, 51, 52, 57, 63, 73, 78,
    91, 95, 142, 157, 158, 166, 177,
    187, 206, 209
Oxford, Worcester & Wolverhampton
    Railway Co., 66

Packet boats, 145 ff.
Paddington, 52
Paddles, 69, 74-5
  flood, 110
Paget, Lord, 140
Painting, boat, 137-8, 172-3, 175
Pall Mall Basin, 47
Parret, river, 30
Passenger boats, 145 ff.
Passing, of horse boats, 143
Pay rates, 179
Peak Forest Canal, 50, 57
  Forest tramroad, 45
Peakirk Drain, 26
Penk, river, 42

Pennines, 37, 47, 48, 85
Pensax (Great) Tunnel, 61, 90
Perry, Capt., 23
Pershore, 71
Peterborough, 25, 27, 28, 34
Pewsey, Vale of, 53, 79, 206
Philips, 58
Pickfords, 176
Piling, 119–20
Pioneer, 131
Platt Lane, 206
Pleasure traffic, 195 ff.
Plot, 70
Pole, Dr., 155
Pollution, river, 103
Pont Cysyllte, 50, 51, 85, 86, 206
Popham, Chief Justice, 25
Popham's Eau, 25
Portals, tunnel, 91
Port Glasgow, 153
Portsmouth, 59
Portsmouth and Arundel Canal, 59
Postilions, 146
Potteries, 57
Pound lock, 68, 70 ff.
Power stations, 104
Pownall, J. F., 105
Precedence, at locks, 143–4
Preston, 50
    Brook, 41, 159, 188
    Brook Tunnel, 88, 93, 94
Priestley, Joseph, 56, 58
Puddle, 121
Pumping stations, 108–9
Punts, 126
    , rudder, 127
    , Severn, 122
Pynock, 35

Quants, 127

Rafts, 125
Railway & Canal Commissioners, 65, 66
    & Canal Traffic Acts (1854, 1873), 65
Railways, competition with, 62 ff.
Rainfall, excess, 109–10
Ramsden's (Sir John) Canal, 48, 49, 96;
    see also Huddersfield Broad Canal
Ramsey, 25
Rates, freight, 64
Reading, 35, 53, 142
Redbridge, 60
Regent's Canal, 55–6, 67, 93, 150, 164, 176
Rennie, John, 24, 27, 46, 48, 49, 53, 61,
    85, 109
Reservoirs, 106–7
Ribble, river, 34

Richard II, 32
Rig, 125
Rimers, 69
Riser, 78
River Boards, 108
River Pollution Prevention Acts, 103
Rochdale, 48
    Canal, 48, 49, 65, 79
Rochester, 59
Rodney boatmen, 150, 178
Romans, 24
Royal Military Canal, 60
Ruabon, 51
Runcorn, 41, 120
Rye, 60

Saddington Tunnel, 93
St. Helens Canal, 38
St. Ives, 28
St. Neots, 28, 30, 32
Salford, 40
Salisbury, 32
Salmon, 122–3
Salter's, Messrs., 148
Saltersford Tunnel, 88, 92, 93, 94
Salter's Lode, 26, 27
Salwarpe, river, 16, 31, 32, 44
Sam's Cut, 26
Sandford, 70
Sandy's Cut, 26
Sandys, William, 31, 71
Saner, J., 81
Sankey Brook, 38
Sankey Canal, 38
Sapperton Tunnel, 53, 89, 91, 182
Saul Lock, 76
Savernake Summit, 109, 205
Savernake Tunnel, 91, 92
Savery & Co., 155
Scott, Sir Walter, 86
Section system, 181
Sedgemoor, 25
Selby, 124
Selly Oak, 51
Semington, 54
Severn, river, 15, 16, 17 ff., 32, 33, 37, 42,
    44, 50, 51, 53, 61, 62, 79, 82, 83, 122,
    128–9, 130, 141, 151
Severn Bridge, 96–7
Sewage conversion, 105
Shalford, 59
Shardlow, 99, 128
Share prices (1824), 56
Sharpness, 54, 96–7, 129, 130, 148
Shearing, 135
Sheffield, 33
Sheffield Canal, 55

Sheffield Mill, 35
Sheffield and South Yorkshire Canal, 65, 129
Shefford, 71
Shire Drain, 26
Shorncliffe, 60
Short boats, 131, 157, 173
Shortwood Tunnel, 90, 93
Shrawley, 33
Shrewsbury, 17, 18, 19, 50, 51, 131
    Canal, 58, 85, 131
    Museum, 122
Shropshire Tub Boat Canals, 33, 82, 131–2
    Union Canal, 64, 66, 72, 74, 81, 95, 98,
        99, 110, 129, 130, 145, 149, 150, 159,
        177, 189, 195, 197, 205, 206, 207, 209
Shropshire Union Canal Carrying Co., 137,
    150
Side pond, 77
Sills, 73
Simpson, L. T., 30, 101
Sirhowey tramroad, 45
Sir Lancelot, 133
Slough, 62
Small, Dr., 152
Smeaton, James, 46, 50, 75 n.
Smeaton, John, 34
Smestow, river, 43
Smethwick, 57
Smiles, Samuel, 48, 120
Smith, George, 150, 176, 178, 179
Smith's Leam, 27
Snatcher, 161
Snubber, 161
Soar, river, 52, 61, 128, 130, 198
Soar Navigation, 79, 142
Somerset Coal Canal, 60
Somerset & Dorset Railway, 60
Sousant Tunnel, 90
Southampton, 46
South Level, 27
South Level Drainage Commissioners, 101,
    102
Sowerby Bridge, 34, 48, 79
Spalding, 22
Speed, 204
Speedwell Mine, 89
Spencer, Arnold, 28, 29, 31
Spinney, 25
Spoon dredgers, 119
Spring-heeled Jack, 188–9
Stafford, 64
Staffordshire and Worcestershire Canal, 34,
    42, 44, 51, 57, 72, 76, 78, 81, 85, 95,
    98, 145, 149, 150, 159, 181, 187, 205,
    207, 209
Stainforth and Keadby Canal, 49
Staircase, 78

Stamford, 22
Standedge Tunnel, 49, 85, 88–9
Stanground, 26
Staunch, 69
Steam haulage, 150, 151, 154–5
Steam power, 60
Steele, 133
Steering, 161–2
Stephenson, George, 48
Stewponey, 159
Stillingfleet, 124
Stockbridge, 60
Stockwith, 44, 124, 129
Stoke Bruerne, 92, 108
Stoke Prior, 79, 84, 117
Stone, transport of, 16, 22
Stony Stratford, 86
Stop grooves, 110
    locks, 80
Stort, river, 61, 141
Story-telling, 183–4
Stour, river, 60
Stour (Canterbury), river, 22
Stour (Essex) Navigation, 74
Stour (Essex), river, 29, 104
Stour (Worcs.), river, 31, 32, 42, 205
Stourbridge (Worcs.), 32
Stourbridge Canal, 51
Stourbridge Fair, 28
Stourport-on-Severn, 34, 42, 99, 129, 130
Stourport Bridge, 61
Stourton Bridge, 51
Strapping post, 73
Stratford-on-Avon, 31, 51
Stratford-on-Avon Canal, 51, 74, 80, 95, 99
Stratford Marsh, 56
Stretford Meadows, 40
Stroud, 35
Stroudwater Canal, 34, 35, 37, 52, 76, 129,
    145
Summit Lock, 77
Surrey Iron Railway, 61
Sutton Weaver, 97
Swale, river, 20
Swansea Canal, 132
Swilgate Brook, 16
Swindon, 54
Swing Bridges, 96–7
Swinton, 49
Symington, William, 152–3

Tamworth, 166
Tardebigge, 77, 79, 83–4, 90, 93, 107,
    205
Taunton, 46, 60, 83
Taylor, John, 20–1
Teifi, river, 122

Telford, Thomas, 46, 50, 52, 57, 58, 61, 85, 86, 88, 99
Teme, river, 16
Teme Valley, 90
Tempsford, 15, 71
Tenbury, 61
Test, river, 60
Tewitfield, 50, 76, 147
Tewkesbury, 18, 124, 129
  Abbey, 16, 31
  , Battle of, 18
  Lock, 62
Thacker, F. S., 35
Thames, river, 16, 23, 42, 52, 54, 59, 62, 70, 72, 124, 126, 130, 133, 140, 141, 142, 148
Thames Ditton, 124
Thames Head Wharf, 89
Thames & Medway Canal, 59
Thames & Severn Canal, 52-3, 54, 62, 64, 89, 99, 182
"Thirty and twelve," the, 79
Thistle, 155
Thorney, 25
Thorneycroft, Messrs., 155
Thurston, E. Temple, 197, 209
Tide locks, 79-80
Tinsley, 34, 55
Tiverton, 60
Tixall, 98
  Wide, 187
Todmorden, 48
Tolls, 63
Tom Pudding, 132
Tone, river, 30, 60
Topsham, 60
Torksey, 20
Tove, river, 108
Towing paths, 141
Towy, river, 122
Tradition, 192-3
Traffic control, tunnel, 94
Traffic rules, 202-3
Trafford Moss, 40, 174, 175, 177
Trench, 131
Trench Inclined Lift, 82-3
Trent, river, 20, 21, 32, 34, 37, 41, 42, 52, 62, 124, 130, 140, 151
Trent Bridge, 52
Trent Junction, 142
Trent & Mersey Canal, 20, 41, 42, 56, 57, 58, 62, 64, 72, 78, 81, 85, 88, 90, 92, 93, 94, 128, 150, 159, 188, 199, 206
Trevithick, 38
Trew, John, 22, 68
Tring, 52
Trows, 18, 19, 124, 126, 128-9

Tub boats, 131-2
Tugs, tunnel, 92-3
Tunnel construction, 91-2
  hooks, 93
Tunnel House, 182
Tunnels, 87 ff.
  , repair, 117-18
Turnrail, 189

Uniformity, lack of, 62-3
Upper Avon Navigation, 51, 66
Upton, 129
Ure, river, 20
Usk, river, 122

Ventilation, tunnel, 94
Vermuyden, Sir Cornelius, 23, 24, 25-7, 28, 105
Vermuyden's Eau, 27
da Vinci, Leonardo, 68
Visconti, Filippo Maria, 68

Wakefield, 33, 49, 132
Wales, 128
  , South, 132
Wallbridge, 52
Walton, Izaak, 187
Walton Summit, 50
Wantage, 54
Wappenshall, 58, 131
Wardle Lock, 58
Warwick, Countess of, 16
Warwick, 166
Warwick & Birmingham Canal, 51, 67, 80, 166
Warwick & Braunston Canal, 51
Warwick & Napton Canal Co., 76
Wash, 153-4
Wash, the, 24
Washlands, 105
Water consumption, of canals, 106-7
  grid, 105
  supply, to canals, 106-8
  supply, domestic, 104
Watford lock, 55
Watt, James, 109, 152
Wattle work, 123
Waveney, river, 32, 34, 127
Weald of Kent Canal, 59-60
Weaver, river, 37, 81, 128, 129, 130
  Navigation, 34, 67, 97, 151
  Trustees, 34
Weddings, 191-2
Wedgwood, Josiah, 39, 41
Weedon, 110, 209
Weeland, 33

Weirs, 69 ff.
  run-off, 110
Welch's Dam, 27
Well, 28
Welland, river, 22, 24, 27
Wellington (Salop), 64
Welsh Canal, 195–6, 197, 206, 209
Welsh Frankton, 50
Welshpool, 17, 51
Wendover, 52
Western barges, 124, 126
West Hill tunnel, 90, 91, 93
West Riding, 103
Weston, Sir Richard, 31, 68
Weston Point, 34
Weston Wharf, 51
Wey, river, 31, 54, 59, 72, 126, 139, 141
Wey & Arun Junction Canal, 59, 60
Wey Navigation, 36, 70
Weymoor Bridge, 54
Wharfe, river, 20
Wherries, 127
Whitchurch, 50, 51, 209
White Horse, Vale of, 54
Whittington Brook, 43
Whittlesea, 26
  Mere, 26
Whitworth, Robert, 43, 46, 47, 49, 52, 53, 60, 61
Whixall Moss, 206
Widbrook, 60
Widdop engine, 157
Wide boats, 131
Wigan, 34, 47, 50, 129, 131, 147, 157
Wilden Ferry, 20, 37, 41, 140
Wilkinson, John, 20, 124
William III, 20, 33

Williams, Sir E. Leader, 81, 87, 155
Wilton Reservoir, 109
Wilts & Berks Canal, 54
Winchelsea, 60
Windlasses, 198–9
Windrush, river, 16
Windsor, Lord, 31, 32
Wings, 92
Winsford Bridge, 34, 37
Wisbech, 25, 26, 27
Wissey, river, 27
Wistow, 124
Witham, river, 20, 21–2, 24
Wolverhampton, 44, 58, 130, 144, 150, 159
Wolverton, 86, 108
Wonder, 127
Woodham, 54
Woodhouse, Mr., 83
Woods, boatbuilding, 133–4
Wootton Bassett, 54
Wootton Rivers, 53, 79, 205
Worcester, 15, 18, 79, 129
  Bar, 80
Worcester & Birmingham Canal, 51, 74, 77, 79, 80, 84, 90, 91, 93, 107, 117, 144, 145, 159, 177, 205, 207, 209
Worsley, 38–9, 40, 41, 43
Wreak & Eye Navigation, 61
Wrenbury, 206
Wye, river, 31, 69, 122, 124, 139
Wynde, 35
Wyre lock, 71
Wyrley & Easington Canal, 51

Yare, river, 34, 127
Yarranton, Andrew, 23, 31, 32, 33
York, 20, 125